Liturgical Resources I

"I Will Bless You and You Will Be a Blessing"

Revised and Expanded Edition

**As authorized by the
78th General Convention
of the Episcopal Church, 2015**

Church Publishing
NEW YORK

Certificate

I certify that this edition of the "Witnessing and Blessing of a Lifelong Covenant" conforms to the version approved for use by the 78th General Convention of The Episcopal Church in 2015.

I further certify that this edition of "The Witnessing and Blessing of a Marriage" and "The Celebration and Blessing of a Marriage 2," from "Liturgical Resources I: I Will Bless You and You Will Be a Blessing, Revised and Expanded 2015" conforms to the version approved for trial use by the 78th General Convention of The Episcopal Church in 2015.

Juan Oliver
Custodian of the Standard Book of Common Prayer
Advent 2015

ISBN-13: 978-0-89869-948-7 (pbk.)
ISBN-13: 978-0-89869-949-4 (ebook)

Church Publishing, Incorporated
19 East 34th Street
New York, New York 10016

www.churchpublishing.org

Table of Contents

I. Introduction to the Revised and Expanded Edition

In 2012, the General Convention of The Episcopal Church commended "Liturgical Resources 1: I Will Bless You, and You Will Be a Blessing" for study and use throughout The Episcopal Church. In the 2013-2015 triennium, the materials were widely used in a number of dioceses, and the Standing Commission on Liturgy and Music (SCLM) invited responses through several avenues. This new volume is the result of this process.

Responses to Liturgical Resources 1

In January 2013, the SCLM asked bishops of The Episcopal Church to report whether they had authorized the liturgy "The Witnessing and Blessing of a Lifelong Covenant," and if so, whether they had authorized any modifications to meet the needs of members of The Episcopal Church. The SCLM received responses from half (fifty-five) of the dioceses, and of these, thirty-eight had authorized use of the resource. In many dioceses in jurisdictions where civil marriage is legal for same-sex couples, the bishop authorized revisions of the liturgy to allow clergy to officiate at a civil marriage of a same-sex couple.

In fall 2013, nearly one thousand people accessed an online survey distributed with the assistance of diocesan contact people and through social media. Responses were overwhelmingly positive to all sections of Liturgical Resources 1. However, a number of respondents expressed frustration or confusion that the liturgy appeared to be a "separate but equal" rite, which therefore was not equivalent to marriage.

The Commission heard similar comments at an international, ecumenical, indaba-style conversation on same-sex marriage that it hosted at Grace and Holy Trinity Cathedral, Kansas City, Missouri, June 3–5 2014. The SCLM invited participation from every diocese of The Episcopal Church and every province of the Anglican Communion where civil marriage is legal for same-sex couples, and from ecumenical partner churches in the United States. Participants at the consultation included fifty-seven people representing twenty-four dioceses of The Episcopal Church, six other churches of the Anglican Communion, and five ecumenical partners, along with the President of the House of Deputies, the Presiding Bishop, and the Secretary of General Convention. Two dioceses of The Episcopal Church and two provinces of the Anglican Communion declined to send representatives. While none of the participants in the consultation was opposed to same-sex marriage, the conversation enabled the Commission to understand more deeply the issues facing clergy and same-sex couples in contexts where civil marriage is legal.

To evaluate the Kansas City consultation, the SCLM asked the Reverend Doctor Paula Nesbitt, a sociologist who has worked extensively in evaluation of the continuing *indaba* process in the Anglican Communion, to interview a selected cross-section of participants. We have included her executive summary of her report as an appendix to this volume.

Faith, Hope, and Love: Theological Resources

In Resolution A049, the 2012 General Convention directed the SCLM to develop the theological resource "with specific attention to further engagement with scripture and the relevant categories and sources of systematic theology (e.g., creation, sin, grace, salvation, redemption, human nature)." The Commission invited responses from theologians representing different disciplines (Scripture, ethics, Church history, systematic theology, missiology) and diverse theological perspectives. These essays are included in this revised and expanded edition; they represent the viewpoint of the individual authors rather than the consensus of the SCLM.

The Church's Canon Law and Laws of the States

Liturgical Resources 1 included a study of the complexities of civil and canon law regarding marriage and civil unions. It offered a number of scenarios, taking into account differences in both civil law and diocesan policy.

Since 2012, dramatic changes in civil law in the United States have reshaped the context. When Liturgical Resources 1 was first published as part of the 2012 Blue Book Report to the 77th General Convention, seven states and the District of Columbia allowed same-sex civil marriage. On June 26, 2015, the Supreme Court of the United States ruled, "The Court, in this decision, holds same-sex couples may exercise the fundamental right to marry in all States. It follows that the Court must also hold – and it now does hold – that there is no lawful basis for a State to refuse to recognize a lawful same-sex marriage performed in another State on the ground of its same-sex character."[1]

Recognizing that resolutions to amend the marriage canon were likely to come before the 2015 General Convention, the SCLM determined that the original section on canon law might no longer be relevant or provide useful guidance. Instead, an appendix to this revised and expanded edition of Liturgical Resources 1 provides a history of the marriage canon prepared by the Task Force on the Study of Marriage for its 2015 Blue Book report. In addition, the definitions of "civil union," "Defense of Marriage Act," and "same-sex marriage" have been revised in the Glossary.

In Resolution A036, the 2015 General Convention revised Canon I.18, and in Resolution A054, the Convention affirmed that the provisions of Canon I.19.3, regarding marriage after divorce, apply to the liturgies in this resource. We have included both the revised Canon I.18 and Canon I.19, which was not revised, in Appendix 2.

Hearing, Seeing, and Declaring New Things: Pastoral Resources

Several participants in the June 2014 consultation on same-sex marriage expressed concern that the pastoral resource portrayed gay, lesbian, bisexual, and transgender people in a negative and stereotypical manner. The SCLM formed an ad hoc task group to recommend revisions. The first half of the resource has been revised accordingly.

The five-session process for preparing couples for a blessing of their covenantal relationship was not revised. Though the SCLM received some suggestions for a different order of the sessions and for other changes, no clear consensus emerged. The content and structure of the sessions is recommended but not required, and the SCLM believes that clergy and lay people trained for preparing couples can adapt the resource to suit their particular approach.

---

1 <u>Obergefell v. Hodges</u>, 576 U.S. _____ (slip op., at 28).

After the 2015 General Convention, the pastoral resource was revised to take account of the revisions of the marriage canon (Canon I.18) and the authorization of trial use of the liturgies for marriage as well as the U.S. Supreme Court decision permitting same-sex marriage throughout the United States.

Liturgical Resources

In response to comments by those who used the 2012 rite, the SCLM made some revisions to the original liturgical resource, "The Witnessing and Blessing of a Lifelong Covenant." The 2015 General Convention authorized this revised liturgy for use "under the direction and with the permission of the bishop exercising ecclesiastical authority" (Resolution 2015-A054).

In addition, heeding the concern that "separate but equal" rites are inherently unequal, the SCLM developed and recommended to the 2015 General Convention an adaptation of the 2012 liturgy that can be used for marriage for any couple, as well as "The Celebration and Blessing of a Marriage 2," a gender-neutral adaptation of the marriage rite in the 1979 Book of Common Prayer. The Convention authorized these rites for trial use, that is, as a proposed revision of the BCP. Resolution 2015-A054 directs that these liturgies be used under the direction and with the permission of the diocesan bishop, and stipulates that bishops exercising ecclesiastical authority or, where appropriate, ecclesiastical supervision will make provision for all couples asking to be married in the Episcopal Church to have access to the liturgies.

Discussion Guide

Some respondents to the survey expressed appreciation for the materials in the discussion guide, while a significant minority indicated that they had not used the materials because they had already done this work.

Given the rapidly changing context, the SCLM believes that the material will continue to be of use in some places. Since the Commission did not receive any strong recommendations for revision of the discussion guide, the primary change to this section of the resource is the addition of an option to present two of the liturgies in this resource. In addition, after the 2015 General Convention minor revisions were made to take account of the decisions of General Convention as well as the U.S. Supreme Court decision on the marriage of same-sex couples.

Terminology

Since 2009, as the SCLM has gone about its work on these resources, terminology has been debated. Should we refer to "same-gender" or "same-sex" couples? As indicated in the Introduction to the first edition, the 2012 General Convention directed that the resource use "same-sex" rather than "same-gender," and the SCLM then determined that "opposite-sex" rather than "different-gender" would be more in keeping with the spirit of Resolution 2012–A049. The task group that reviewed the pastoral resource recommended that the resource refer to LGBT (lesbian, gay, bisexual, and transgender) people. The terms reflect growing awareness of the complexity of sexual orientation and gender identity.

The Commission consulted with scholars working in the area of gender studies and learned that the term "gender and sexual minorities" (GSM) is increasingly preferred as an all-encompassing term. We have introduced that term in the section "Hearing, Seeing, and Declaring New Things: Pastoral Resources for Preparing Couples for a Liturgy of Blessing or Marriage" and included a discussion of sexual orientation and gender identity. In addition, recognizing the complexity of gender and sexuality, we have used the term "different-sex" rather "opposite-sex" throughout this revised and expanded edition.

Conclusion

We offer this revised and expanded edition with gratitude for all who have offered their feedback, and in the hope that these resources will continue to strengthen our shared witness to the gospel.

Ruth A. Meyers
on behalf of
The Standing Commission on Liturgy
and Music and The Special Legislative
Committees on Marriage of the
78th General Convention
July 2015

II. Introduction to the First Edition (2012)

As members of the Standing Commission on Liturgy and Music (SCLM) of the Episcopal Church, we give thanks for the many and various ways that the grace of God in Christ is made manifest in our Church and throughout the world. Whenever the Church pronounces God's blessing, it does so with such gratitude always in mind.

For more than thirty years, the Episcopal Church has been responding to the call to seek and serve Christ in its members who are gay and lesbian. In 1976, a resolution of General Convention affirmed that "homosexual persons are children of God who have a full and equal claim with all other persons upon the love, acceptance, and pastoral concern and care of the Church."[2] Since then, we have been in a churchwide discernment process about how we live out that resolution. Some congregations and their clergy have welcomed same-sex couples and offered liturgical blessings of their relationships, and some dioceses have developed guidelines for such blessings. Resolution C051 of the 2003 General Convention recognized "that local faith communities are operating within the bounds of our common life as they explore and experience liturgies celebrating and blessing same-sex unions." Six years later, General Convention called for the collection and development of resources for those blessings. The materials presented here respond to that call.

Resolution C056 of the 2009 General Convention of the Episcopal Church directed the Standing Commission on Liturgy and Music to "collect and develop theological and liturgical resources" for the blessing of same-sex relationships. This resolution instructed the Commission to work in consultation with the House of Bishops and to "devise an open process for the conduct of its work, inviting

---

2 The text of Resolution 1976–A069 and other General Convention legislation concerning same-sex relationships is included in an appendix to these resources.

participation from provinces, dioceses, congregations, and individuals who are engaged in such theological work, and inviting theological reflection from throughout the Anglican Communion." We have understood the process for our work to be as important as the resources themselves.

The Scope of Our Work

Because Resolution 2009–C056 directed us to "collect and develop" resources, we have not debated whether the Church should bless same-sex relationships. Nonetheless, we recognize that Episcopalians and Christians throughout the Anglican Communion have disagreed about whether such blessings are a legitimate development within Christian tradition or an unacceptable departure from biblical teaching. Resolution 2009–C056 acknowledged this dispute in the resolve "that this Convention honor the theological diversity of this Church in regard to matters of human sexuality," and previous General Convention resolutions have also recognized this disagreement. In the theological essay "Faith, Hope, and Love" we acknowledge these differences, and offer an approach to blessing same-sex relationships that reflects the centrality of Scripture in Anglican tradition, interpreted in concert with the historical traditions of the Church and in the light of reason. The discussion guide included in these resources is intended to enable all congregations and dioceses to explore the materials, whether or not they believe the Church should bless same-sex relationships.

As we developed the resources, many people asked whether we were actually preparing a rite for same-sex marriage. In accord with Resolution 2009–C056, the Commission has understood our charge to be the development of a liturgy of blessing, not marriage. Nonetheless, there are a number of parallels to opposite-sex marriage, as General Convention Resolution 2000–D039 suggested when it acknowledged that "there are currently couples in the Body of Christ and in this Church who are living in marriage and couples in the Body of Christ and in this Church who are living in other life-long committed relationships." That 2000 resolution then set forth the expectation that "such relationships will be characterized by fidelity, monogamy, mutual affection and respect, careful, honest communication, and the holy love which enables those in such relationships to see in each other the image of God," and denounced "promiscuity, exploitation, and abusiveness in the relationships of any of our members." These expectations have defined the Commission's understanding of the same-sex relationships for which we have developed resources. While the liturgy we have developed is not called "marriage," we recognize significant parallels: two people publicly make a lifelong, monogamous commitment to one another with the exchange of solemn vows in a ritual that pronounces God's blessing on their life together.

The question of marriage is complicated by ongoing changes in American civil law. As of August 2011, six states and the District of Columbia issue marriage licenses to same-sex couples, five states allow civil unions, and seven recognize some form of domestic partnership; on the other hand, thirty states have adopted constitutional language defining marriage as between one man and one woman and thirty-nine states have statutes defining marriage in this way.[3] Civil law in other countries where the Episcopal Church is located adds further complexity. Both the Book of Common Prayer and the Canons of the Episcopal Church require clergy to conform to the laws of the state regarding marriage and describe marriage as being between a man and a woman. To address this complexity, these resources include an essay on canon law that discusses scenarios likely to arise as same-sex couples request an authorized liturgy for blessing of their relationship and/or civil marriage (or union) in the Church.

In addition to questions about the term "marriage," we received many comments about the terms "gender" and "sex." Following the wording of Resolution 2009–C056, in the resource presented to the 2012 General Convention, the Commission used the term "same-gender" to describe these relationships and "different-gender" as the comparable term. However, the 2012 General Convention directed that the term "same-sex" be used rather than "same-gender," and the published resource makes this change. In addition, as the Commission reviewed the resource for publication, it determined that the use of the term "opposite-sex" rather than "different-gender" was in keeping with the spirit of the 2012 General Convention resolution, and so the published resource makes this change as well. This is more than a linguistic question. As the Commission worked on these resources, we acknowledged but did not address the complexity of contemporary social and academic conversations about the categories of "sex" and "gender." The pastoral resources for preparation of couples prior to a liturgy of blessing offer ways to work with individuals who identify themselves as bisexual or transgender. The resources expect that a bisexual or transgender couple who seeks the Church's blessing of their relationship will commit to monogamy and lifelong faithfulness, the same commitment asked of every other same-sex and opposite-sex couple.

---

3 This information is from the website of the National Conference of State Legislatures, www.ncsl.org.

Collecting Resources

The Commission has gathered a vast amount of materials, including official studies, service leaflets from liturgies of blessing, and diocesan and provincial guidelines for these blessings. The Archives of the Episcopal Church established a digital archive for the project, http://www.episcopalarchives.org/SCLM/, where anyone may review the materials we have gathered.

Resolution 2009–C056 allows bishops to "provide generous pastoral response" to meet the needs of the Church's members, so in December 2009, the chair of the Commission asked all diocesan bishops to report what provisions they were making and what resources they were commending to their dioceses. Twenty-seven bishops responded to this request, and a number of these bishops included theological, pastoral, teaching, and/or liturgical resources. Seven other dioceses subsequently submitted materials. All diocesan materials that we received are available for review in the digital archive for Resolution 2009–C056.

We gathered liturgical resources from many places. Clayton Morris, who served as Liturgical Officer for the Episcopal Church until 2009, had accumulated numerous materials over the course of nearly two decades. The Commission received resources from lay and ordained Episcopalians throughout the Church, including some of our own members. Commission members reviewed all of these as we began the process of developing liturgies. A representative sampling of the resources is posted on the digital archive, and all of the resources will be permanently housed at the Archives of the Episcopal Church.

Developing Resources

At our March 2010 meeting, the Commission began our work in response to this resolution with a day of theological reflection. That conversation resulted in a brief outline of the resources to be developed:

- one or more essays setting forth scriptural and theological foundations for blessing same-sex relationships;

- one or more rites for blessing same-sex relationships;

- pastoral and teaching resources to assist clergy and congregations as they consider these blessings; and

- resources designed to help communities understand and address canonical and legal matters.

This proposed outline became the basis for four task groups formed to develop materials. These groups were advisory to the Commission, which made the final decision about the resources to be reported to the 77th General Convention in 2012.

In forming the task groups, the Commission sought the wisdom and experience of lay people and clergy from both academic and congregational contexts. Members of the task groups reflected the diversity of the Episcopal Church in terms of age, gender, race/ethnicity, geography, and sexual orientation. The task groups met four times in 2010 and 2011, and the chairs of the task groups met monthly by telephone or video conference. The Commission discussed the work at each of its five meetings during the triennium.

An Open Process ... Inviting Participation

Consultation with the House of Bishops

In September 2010, the chair of the Commission and four of the task-group chairs presented to the House of Bishops a draft of theological and liturgical principles that would guide this work. Responses from the bishops helped refine those principles. At the March and September 2011 House of Bishops meetings, bishops serving on the Commission and/or the task groups updated their colleagues. At the September 2011 meeting, bishops had an informal opportunity to discuss the final draft of the theological essay and the liturgy with the bishops who are members of the Commission.

Province I Hearing

In October 2010, the Commission meeting in New Hampshire included a hearing with bishops, other clergy, and same-sex couples from each of the seven dioceses in Province I, which comprises the six New England states. The evolving legal status of civil unions and marriage equality in those states has meant that many of the dioceses have been addressing questions of blessing same-sex relationships for many years. Province I is the only province of the Episcopal Church to develop a resource for clergy ministering to same-sex couples, and a majority of the dioceses in this province have guidelines for blessing these relationships. Thus, our meeting in one of the dioceses of Province I offered a good opportunity to consult with those engaged in this work, as directed in Resolution 2009–C056.

At the hearing, thirty-three people, lay and ordained, testified about their experiences. Many told the Commission that congregations were transformed when they joined in the celebration of a blessing. For some congregations and couples, the blessing of a civil union as part of the regular Sunday liturgy was an especially powerful expression of the Church's acceptance and care for the couple. Clergy and couples alike were surprised at how jubilant congregations were. We also heard about the cost of secrecy in places where relationships had to be hidden and blessings could not be openly celebrated. Couples and clergy spoke of the joy that came when relationships could be openly acknowledged. A few couples told powerful stories of reconciliation that happened within their families when their relationship was celebrated and blessed in a Church liturgy.

Church-wide Survey Regarding Pastoral and Teaching Materials

In October 2010, the Task Group on Pastoral and Teaching Resources created a Web-based survey asking what resources congregations were using to prepare same-sex couples who came to the Church seeking a blessing, and what teaching materials and resources were used or would be needed to help congregations in a discernment process about welcoming the blessing of same-sex relationships. The Commission used both official and unofficial channels to invite responses to the survey: a press release sent to diocesan communicators, a letter to all members of the 2009 House of Deputies and the House of Bishops, invitations on the unofficial list-serve for bishops and deputies, and networking by members of the Commission and the task groups.

Between October 2010 and January 6, 2011, we received 1,131 responses to the survey from 111 dioceses and all nine provinces of the Episcopal Church. Twenty-three percent of the respondents stated that the blessing of same-sex relationships already occurs in their congregations, and of these, 55 percent confirmed that their congregations had engaged in an educational and/or discernment process before the blessing of same-sex relationships began. With regard to preparing same-sex couples, 32 percent of respondents said that their preparation differed from that provided for opposite-sex couples, and 43 percent expressed a need for additional resources. The data from this survey helped guide the development of the pastoral and teaching resources.

Churchwide Consultation

The Commission invited every diocese in the Episcopal Church to send two General Convention deputies, one lay and one clergy, to an overnight consultation at the conclusion of its March 2011 meeting in Atlanta, Georgia. Three goals were set forth:

- to *inform* the deputies about the work of the Standing Commission on Liturgy and Music in response to Resolution 2009-C056;

- to *engage* the deputies in theological reflection in response to the Commission's work, and to solicit feedback that would inform the Commission and its task groups as they continued their work;

- to *equip* the deputies to report to the rest of their deputations and engage them in ongoing theological reflection about the blessing of same-sex relationships.

Materials distributed to participants at the consultation are available for review in the SCLM digital archive, which also includes a link to the webcast of the entire consultation.

One hundred ninety-five deputies from ninety-eight dioceses registered for the gathering. Most responded enthusiastically to the process. A significant majority stated on the evaluation form that they felt either "completely equipped" or "somewhat equipped" to discuss this work in their dioceses and at the 2012 General Convention. When asked what they valued most, one responded, "the thoughtful and prayerful way that people with differing opinions were able to discuss this important work." Another deputy noted "the opportunity to speak and listen to other people and the broader perspective I gained from those interactions; the opportunity to engage the process, principles and issues that are in play as we do this work together; the real and abiding sense that we are doing this work 'together.'" A few deputies commented on the absence of opposing viewpoints in the plenary sessions. One wrote, "The only thing lacking for me was an opportunity for those who are new to engaging this conversation or who are opposed to have enough space to express their reservations, be heard, and maybe to hear constructive, respectful responses."

Review of Draft Resources

After the task groups presented a complete first draft of the resources to the Commission in June 2011, we made the drafts available to a group of consultant reviewers. During July 2011, 133 people, lay and ordained, representing all nine provinces of the Episcopal Church, offered thousands of comments on the draft resources. In August, the task groups' extensive revisions led to final drafts for the Commission.

Inviting Reflection from throughout the Anglican Communion

In addition to the direction of Resolution 2009–C056, the Commission was mindful that the 2004 *Windsor Report* urged "all provinces that are engaged in processes of discernment regarding the blessing of same sex unions to engage the Communion in continuing study of biblical and theological rationale for and against such unions" (par. 145).

Knowing that the Anglican Church of Canada has been addressing this subject for many years, we requested and received liturgies from several of the Canadian dioceses. The digital archive includes, under "Church-Wide Resources," an issue of *Liturgy Canada* that gives an overview of the history and summarizes the guidelines and rites available on diocesan websites in the Anglican Church of Canada.

International Anglican Liturgical Consultation (IALC)

The IALC, a biennial gathering, includes liturgical scholars, representatives nominated and sent by provinces of the Anglican Communion, and members of liturgical commissions of Anglican provinces. Since provinces may refer matters to the Consultation, the Standing Commission on Liturgy and Music requested time on the agenda of the August 2011 meeting. The IALC Steering Committee not only granted a half-day for this discussion, but also met in March 2011 with representatives of the Commission to learn more about the work and to prepare for the discussion in the full Consultation.

The IALC meeting included fifty-five people from nineteen provinces of the Anglican Communion. The official representatives of the Episcopal Church, Ruth Meyers (Chair of the Standing Commission on Liturgy and Music) and Thomas Ely (Bishop of Vermont and a member of the Commission), presented a summary of the theological rationale and liturgical principles guiding the development of resources, along with a draft of the liturgy. Not all participants in the IALC meeting supported the Episcopal Church's decision to develop these resources, but all joined in respectful conversation in a small-group format. In the written notes submitted from the small groups, some stated that the work of the Episcopal Church would be helpful for their own province, while others indicated that blessing same-sex relationships is not on the agenda for them.

Participants in the IALC conversation asked for development of the scriptural foundations for blessing same-sex relationships and clarification of the concepts of blessing and covenant. They urged that the theological and liturgical resources make clear that the Episcopal Church is envisioning these relationships as monogamous and lifelong. Many found the liturgy to be strikingly similar to marriage. They encouraged greater clarity in the liturgy about the nature of the covenant and a more robust form of blessing.

The task groups received a detailed report of the comments from the IALC meeting and took account of them as they prepared the final draft of the resources.

Conclusion

"I will bless you," God declared to Abraham, "so that you will be a blessing" (Genesis 12:2). The Commission and its task groups have been reminded, at every step in this process, of the many blessings God has bestowed on our Church. The unprecedented opportunities we have had to engage with our sister and brother Episcopalians in every province of the Episcopal Church and with Anglicans from the wider Anglican Communion have illustrated for us the rich diversity of our life together in the Body of Christ. This work has been a divine gift and a blessing to us, which we are eager to share.

We offer these resources with the hope that they will strengthen our shared witness in the Episcopal Church to the love and grace of God in Christ. As in every other aspect of our life together as God's people, we offer these resources, not relying on ourselves alone, but on God, who "is able to accomplish abundantly far more than all we can ask or imagine," and always for the sake of God's glory in Christ Jesus (Ephesians 3:20–21).

The Standing Commission on
Liturgy and Music
November 2012

III. Faith, Hope, and Love

Theological Resources for
Blessing Same-Sex Relationships

Contents

Preface

The Episcopal Church has been seeking, in various ways and over the last thirty years, to celebrate the goodness of God, the grace of Christ, and the gifts of the Holy Spirit in the lives of our brothers and sisters who are gay and lesbian. A series of General Convention resolutions during that time (1976–A069; 1985–D082; 1991–A104; 1994–C020; 1994–C042; 1997–C003; 2000–D039; 2003–C051) has now led the Church to ask the Standing Commission on Liturgy and Music to "collect and develop theological and liturgical resources" for the blessing of same-sex relationships (Resolution 2009–C056). In response to that call, we offer this essay as a theological resource and invite the wider Church to reflect with us on how God is working today in the committed relationships of same-sex couples.

For generations the Church has celebrated and blessed the faithful, committed, lifelong, monogamous relationships of men and women united in the bonds of Holy Matrimony. In the Episcopal Church, the marriage relationship is held in high regard, included as a "sacramental rite" by some,[4] and as one of the seven sacraments by others. The Commission has discovered in its work in response to Resolution 2009–C056 that any consideration of the blessing of faithful, committed, lifelong, monogamous relationships of same-sex couples cannot ignore the parallels to marriage, whether from practical, theological, or liturgical perspectives. While this reality may well be inviting the Church to deeper conversation regarding marriage, the similarities between marriage and the blessing of same-sex unions also illuminate our discussions in this resource.

For some Episcopalians, this material will resonate well with their long-standing experience and theological reflection; for others, the

---

4 "An Outline of the Faith," *The Book of Common Prayer* (New York: Church Hymnal Corporation, 1979), 860. Hereafter this edition of the Prayer Book is cited as BCP.

call from the 2009 General Convention represents a new and perhaps perplexing moment in the life of our Church. We take that difference seriously. To the best of our ability, given the mandate of Resolution 2009–C056 to "collect and develop theological and liturgical resources" for the blessing of same-sex relationships, we address those who are eager to receive this theological resource while also acknowledging that others have deep reservations about proceeding in this direction. All of us belong equally to the Episcopal Church and to the worldwide Anglican Communion and, most of all, to the universal Body of Christ. This theological resource honors the centrality of Scripture among Anglicans, interpreted in concert with the historical traditions of the Church and in the light of reason.

An overview introduces and summarizes questions and major theological themes. Four sections follow the overview, each expanding on the themes. While readers may engage with this material in a number of ways, the order of the four sections, which we recommend following, reflects a particular theological approach to this work. Section one affirms the understanding that everything we do as Christians is meant to express the Church's call to participate in God's own mission in the world. The second section offers theological reflections on blessing. The third considers blessing same-sex couples within the broader sacramental life of the Church, especially in light of the theological significance of covenantal relationship. The fourth section reflects on the challenge of living into our baptismal bond with each other in the midst of disagreements over biblical interpretation.

In researching and preparing this essay, we discovered and recalled an abundance of resources in Scripture and the traditions of the Church that have informed our response to Resolution 2009–C056. We now invite the wider Church to further study and conversation, mindful that the apostle Paul described our shared life in Christ as one marked by faith, hope, and love, the greatest of these being love (1 Corinthians 13:13).

Overview: Theological Reflection on Same-Sex Relationships

> I give thanks to my God always for you because of the grace of
> God that has been given you in Christ Jesus, for in every way
> you have been enriched in him, in speech and knowledge of
> every kind—just as the testimony of Christ has been strengthened
> among you—so that you are not lacking in any spiritual gift as
> you wait for the revealing of our Lord Jesus Christ.
>
> — 1 Corinthians 1:4-7

In 2009, the General Convention of the Episcopal Church asked for theological and liturgical resources for the blessing of same-gender relationships (Resolution C056). In response to that call, we invite the Church to reflect on the theological material collected and developed here for that purpose. In our theological reflection, we have kept in view more than thirty years of deliberation at General Convention on these matters, especially Resolution 2000–D039, which identified certain characteristics the Church expects of couples living in marriage and other lifelong, committed relationships: "fidelity, monogamy, mutual affection and respect, careful, honest communication, and the holy love which enables those in such relationships to see in each other the image of God."[5] We understand couples who manifest this manner of life, with God's grace, to have entered into a covenant with each other, which presents a rich opportunity for theological reflection.[6]

---

5 Texts of these resolutions are included in the appendix to these resources. For a fuller discussion of the history of General Convention resolutions and reports on these issues, see the appendix in *To Set Our Hope on Christ: A Response to the Invitation of* Windsor Report ¶135 (New York: The Office of Communication, The Episcopal Church Center, 2005), 63–121.

6 As Paul Marshall points out, the marriage rite of the 1979 *Book of Common Prayer* uses the language of "covenant" (423). Marshall notes that covenant-making is a key biblical motif, which makes it useful in our theological reflection on the committed relationships of all couples (*Same-Sex Unions: Stories and Rites* [New York: Church Publishing, 2004], 40).

The theological themes in this resource, rooted in baptism, eucharist, and the paschal mystery of Christ's death and resurrection, offer ways to consider how the Church may appropriately bless lifelong, committed covenantal relationships of same-sex couples. Such covenantal relationships can reflect God's own gracious covenant with us in Christ, manifest the fruits of the Spirit in holiness of life, and model for the whole community the love of neighbor in the practice of forgiveness and reconciliation.

As the Commission responded to the charge to collect and develop theological resources, we focused our attention on four areas of consideration. The first is *mission*: what does the Church believe these blessings will contribute to God's own work of redeeming and reconciling love in the world? Second, what does the Church believe is happening when it pronounces God's *blessing*? Third, what does the Church believe are the distinguishing marks of a holy *covenant*? And, finally, what is the relationship between *Christian unity* and our differing approaches to *biblical interpretation* regarding same-sex relationships? This overview introduces and summarizes these areas, and the subsequent sections expand on each of them in turn.

A Focus on Mission

Our starting point is Holy Baptism, which incorporates us into the Body of Christ and commissions us to participate in God's mission of reconciliation in the world (2 Corinthians 5:17–19). The purpose of this reconciling mission is nothing less than the restoration of all people to "unity with God and with each other in Christ."[7] One of the ways Christians participate in this mission is by witnessing to Christ in how we live in our closest relationships. "By this everyone will know that you are my disciples," Jesus said, "if you have love for one another" (John 13:35).

As Christians, then, our closest relationships are not solely private. The Church has always affirmed the public and communal dimension of our covenantal relationships. The character of our love, both its fruitfulness and its failures, affects others around us. The Church, therefore, commissions a couple bound by sacred vows in Holy Matrimony to participate in God's mission of reconciliation. Such relationships are set apart for precisely that divine purpose: to bear witness to and participate in the creating, redeeming, and sustaining love of God.

---

7 "An Outline of the Faith," BCP, 855.

This missional character of covenantal blessing, reflected in both Scripture and the historical traditions of the Church, deserves renewed attention today. The 2000 General Convention contributed to this renewal when it passed Resolution D039, which identified monogamy, fidelity, holy love, and other characteristics of lifelong, committed relationships. Significantly, that resolution was framed as a way to enable the Church to engage more effectively in its mission. Many in the Episcopal Church have witnessed these characteristics in the committed relationships of same-sex couples. That recognition can, and in many places already has, broadened the understanding of the Church's mission of participating in God's reconciling work in the world.

A Theology of Blessing

We understand the celebration and blessing of committed, monogamous, lifelong, faithful same-sex relationships as part of the Church's work of offering outward and visible signs of God's grace among us. "Blessing" exhibits a multifaceted character, yet the Church has always affirmed that blessing originates in God, the giver of every good gift. The Church participates in God's blessing of committed, covenantal couples in three intertwined aspects: first, we thank God for the grace already discerned in the lives of the couple; second, we ask God's continual favor so that the couple may manifest more fully the fruits of the Spirit in their lives; and third, we seek the empowerment of the Holy Spirit as the Church commissions the couple to bear witness to the gospel in the world.

This threefold character of blessing, therefore, acknowledges what is already present—God's goodness. The Church's blessing also sets the relationship apart for God's purposes and prays for the divine grace the couple will need to fulfill those purposes. Just as the blessing of bread and wine at the eucharist sets them apart from ordinary usage and designates them for a particular, sacred purpose, so the public affirmation of divine blessing in a covenantal relationship sets that relationship apart from other types of relationship.

The Church expects the blessing of a covenantal relationship to bear the fruits of divine grace in particular ways—and always with God's continual help and favor. This makes the couple accountable to the community of faith as well as to God and to one another. The community, in turn, is held accountable for encouraging, supporting, and nurturing a blessed relationship as the couple seeks to grow together in holiness of life. Through its participation in the blessing

of covenantal relationships, the Church is blessed by the goodness
of God, who continues to offer blessings in abundance, regardless of
merit or circumstance. As we live more fully into our call to discern,
pronounce, seek, and return blessing wherever it may be found, we
find that we ourselves are blessed with joy.

Covenantal Relationship

Reflecting theologically on same-sex relationships can become an
occasion for the Church to reflect more broadly on the significance
of covenantal commitment in the life of faith. Both Scripture and
our theological traditions invite us to consider, first, the *sacramental
character* of covenantal relationships; by this we mean the potential of
such relationships to become outward and visible signs of God's grace.
And second, covenantal relationships can both reflect and inspire the
eschatological vision of Christian life. The covenantal commitments
we make with each other, in other words, can evoke our desire for
union with God, which is our final hope in Christ.

Our understanding of covenant thus derives first and foremost from
the gracious covenant God makes with us in Christ. The many types
of relational commitments we make carry the potential to reflect and
bear witness to that divine covenant. Here we have especially in mind
the covenants made by intimate couples in the sacred vows they make
to enter into a public, lifelong relationship of faithful monogamy.

Scripture and Christian tradition encourage us to see in these intimate
relationships a reflection of God's own desire for us. The long
tradition of commentary on the biblical Song of Songs, for example,
illustrates this spiritual significance of sexual relationships. Hebrew
prophets likewise turned frequently to the metaphor of marriage
to describe God's commitment to Israel (Isaiah 62:5), an image the
Pauline writer also used to describe the relationship of Christ and the
Church (Ephesians 5:21–33).

Covenantal commitments are thus shaped by and can also reflect
the paschal mystery of Christ's death and resurrection, which the
Church celebrates in baptism and eucharist. Intimate couples who
live in a sacred covenant find themselves swept up into a grand and
risky endeavor: to see if they can find their life in God by giving it
to another. This dynamic reflects the baptismal life all of us share as
Christians. As we live out our baptismal vows throughout our lives,
we are called to follow this pattern of God's self-giving desire and
love.

In the eucharist, we recall Christ's willingness to give his life for the world: "This is my body, given for you." When two people give their lives, their bodies, to one another in a lifelong covenant, they can discover and show how in giving ourselves we find ourselves (Matthew 16:25). When the Church pronounces God's blessing on the vows of lifelong fidelity—for different-sex and same-sex couples alike—the Church makes a bold claim: the paschal mystery is the very root and source of life in the couple's relationship.

This sacramental framework in which to reflect on same-sex relationships has, in turn, led us to consider more carefully several other key theological themes: the *vocational* aspect of covenantal relationship; how such a vocation is lived in Christian *households*; the *fruitfulness* of covenantal relationships in lives of service, generosity, and hospitality; and *mutual blessing*, as God's blessing in covenantal relationship becomes a blessing to the wider community.

Christian Unity and Biblical Interpretation

Baptism binds us to God by binding us to one another. Salvation is inherently social and communal. This bond, furthermore, does not depend on our agreement with one another but instead relies on what God has done and is doing among us. In fact, our unity in God gives us room to disagree safely, ideally without threat of breaking our unity, which is God's own gift. This principle is the very foundation of all covenants, beginning with the covenant between God and God's people, exemplified in baptism, reflected in ordained ministry, lived in vowed religious life and marriage, and encompassing the life of the Church. Our common call as God's people is not to find unanimity in all matters of faith and morals, but to go out into all nations as witnesses to the good news of God in Christ.

Most Christians would, nonetheless, recognize limits to acceptable and legitimate differences. Beyond such limits, unity becomes untenable. Those limits then pose difficult questions: How far is too far? What kind of difference would constitute essential disunity? In the debate over same-sex relationships and biblical interpretation, Episcopalians and other Christians throughout the Anglican Communion have disagreed about the answers to these questions. Some Episcopalians have concluded that blessing such relationships has gone too far and, acting on their conscience, have parted company with the Episcopal Church, while others who disagree have chosen to remain. As a Church, we continue to take different approaches to interpreting Scripture as we consider same-sex relationships.

We who differ profoundly and yet desire unity more profoundly recall that the Church has held this creative tension in the past. In Acts 15, we see that Paul differed from the community in Jerusalem over whether circumcision and the observation of dietary laws should be required of Gentiles in order for them to be baptized into Christ's Body. This difference was a matter of biblical interpretation. As Church members held the tension between their essential unity and their differences in how they understood Scripture, they found themselves guided by the Holy Spirit.[8]

Since then, the Church has faced many other similar times of wrestling over differing views of Scripture concerning a wide range of questions: whether vowed religious life takes priority over marriage, the prohibition on lending money at interest, polygamous households, divorce and remarriage, contraception, the institution of slavery, and the role of women in both Church and society, to name just a few. In all these times, the Church has sought to follow the apostolic process of prayerful deliberation, which respects the centrality of Scripture and attends carefully to the Spirit's work among us. This process will not resolve all of our disagreements, but we continue to trust in the unity that comes not from our own efforts but as God's gift to us and for which Christ himself prayed (John 17:11).

⤫

The following four sections expand on all of these theological themes and considerations, and we offer them to the wider Church for ongoing, shared discernment as the Body of Christ. No one perspective or community can fully capture the fullness of the truth into which the Spirit of God continually leads the Church. In this work, then, as in every other matter of concern for the Church's life and mission, we take to heart Paul's reminder that now "we know only in part" while awaiting that day when "the partial will come to an end" (1 Corinthians 13:9–10). In that spirit of humility, in which no one knows fully, we offer this theological resource on the blessing of same-sex relationships, trusting that it reflects a shared faith in the gospel of Jesus Christ, inspires hope for that union with God which Christ has promised, and, above all, expresses that love which shall not end (1 Corinthians 13:8).

---

8 This process of discernment over scriptural interpretation guided by the Holy Spirit has shaped every era in Christian history, including Anglican approaches. See "An Outline of the Faith," BCP, 853–54.

1. The Church's Call: A Focus on Mission

> If anyone is in Christ, there is a new creation: everything old
> has passed away; see, everything has become new! All this is
> from God, who reconciled us to himself through Christ, and
> has given us the ministry of reconciliation; that is, in Christ
> God was reconciling the world to himself, not counting
> their trespasses against them, and entrusting the message of
> reconciliation to us.
>
> — 2 Corinthians 5:17-19

The meaning and character of blessing play an important role in our
shared calling to participate in God's own mission of reconciling
love in the world. Pronouncing divine blessing takes many forms
covering a wide range of occasions. When the Church gathers to
bless the exchanging of sacred vows in a covenantal relationship, the
blessing reflects a threefold action. First, the Church gives thanks for
the presence of the Spirit discerned in the lives of the couple. Second,
the Church prays for the divine grace and favor the couple will
need to live into their commitment to each other with love, fidelity,
and holiness of life. And third, the Church commissions the couple
to participate in God's own mission in the world. This missional
character of covenantal blessing, reflected in both Scripture and the
historical traditions of the Church, deserves renewed attention today.
While the Church gives thanks for God's presence and blessing, the
public affirmation of the blessing of a covenantal relationship also sets
that relationship apart for a sacred purpose: to bear witness to the
creating, redeeming, and sustaining love of God.

God's promise to Abraham sets the tone for this missional
understanding of blessing: "I will bless you, and make your name
great, so that you will be a blessing" (Genesis 12:2b). Through Moses,

God's promise extends to the divine covenant with Israel, a people
God chooses to receive divine gifts of protection, guidance, and
fruitfulness. In this covenantal relationship, God makes the people of
Israel the stewards of these gifts, not for their sake only, but to become
a blessing for the world. As God declared to Jacob: "All the families
of the earth shall be blessed in you and in your offspring" (Genesis
28:14b). And as God also declared through Isaiah: "It is too light a
thing that you should be my servant to raise up the tribes of Jacob and
to restore the survivors of Israel; I will give you as a light to the
nations, that my salvation may reach to the end of the earth" (Isaiah
49:6).

The earliest Christians likewise adopted this missional understanding
of covenantal blessing as they recognized that the grace they received
in Christ was not for themselves alone but so that they could bear
witness to that grace "in Jerusalem, in all Judea and Samaria, and to
the ends of the earth" (Acts 1:8). Jesus urged this view of the life of
faith by reminding his listeners that "no one after lighting a lamp puts
it under the bushel basket, but on the lampstand, and it gives light
to all in the house" (Matthew 5:15). In John's Gospel, Jesus models
this divine mission by washing his disciples' feet. This act of intimate
service provided the example his disciples were to follow in blessing
others with the same life of service (John 13:14–15); the love God
shows for us in Christ, in other words, becomes a blessing for mission
and ministry. The covenant of grace God has made with us in Christ
thus calls all of us to that life of service: "Like good stewards of the
manifold grace of God, serve one another with whatever gift each of
you has received" (1 Peter 4:10).

Worship and Mission: An Eschatological Vision

Whenever the people of God gather for worship, we return to this
foundational view in Scripture: God continues to bless us through
our covenantal relationship with Christ, and this blessing enables and
empowers us to provide a blessing to others. In all of the Church's
rites, from the Daily Office to the Holy Eucharist, we give thanks for
God's blessings, and we pray for the grace we need to manifest that
blessing in the world, to "do the work [God has] given us to do."[9]
This pattern appears in the marriage rite as well, which celebrates
God's blessing on loving commitment, not for the sake of the couple
alone, but for the world, which stands in need of such witness to love
and faithfulness. In that rite, the assembly prays for the couple, that
God will "make their life together a sign of Christ's love to this sinful

---

9 Postcommunion Prayer, BCP, 366.

and broken world, that unity may overcome estrangement, forgiveness heal guilt, and joy conquer despair."[10] God's covenantal blessing empowers the couple as missionaries of grace.

Moreover, the Church blesses and sends in order to lay claim to our part in the fulfillment of salvation history; we collaborate with God as both proclaimers of and instruments for the new creation God is bringing about. "The redemption of the world is not finished, and so human history is not finished. History is going somewhere, and it is not there yet," one theologian reminds us. "The church exists to be the thing that God is doing, and to become the thing that God will be doing until the End." What God has done and will continue to do in the life of the Church manifests "not just the inherent goodness of creation but the possibility of *new* creation, of healing and justice and forgiveness." And so the Church blesses in order to fulfill its "'eschatological' project of becoming the kingdom."[11]

This eschatological vision of the Church's life of worship and mission carries the potential to deepen our shared reflection on the meaning of blessing itself. In blessing and being blessed, we join in the great work of redemption that God has always been doing, is doing now, and will do until the End. Indeed, this expansive view of blessing, rooted deeply in the covenant God has made with us in Christ, led Paul to declare that God's own mission of reconciliation has been entrusted to all those who have been blessed by this promise of a new creation (2 Corinthians 5:17–19).

Same-Sex Relationships and the Church's Mission

In responding to the call to participate in God's mission in the world, the Church must attend carefully to the particular cultural circumstances in which it proclaims the hope of the gospel. Over the last sixty years in the United States (among other places), social, psychological, and biomedical sciences have contributed to a gradual shift in cultural perspectives on the complexity of sexual orientation and gender identity. The American Psychiatric Association, for example, no longer considers homosexuality to be a pathological condition,[12] which it did in the mid-twentieth century. Gay and lesbian

---

10 BCP, 429.

11 Charles Hefling, "What Do We Bless and Why?" *Anglican Theological Review* 85:1 (Winter 2003): 91–93.

12 "All major professional mental health organizations have gone on record to affirm that homosexuality is not a mental disorder. In 1973, the American Psychiatric Association removed homosexuality from its official diagnostic manual, the *Diagnostic and Statistical Manual of Mental Disorders (DSM)*." From "Let's Talk Facts about Sexual Orientation," produced by the American Psychiatric Association, http://www.healthyminds.org/

people now participate openly in nearly every profession and aspect of life. Many openly form stable and enduring relationships and some also raise children in their families. Many churches, including the Episcopal Church, have also discerned in same-sex relationships the same possibility of holiness of life and the fruits of the Spirit that we pray for in those who seek the commitment of marriage and its blessings.[13]

This cultural shift concerning human sexuality bears on the Church's pastoral care and also on its mission. The 2000 General Convention, for example, identified certain characteristics that the Church expects of all couples in lifelong, committed relationships: "fidelity, monogamy, mutual affection and respect, careful, honest communication, and the holy love that enables those in such relationships to see in each other the image of God."[14] Significantly, the Convention framed that resolution as a matter of *mission*. Witnessing the Spirit at work in same-sex relationships, just as we do in different-sex relationships, can and in many places already has broadened the Church's understanding of how it participates in God's own reconciling work in the world.

Many gay and lesbian people (among others) who see same-sex couples exchange vows and receive a blessing are moved, likewise, to seek the Church's support for deepening their own commitments and faithfulness. They, in turn, offer their gifts for ministry to the wider community, gifts that contribute to the Church's mission to "restore all people to unity with God and each other in Christ."[15] When the Church pronounces God's blessing on same-sex couples who are also raising children, those children can understand better the sanctity of their own family, and the family itself can receive the same support and encouragement from the Church that different-sex couples receive for their families. The blessing of same-sex relationships in the community of faith can also become an occasion for reconciliation among estranged family members, including those who have not understood or have even rejected their lesbian and gay relatives.

Heterosexual people may also find their own vocations and ministries strengthened and empowered in those moments of blessing, as they

Document-Library/Brochure-Library/Lets-Talk-Facts-Sexual-Orientation.aspx?FT=.pdf.

13 *To Set Our Hope on Christ,* 24–25. For a broader overview and analysis, see the collection of essays edited by Walter Wink, *Homosexuality and Christian Faith: Questions of Conscience for the Churches* (Minneapolis: Fortress Press, 1999).

14 General Convention Resolution 2000–D039. Scripture reflects a similar approach to discerning evidence of divine grace and the Spirit's work when, for example, Jesus uses the analogy of assessing the goodness of a tree based on the kind of fruit it bears (Matthew 7:16–18 and Luke 6:43).

15 "An Outline of the Faith," BCP, 855.

may do at the celebration of a marriage, or at the public profession
of commitment to a particular ministry or community. In other
words, the gifts lesbians and gay men discern in their own lives
and committed relationships are not just for themselves alone. One
Episcopal priest has observed, "Over and over again, we see lesbians
and gay men, people who would have been hiding in the shadows
of our church a generation ago, now coming forward to contribute
their gifts, their strength and loyalty and wisdom, freely and openly
to the whole community of faith. And heterosexual people who have
seen this happening have also been freed to give more generously of
themselves."[16]

Friends of same-sex couples and many others in the general public also
take note of these moments of blessing, encountering the expansive
and generous reach of gospel welcome. As friends witness the grace
of these covenantal commitments, and the generosity of the Church's
embrace, many of them will be drawn to the community of faith,
perhaps for the first time or after having left. Such has already been
the case in many congregations and dioceses in the Episcopal Church.

The Challenge of God's Blessing for Mission

Scripture attests to significant moments in which biblical writers
challenged their communities to expand their vision of God's saving
work in the world or in which the writers were themselves challenged
by that divine word to see past their present horizons. The ancient
Israelites, for example, had to struggle with how far the blessing of
their covenantal life would reach. Isaiah urged them to see all the
nations—not just their own—streaming to God's holy mountain
(Isaiah 2:1–4). The early Church was no exception to this struggle.

In the Acts of the Apostles, we read about Peter's hesitation to cross
traditional boundaries between the clean and the unclean in his
encounter with Cornelius, a Roman centurion (Acts 10). In a vision,
Peter heard God urging him to eat certain unclean animals in direct
disobedience to the injunctions found in Leviticus 11. This vision led
Peter to consider anew whether God's saving work and blessing might
be found in places and among particular people he had not before
considered possible. When challenged about this expansive vision,
Peter declared, "God has shown me that I should not call anyone

---

16 L. William Countryman, "The Big House of Classic Anglicanism," from a speech given
   at the Claiming the Blessing Conference in St. Louis, Missouri, in November 2002 and
   quoted in *Claiming the Blessing*, the theology statement of the Claiming the Blessing
   coalition, page 11; http://www.claimingtheblessing.org/files/pdf/CTBTheology_Final_.pdf.

profane or unclean" (Acts 10:28). To those who were startled and
perhaps scandalized by the extension of the gospel to Gentiles, Peter
asked, "Can anyone withhold the water for baptizing these people
who have received the Holy Spirit just as we have?" (Acts 10:47).[17]

Time after time in the history of Israel and in the early Church,
responding to the challenge of God's extravagant grace and the
richness of divine blessing has expanded the mission of God's people
in the world, even beyond where many had previously imagined.
The loving faithfulness and covenantal commitment of lesbian and
gay couples presents a similar challenge to the Church today. Many
throughout the Episcopal Church and other Christian communions
have recognized and discerned the Spirit's presence and work in these
same-sex relationships, and are asking God's people to ponder why
we would withhold a public affirmation and declaration of blessing
from those who have received the Holy Spirit just as others have.
More importantly, however, this moment in the Episcopal Church's
life calls all of us to consider anew the rich blessings we receive by
God's grace in Christ and through the Holy Spirit. These blessings, in
turn, animate the ministry of reconciliation that God has given us as
ambassadors of the new creation that is unfolding, even now, in our
midst.

---

17 Paul describes his confrontation with Peter about these very issues in Galatians 2:1–21.

2. The Church's Joy: A Theology of Blessing

Whoever invokes a blessing in the land shall bless by the God of faithfulness.

— Isaiah 65:16

The disciples were continually in the temple blessing God.

— Luke 24:53

"Blessed are you, Lord God, ruler of the universe, who created everything for your glory!" This classic blessing in Jewish tradition sets the tone for any theological reflection on what it means to bless and to receive a blessing. Rather than ourselves, other people, animals, places, or things, God's people first and foremost bless God, the giver of life and creator of all. Discerning and giving thanks for the countless reasons that we can and should bless God are, therefore, at the heart of the Church's work in the world. Indeed, at the heart of Christian worship is the eucharist, or "thanksgiving," in which we lift up the "cup of blessing" (1 Corinthians 10:16).

In Anglican contexts, the Church's work in the world is shaped by common prayer and worship. In addition to reading the Scriptures and prayerful meditation, Anglicans have always relied on our shared liturgical life for discerning where God is present and how God is calling us to live in the world as witnesses to the gospel of Jesus Christ in the power of the Holy Spirit. While God is active always and everywhere, the community of faith gathers to discern God's activity and make it ever more visible.

Although ordained ministers are called to the Church's work in a particular way, they share the work with the whole community of the baptized. In their sacramental vocation, ordained ministers lead the community in offering outward and visible signs of the inward and spiritual grace that is present among God's people. Clergy do not, in other words, "create grace" where there was none to be found already; rather, the whole Body of Christ, in many and various ways, proclaims God's gracious activity in our midst. This proclamation offers the assurance of God's grace promised to us in Christ Jesus and offers support as we strive to manifest the fruits of the Spirit in our daily lives.

Many in the Episcopal Church and other Christian communions believe that the celebration and blessing of the covenantal commitment of a same-sex couple also belongs in the Church's work of offering outward and visible signs of God's grace. While "blessing" exhibits a multifaceted meaning, it always originates in God, which the Church rightly and daily acknowledges: "We bless you for our creation, preservation, and all the blessings of this life; but above all for your immeasurable love in the redemption of the world by our Lord Jesus Christ; for the means of grace, and for the hope of glory."[18]

The Church participates in this fundamental, divine blessing in three related ways: thanking God for God's goodness and favor; seeking God's continued favor and grace so that we may manifest more fully that gratitude in our lives; and receiving power from the Holy Spirit to bear witness to that grace in the world. This threefold character of blessing acknowledges what is already present, God's grace, but it does something more as well: it establishes a new reality. Bread and wine, for example, when blessed at the eucharistic table, are set apart from their ordinary use and designated for a particular, sacred purpose. Similarly, the public affirmation of divine blessing in a covenantal relationship sets that relationship apart from other types. God's people expect such a blessing to bear the fruits of God's grace in particular ways, making a couple in such a blessed covenant accountable to the community of faith, as well as to God and to each other. The community, in turn, is held accountable for encouraging, supporting, and nurturing a blessed relationship as the couple seeks to grow together in holiness of life.

In short, the grace and blessing of God already discerned in a couple's relationship does not thereby render a liturgical rite of blessing redundant. To the contrary, the Church's blessing performs what it declares, thus changing the couple and the Church. The couple becomes more fully aware of God's favor and also receives a particular role, as a couple, in the Church's mission in the world; the Church is likewise changed, as holiness of life is made more visible and as it receives and accepts its commission to support the couple in their life and ministry.

18 "The General Thanksgiving," BCP, 125.

Scripture guides us in this understanding of blessing by placing it in relation to both creation and covenant. In Genesis, God declares the whole creation good, a source of blessing for which we thank God, the giver of every good gift. This blessing is manifested in more particular ways in the covenant God makes with Noah and, by extension, the whole of the creation (Genesis 9:8–16), with Abraham (Genesis 12:2–3), and, through Moses, with the people of Israel (Deuteronomy 7:12–14). Likewise, the New Testament reflects God's blessing on all creation, as the Word of God becomes flesh in Jesus; it reflects the blessing of covenant as well, as the life, death, and resurrection of Jesus reconcile us with God and assure us of God's loving faithfulness toward us and the whole creation. In his final meal with his disciples, Jesus blessed God for the bread and cup as signs of the new covenant (Matthew 26:26–29). The blessing we receive by participating in that meal at the eucharistic table strengthens us to live out in all of our relationships the forgiveness and reconciliation to which that meal calls us.

Scripture bears witness to the relational character of blessing: being in relationship with God is not only a blessing for us, but becomes a blessing to others as well. God's covenant with Israel becomes a blessing not for Israel alone but for "all the nations." This is the very promise made to Abraham: "in you all the families of the earth shall be blessed" (Genesis 12:3b). The extent of this divine blessing unfolded in Israel's self-awareness over time and in various ways. "All the nations" referred, of course, to Gentiles, the very ones many in Israel had not expected to share in God's promises. God's blessing thus expands the reach of welcome and hospitality not only to the near and familiar neighbor, but also to the distant stranger, who is made neighbor because of God's own generosity. As Paul noted, through faith "in Christ Jesus the blessing of Abraham might come to the Gentiles, so that we might receive the promise of the Spirit through faith" (Galatians 3:14). The blessing of God's covenant with us in Christ empowers us, through the Spirit, to offer such expansive and generous blessing to the world, in thought, word, and deed. God's blessings inspire us in countless ways to live as emissaries of divine blessing in all that we do—in our work, our play, and our relationships. In all of this, God's goodness in our lives becomes a blessing to others, to neighbors both near and far.

As Christians, baptism and eucharist focus our attention on the particular blessings of the paschal mystery of Christ's death and resurrection. Those blessings, in turn, encourage us to discern the many other ways God's blessing is manifested in both creation and covenant. The goodness of God makes everything in creation a potential vehicle for blessing, including the love and faithfulness of covenantal relationship, in which we experience our call to manifest divine goodness. Thus, the Church is continually discerning where the goodness of God, the grace of Christ, and the gifts of the Holy Spirit are urging the Church to manifest God's blessing for others and, in response, to bless God with hearts and lives marked by gratitude and praise.

Another aspect of the biblical witness deserves attention as well: the emphasis on *abundance*. In the midst of desert wanderings, Moses struck a rock and "water came out abundantly" for the people of Israel (Numbers 20:11). "Like the vine," we read in Ecclesiasticus, "I bud forth delights, and my blossoms become glorious and abundant fruit" (Ecclesiasticus 24:17). "You prepare a table before me," declares the psalmist, and "my cup overflows" (Psalm 23:5). "Give," Jesus says, "and it will be given to you. A good measure, pressed down, shaken together, running over, will be put into your lap" (Luke 6:38). And to the Christians in Corinth, Paul declares, "God is able to provide you with every blessing in abundance, so that by always having enough of everything, you may share abundantly in every good work" (2 Corinthians 9:8). Scripture invites us, in other words, to see the blessing of God's goodness, not as a scarce commodity either to hoard or to protect, but rather as an unending font of deathless love and perpetual grace—a veritable embarrassment of divine riches. In sacred covenantal relationship, God's abundance is exhibited in many ways, including the companionship, friendship, and mutual joy of intimacy. By affirming and publicly acknowledging that blessing of abundance already present in vibrant covenantal relationships, including same-sex relationships, the Church expects those relationships to manifest the grace of God, the gifts of the Spirit, and holiness of life.

Jesus' iconic parable about the prodigal son adds a further layer to this biblical witness to God's abundant love and grace. In this story, God pours out the abundance of divine blessing on all, regardless of merit or circumstance. When the prodigal son decides at last to return to his father's house, hoping to be granted, at best, the status of a slave, his father rushes to meet him and welcome him home, and even prepares a lavish feast in his honor. "While he was still far off," Jesus says, and thus well before the son could speak any words of repentance, "his father saw him and was filled with compassion; he ran and put his arms around him and kissed him" (Luke 15:20). In our lives, as in the parable, God showers us with blessings so that we may receive life abundantly, even though we have in no way earned these blessings.

This parable suggests that the abundance of this household is more than sufficient to open outward to receive the younger son. The abundance of this household is even more than sufficient for the resentful elder son, who begrudges such celebration for his wayward brother. The household brims with abundance, if only the elder son would open his heart to receive it (Luke 15:29–31). Both sons in Jesus' parable stand as potent reminders that the blessing of divine goodness does not automatically transform lives: we must be willing to receive such blessing. And yet even when we are not willing, God will continue to offer blessings in abundance. The teachings of Jesus return to this theme repeatedly, as in the parables of the sower (Mark 4:3–8) and the wedding banquet (Matthew 22:1–10), as well as the feeding of more than five thousand with just five loaves of bread and two fish (Luke 9:12–17).

The Church's participation in divine blessing can help each of us in various ways to be open to God's abundant goodness. The Church's liturgical life, that is, our practice of common prayer and worship, can create space for God's people to open their hearts and minds to receiving the blessing God offers. For those in a covenantal relationship, that intentional space (for both hearing the word of blessing in their lives and blessing God in return) marks a significant, even an essential deepening and strengthening of their lives with each other, with their community, and with God. In blessing covenantal relationships, just as in the eucharist, we give thanks for God's abundant goodness and pray for the continued presence of the Spirit to empower us to do the work God has given us to do in the world. The blessing of the eucharistic table sets us apart as the Body of Christ in the world, called and empowered to proclaim the gospel, just as the blessing of a covenantal relationship sets that relationship apart as "a sign of Christ's love to this sinful and broken world, that unity may overcome estrangement, forgiveness heal guilt, and joy conquer despair."[19]

Discerning, pronouncing, seeking, and returning blessing describe well the Church's work. Even more, it is the Church's *joy*. Paul urged the Christians in Rome to "rejoice with those who rejoice, weep with those who weep" (Romans 12:15). The early Christians gave themselves to such rejoicing, as they were "continually in the temple blessing God" in their celebration of Christ's victory over death (Luke 24:53). Whenever and wherever the Church discerns particular instances of God's abundant goodness, the Church rightly thanks God for such a gift. We also ask God for the grace to live into that gift more fully, as we joyfully bear witness to that blessing in the world.

---

19 The Celebration and Blessing of a Marriage, BCP, 429.

3. The Church's Life: Covenantal Relationship

Do you not know that all of us who have been baptized into Christ Jesus were baptized into his death? Therefore we have been buried with him by baptism into death, so that, just as Christ was raised from the dead by the glory of the Father, so we too might walk in newness of life.

— Romans 6:3-4

Creation, Baptism, and Eucharist

Covenants have taken many different forms across time and in diverse cultural contexts. Both Scripture and Christian history exhibit that diversity as well. The most familiar covenantal relationship is marriage, to which both the Hebrew prophets and New Testament writers turned as a way to describe God's desire and commitment to be in relationship with us (Isaiah 62:5, Ephesians 5:21–33). Marriage itself has exhibited a variety of forms over the centuries yet still provides a pattern for a number of significant covenantal relationships, such as the vowed religious life or ordained ministry.

In 2000, General Convention identified certain characteristics that the Church expects to see in lifelong, committed relationships: "fidelity, monogamy, mutual affection and respect, careful, honest communication, and the holy love which enables those in such relationships to see in each other the image of God" (Resolution D039). These characteristics describe well what we mean by "covenant" as we have reflected theologically on same-sex relationships. A couple enacts their decision to enter into a lifelong commitment of fidelity and accountability in the context of God's household, the Church, by exchanging vows, and the Church responds by pronouncing God's blessing. Covenantal relationship then carries the potential to reflect for the Church the gracious covenant God has made with us in the paschal mystery of Christ's death and resurrection, which the Church celebrates in baptism and eucharist.

Some will find this kind of theological reflection on same-sex relationships unfamiliar and perhaps unwarranted. Many different-sex couples would likewise find this to be a new way of thinking about their own marital vows. Thus, General Convention Resolution 2009–C056, which called for these theological resources, becomes an opportunity for reflecting more broadly on the role of covenantal relationship in the life of the Church. In doing so, the blessing of same-sex relationships can then be understood within the broader framework of the Church's sacramental life and its mission in the world.

The framework for covenantal relationship begins with God's own declaration of the goodness of creation (Genesis 1:31). That goodness inspires us to give thanks to God, the creator of all things. The heavens declare God's glory, the psalmist reminds us, and the earth proclaims God's handiwork (Psalm 19:1). Thus, even in creation's fragility, limitation, and affliction, the biblical writers discerned signs of God's providential power, sustaining love, and saving grace. The Church celebrates God's goodness in worship and with sacramental signs of God's blessing. These "outward and visible signs of inward and spiritual grace" manifest God's transforming presence and so are "sure and certain means by which we receive that grace."[20] Chief among these signs are baptism and eucharist, which derive directly from the life and ministry of Jesus Christ. Reconciliation, confirmation, marriage, ordination, and unction also manifest the grace of God at key moments in Christian life, each in its own way, yet these are by no means the only occasions that do so.[21] As disciples of Jesus, the incarnate Word of God, we are called to make God's creating, redeeming, and sustaining love known in all things, in all circumstances, and throughout our daily lives and relationships. The sacramental life of the Church focuses that calling in particular ways.

Baptism and eucharist recapitulate the arc of salvation history in creation, sin, judgment, repentance, and redemption, or the fulfillment of the whole creation in the presence of God.[22] In baptism, we are incorporated into the paschal mystery of Christ's death and resurrection, and we are empowered by the Holy Spirit to live

---

20 "An Outline of the Faith," BCP, 857.
21 "An Outline of the Faith," BCP, 857–58, 861.
22 See "Thanksgiving over the Water," BCP, 306–307; Romans 8:18–25; and 1 Corinthians 15:28.

more fully into the holiness of life to which God calls all of us. This sacramental act manifests the eternal covenant God has made with us, declaring that we are God's own beloved, inheritors of God's promises, and God's friends;[23] we are sealed by God's own Spirit and marked as Christ's own forever.[24] This sign of God's covenant is irrevocable, not relying on our adherence to the covenant but rather on the grace and goodness of God in Christ Jesus. As members of the Body of Christ, we commit ourselves to live in the manner of life appropriate to the body to which we belong. This manner of life is summed up in the two great commandments: to love God with our whole being and to love our neighbors as ourselves.[25] Even though we inevitably fall far short of this commitment, God's steadfast love maintains the covenant God has made, and God both seeks and graciously enables our return to fidelity.

In the Episcopal Church, the significance of baptism for Christian faith and life became even clearer with the ratification of the 1979 *Book of Common Prayer*. The Baptismal Covenant shapes the rite of Holy Baptism by beginning with an affirmation of faith (the Apostles' Creed), followed by five distinct promises made by (or on behalf of) those being baptized: to continue in the apostles' teaching and fellowship; to persevere in resisting evil; to proclaim the Good News of God in Christ; to seek and serve Christ in all persons; and to strive for justice and peace, respecting the dignity of all persons.[26] The rite begins, in other words, with God's own Trinitarian mission of creating, redeeming, and sustaining love in the world. The promises we make are in response to that divine mission and constitute our vowed commitment to participate in that mission—and always "with God's help." This approach to baptismal theology continues to guide and inform our prayerful discernment as Episcopalians, which is rooted first and foremost in the covenant God makes with us through the Word of God made flesh (John 1:14).[27]

In the redemptive work of the Incarnation, God draws the whole creation back into union with God, lifting it up through the resurrection and ascension of Christ toward its perfection, when God will be all in all (1 Corinthians 15:28). In the eucharist we celebrate this transformative action, accomplished through Christ's self-giving

---

23 "I do not call you servants any longer, ... but I have called you friends" (John 15:15). See also Gregory of Nyssa, who understood our incorporation into the Body of Christ to make us God's own "friends" (*Orat. in 1 Cor. xv.28*).

24 Holy Baptism, BCP, 308.

25 See Deuteronomy 6:5, Leviticus 19:18, and Matthew 22:37–40.

26 BCP, 304–305.

27 See Louis Weil, *A Theology of Worship*, The New Church's Teaching Series, vol. 12 (Cambridge, MA: Cowley Publications, 2002), 11–22.

of his own Body and Blood, which nourishes our bodies and souls, equipping us to participate in God's own mission of reconciliation in the world.

In the eucharist, our fragmented lives are gathered together into one offering to God, the giver of all good things. As a community gathered in prayer, we reaffirm our participation in God's covenant as we hear God's holy word, confess and receive forgiveness of our sins, and join with the whole company of saints in prayer for the Church and the world. God receives the gifts we bring, limited and flawed as they may be, blesses them, and then returns them to us as bread from heaven. As we are nourished by the Body and Blood of Christ, we are formed ever deeper in holiness of life, conforming to the likeness of Christ. At the table, we are given a foretaste of the heavenly banquet in which all are gathered to God, a foretaste that clarifies and strengthens our longing to witness to God's love. As we are blessed and sent out, we are empowered by the Holy Spirit to participate in God's work of bringing all things to that sanctification and fullness for which God created them. Moreover, as we celebrate eucharist together, we recall all the other tables that we gather around in our various households and come to see them as places where Christ is present. This eucharistic pattern—often described with the actions *take, bless, break,* and *give*—shapes all the relationships that we bring into our baptismal life with God. We *take* these relationships, *bless* God for their goodness, ask God to bless them and *break* them open further to divine grace, so that we may *give* them to the world as witnesses to the gospel of Jesus Christ.

Baptism and eucharist, as sacraments of God's covenant of creating, redeeming, and sustaining love, shape our lives as Christians in relation to God and to God's creation; this calls us to live with love, compassion, justice, and peace toward all creatures, friend or foe, neighbor or stranger. We are not only called to live in this way but also strengthened to do so by our participation in these sacramental acts. The sacramental life of the Church strengthens us to give ourselves and to receive others as we contribute to the coming of God's realm "on earth as it is in heaven" (Matthew 6:10) and proclaim Christ until he comes again (1 Corinthians 11:26).

Through baptism and eucharist we are brought into and sustained in all these many and various relationships. First and foremost among them is our relationship with the God who creates, redeems, and sustains us. We also participate in countless other relationships with the many diverse people, communities, and institutions that we encounter throughout the world. All of these relationships call us to bear witness to the gospel precisely because our lives as creatures of God are constituted in relation; we are created in the Trinitarian image of God, an image that is inherently relational and rooted and grounded in love.[28]

Accordingly, same-sex relationships belong in that extensive network of relations in which we are called to bear witness to the gospel. In the next section, we consider the blessing of same-sex relationships in that broader context, beginning with the fundamental call all of us share to love our neighbors as ourselves. Since God calls us into particular forms of loving commitments with others, we turn in the following sections to three interrelated aspects of that calling: covenant-making, intentional Christian households, and faithful intimacy.

Loving Our Neighbors as Ourselves

Christians strive to model all of our relationships on the love, grace, and compassion of Christ, loving our neighbors, both near and distant, as we love ourselves. Loving others is possible only because of the grace of God, who first loved us (1 John 4:19). Baptism and eucharist continually send us out to all our neighbors, where we learn again and again the blessing of offering ourselves and receiving others in gospel hospitality.

Hospitality means more than good manners. Scripture regards hospitality toward both friend and stranger as evidence of covenantal obedience and fruitfulness.[29] The story of Sodom's destruction in Genesis 19, a particularly dramatic biblical reminder of the importance of hospitable relations, has been frequently cited by opponents of blessing same-sex relationships. However, such interpretations of this passage rely less on the biblical story itself than on the cultural reception of this story over many centuries of European history.[30]

The narrative in this passage turns on whether certain visitors to Sodom will be received graciously and hospitably by the city's

---

28 "An Outline of the Faith," BCP, 845.
29 See Exodus 22:21, Leviticus 19:34, Deuteronomy 24:19–21, Malachi 3:5, and Hebrews 13:2, among many others. For an overview and analysis of the centrality of hospitality in Scripture and in early Christianity, see Amos Yong, *Hospitality and the Other: Pentecost, Christian Practices, and the Neighbor* (Maryknoll, NY: Orbis Books, 2008).
30 The term "sodomy," for example, does not appear in Scripture, and what it has come to mean (including within North Atlantic jurisprudence) is not supported by the biblical references to it. See Jay Emerson Johnson, "Sodomy and Gendered Love: Reading Genesis 19 in the Anglican Communion," in *The Oxford Handbook of the Reception History of the Bible*, ed. Michael Lieb, Emma Mason, and Jonathan Roberts (Oxford: Oxford University Press, 2010), 413–34; and Michael Carden, *Sodomy: A History of a Christian Biblical Myth* (London: Equinox Publishing, 2004).

inhabitants or instead will be exploited and even raped. The sin of
Sodom's citizens thus refers explicitly to the codes of hospitality in the
ancient Near East rather than to same-sex sexual relations.[31] Other
biblical writers who refer to Sodom never highlight sexuality—or
mention it at all. Ezekiel's interpretation, for example, is quite direct:
"This was the guilt of your sister Sodom: she and her daughters had
pride, excess of food, and prosperous ease, but did not aid the poor
and needy" (Ezekiel 16:49).[32] Jesus evokes the story of Sodom not to
teach about sexual ethics but in the context of sending out his disciples
to minister. Those who do not receive his disciples, he promises, will
suffer a fate worse than the citizens of Sodom (Matthew 10:15). The
threat underscores the centrality of hospitality in that ancient story.[33]

As early as the 1950s, biblical scholars attempted to place Genesis 19
in its original cultural context and to revive an interpretive approach
to that story that resonated with the intrabiblical witness to it.[34] In
this interpretation, Genesis 19 applies to all people rather than only to
some, and the lesson for all is the primacy of hospitality, or the love
of neighbor, as Jesus himself commanded.[35] We manifest this love of
neighbor in countless ways, each instance shaped by the particular
individual or community we encounter, whether in our own family, or
with coworkers, or strangers.

Relationships, in other words, take many different forms. At times, we
choose particular relationships based on our own preferences, needs, or

---

31 The definition of "sodomy" varied widely throughout Christian history and coalesced
     exclusively around a particular sexual act between men only in the eleventh century; see
     Mark D. Jordan, *The Invention of Sodomy in Christian Theology* (Chicago: University of
     Chicago Press, 1997).
32 Ezekiel's description represents the approach most often taken by writers in the Hebrew
     Bible, in which the sin of Sodom is always associated with violence or injustice; see
     Robin Scroggs, *The New Testament and Homosexuality: Contextual Background for
     Contemporary Debate* (Philadelphia: Fortress Press, 1983). In the New Testament, Jude 7
     is sometimes cited as well, yet that verse does not describe "sexual immorality" precisely
     (it could refer to rape, for example); the "unnatural lust" of Sodom's inhabitants could
     also mean that the strangers sent to Sodom were actually angels (see Genesis 6:4).
33 Patristic writers viewed hospitality as central. See, for example, Origen, *Homilia V in
     Genesim* (PG 12:188–89): "Hear this, you who close your homes to guests! Hear this,
     you who shun the traveler as an enemy! Lot lived among the Sodomites. We do not read
     of any other good deeds of his ... [save] he opened his home to guests"; Ambrose of
     Milan, *De Abrahamo* 1:6:52 (PL 14:440): Lot "placed the hospitality of his house—sacred
     even among a barbarous people—above the modesty [of his daughters]." Cited by John
     Boswell, *Christianity, Tolerance, and Homosexuality: Gay People in Western Europe from
     the Beginning of the Christian Era to the Fourteenth Century* (Chicago: University of
     Chicago Press, 1980), 98.
34 One of the earliest examples of this approach was Derrick Sherwin Bailey, *Homosexuality
     and the Western Christian Tradition* (London: Longmans, Green, 1955).
35 Some biblical scholars continue to interpret the story as a condemnation of homosexual
     behavior. See, for example, Robert A. J. Gagnon, *The Bible and Homosexual Practice:
     Texts and Hermeneutics* (Nashville: Abingdon Press, 2001), 71–91.

desires; at other times, we are in relationships without a lot of choice, as with colleagues at work or fellow travelers. No matter which, the "neighbor" offers us an occasion for manifesting the love of God in Christ. The gospels proclaim not only the self-giving love Jesus showed to the disciples he chose, but also the love Jesus urged for the stranger encountered by chance, as in the parable of the good Samaritan (Luke 10:29–37). Christ sets the example for us to follow in all of our many and varied relationships, a model that respects the dignity of every person and that encourages giving oneself for the good of the other.[36] Relationships are "schools for virtue" and formation, that is, opportunities for us to form dispositions and habits that manifest Christ-like love.

As people joined with God and to each other by baptism and eucharist, we are called to embody in all of our relationships—those we may consider personal or private *and* those we consider corporate or public—a love that is both self-giving and other-receiving. As we endeavor to respond to this calling, we depend on God's grace as we are gradually brought by the Spirit into that union with God for which Christ himself prayed (John 17:11). We also serve as living proclamations of God's creative, redeeming, and sustaining love for the world. Given our limitations, that witness is inevitably imperfect and sometimes ambiguous, yet we continue to trust that all things are working together for good (Romans 8:28) as we shape our lives and relationships to the pattern of God's own love for us and for the world. That pattern may then lead into particular forms of commitment in which we discern a call to covenantal relationship.

Called into Covenant

Some loving relationships with our neighbors exhibit a particular depth of commitment, which can lead to an intentional covenant with another person or with a community. Scripture bears witness to the significance of covenant-making in many ways but especially as an expression of God's blessing, such as the covenant God makes with the whole of creation through Noah (Genesis 9:9–13) and with the people of Israel through Abraham (Genesis 12:2–3). Christians celebrate the covenant that Jesus proclaimed and enacted at the final meal he shared with his disciples (Luke 22:20) and which we mark with the "cup of blessing" (1 Corinthians 10:16) at the eucharistic table.

Scripture invites us, in other words, to see our covenantal commitments with each other as particular expressions of the love of both God and neighbor as well as expressions of God's blessing. As we

---

36 "The Baptismal Covenant," BCP, 305.

commit ourselves to the good of the other, we offer that commitment as a witness to God's covenantal love for the world. We discover God's blessing in these covenantal commitments as we are able, more and more, to manifest consistent regard and respect for the other, even as we struggle with our own limitations and flaws. We discover God's blessing even further as we realize, in ever newer ways, how a covenantal relationship can enhance and contribute to the well-being of others, of neighbors, strangers, the Church, and the world.

People who enter a covenant promise each other, a community, and God that their shared future will take a particular shape, one for which they intend to be held accountable, not only by their covenant partners but also by the wider community.[37] While the Canons of the Episcopal Church describe marriage as a union of a man and a woman, the patterns of marriage can help us understand other kinds of covenantal relationship, such as vowed religious life and the commitments of same-sex couples. In all of these covenantal relationships, the partners promise to be trustworthy, to remain faithful to one another despite other demands on their time and energy or possibilities for engagement with others. The partners promise to accompany and assist each other in faithfulness; they pledge their support for the well-being of the other. These relationships are directed toward vitality and fruitfulness as they contribute to human flourishing, within and beyond the relationship. The depth of this covenantal commitment means it is a *vocation*, a life of faithfulness to which some are called by God and which God blesses, so that, by God's grace, that blessing will be made manifest to the world.

Recognizing God's blessing and the work of the Spirit in relationships of lifelong commitment, the Church rightly celebrates these moments of covenantal vocation. This divine calling, discerned by a couple and their faith community, draws the Church deeper into God's own mission of redeeming and sanctifying love in the world. Christians express this calling in the ways we live our lives with others. Two of these ways deserve attention here: shaping households and deepening faithful intimacy.

The Vocation of Households

Households today are most often associated with marriage and child-rearing, yet this has not always been the case. The history of the Church offers a broader view of how households can bear witness to

---

37 See Margaret A. Farley, *Personal Commitments: Beginning, Keeping, Changing* (New York: HarperCollins, 1990).

the gospel. Since it is finally God, and not another human being or anything else in creation, that fulfills and completes us, some people feel called to remain unmarried or single. A single life, which is not necessarily the same as a solitary life, can be lived in households of various types. Living in this way can allow individuals to be more available as friends and companions; this is often the case with vowed religious life, such as a monastic calling. Indeed, for the first half of its history (more than a thousand years), the Church understood vowed religious life as a calling higher than marriage, a view that changed decisively only during the Protestant Reformation. The diverse forms of an intentional single life may afford greater opportunity for contemplation, service, and mission, which some people understand as a particular vocational calling into deeper relationship with God and the world. This seems to be Paul's understanding of the spiritual significance of remaining unmarried (1 Corinthians 7:25–32).

Paul also discusses human sexuality in relation to God's gracious covenant with us in Christ in the first chapter of his letter to the Romans. This chapter, especially verses 26–27, has been used to support the Church's reluctance to embrace the loving faithfulness of same-sex couples and continues to influence conversation in Christian communities.

In interpreting this Pauline passage, it is difficult to know precisely what Paul meant by "unnatural" in those verses and to whom he was addressing these concerns.[38] Significantly, Paul's description of sexual behavior in the first chapter appears in direct relation to his condemnation of idolatry. For Paul, the consequence—not the cause—of worshiping false gods is a distorted understanding of sexuality, its purpose and goal (Romans 1:22–23). In the Greco-Roman world of the first century, those distortions of sexuality with which Paul was most likely familiar included a range of practices associated with cults devoted to fertility gods and goddesses. Some interpreters have claimed that these cultic rituals may have included self-castration, drunken orgies, and sex with young male and female temple prostitutes.[39] Christians rightly condemn all those behaviors as

---

38 See L. William Countryman, *Dirt, Greed, and Sex: Sexual Ethics in the New Testament and Their Implications for Today*, revised edition (Minneapolis: Fortress Press, 2007), 119–123. See also Dale B. Martin, "Heterosexism and the Interpretation of Romans 1:18–32," in *Sex and the Single Savior: Gender and Sexuality in Biblical Interpretation* (Louisville: Westminster John Knox Press, 2006), 51–64. Some interpreters have noted that Paul uses the phrase often translated as "contrary to nature" in Romans 1 again in Romans 11:24 to describe the love of God in saving those same Gentiles; see William Stacy Johnson, *A Time to Embrace: Same-Gender Relationships in Religion, Law, and Politics* (Grand Rapids: Eerdmans Publishing Company, 2006), 98–99.

39 For the controversy over ancient fertility cults and the alleged sexual practices associated with them, see Robert A. Oden, Jr., *The Bible Without Theology: The Theological*

48

violations of the human body, the very temple of the Holy Spirit, Paul insisted (1 Corinthians 3:16–17). Moreover, some interpreters say, those alleged ancient cultic practices have nothing to do with today's same-sex Christian couples.[40]

Paul's broader insight, however, still compels the Church to continual discernment and assessment of its common life: proper worship corresponds directly to proper sexual relations. This insight can shed even further light on Paul's recommendation to the Christians in Corinth that they remain unmarried.

In the end, human sexual relationships of any kind are not the purpose or goal of human life. Instead, union with God in Christ is the goal for all, including the whole created order, as the rest of Paul's letter to the Romans makes clear (Romans 8:18–25). At their best, human relationships can only point us toward that final fulfillment. People who make an intentional decision to remain unmarried place important signposts on that spiritual journey to which all of us are called and in which nothing, including marriage, should supplant our primary devotion to God and to God's household, the Church.

Other types of relationships teach us that to prepare us for life with God, God can bind us with another for life. Thus, some (though not all) covenantal commitments are enacted in households, those intimate spaces where people encounter each other as their nearest neighbors daily and continually.[41] Clearly, the character, shape, and form of a household have varied enormously over time, from the patriarchal and polygamous families of ancient Israel to the family Jesus created between his mother and his beloved disciple (John 19:26–27) and the economic reordering of familial relations among early believers (Acts 4:32–37, 5:1–7). What "household" means and how people may be called, as a vocation, into covenantal households matter not only in light of historical differences but also in the midst of the wide range of household customs and organizational patterns found throughout the world today.

Appreciating the significant cultural differences between the households of ancient Israel and today's Western, nuclear families can also inform our interpretation of two biblical passages cited as a scriptural warrant for rejecting the loving faithfulness of same-sex

---

Tradition and Alternatives to It (San Francisco: Harper and Row, 1987), especially chapter 5, "Religious Identity and the Sacred Prostitution Accusation," 131–153.

40 See Martti Nissinen, Homoeroticism in the Biblical World: A Historical Perspective (Minneapolis: Fortress Press, 1998), 103–113.

41 Thomas E. Breidenthal, Christian Households: The Sanctification of Nearness (Eugene, Oregon: Wipf and Stock, 2004).

couples: Leviticus 18:22 and its analogue, 20:13. These two verses belong to an extensive array of dietary restrictions, commandments, and ritual practices often referred to as the "Levitical holiness code." Two features of ancient Israelite society are important in interpreting these difficult passages: the process of constructing a religious identity for Israel distinct from its surrounding cultures, and the strict gender hierarchy of the ancient Mediterranean world.[42]

Leviticus 18:22 condemns sex between men, and, more particularly, treating a man like a woman. The Hebrew word used for this condemnation, translated as "abomination," appears most often with reference to the cultic practices associated with the worship of foreign gods; similar condemnations of child sacrifice and bestiality in Leviticus 18 strengthen the connection to idolatrous rituals.[43] Equally important, patriarchy placed a high premium on male privilege. Sexual practices reflected this gendered ordering as men were expected to take an active role and women a passive one, reflecting and perpetuating male dominance in all other spheres of cultural and religious life and reinforcing the treatment of women as property. Sexual relations in the ancient Near Eastern cultural context were defined by who had power over whom. So, according to this worldview, sex between men would violate male privilege and disrupt the patriarchal ordering of society.[44]

Ancient Israelite culture, which the Levitical holiness code was meant to uphold, differs significantly from the egalitarian ideals toward which many Christian families strive in modern Western culture (and indeed in other locales as well).[45] Likewise, the distinctive concerns shared by both the ancient Israelites and Paul to reject the sexual practices associated with idolatrous cults are in no way applicable to the lives of faithful Christians today who identify themselves as

---

42 Insights from Jewish commentators and scholars on these and other important aspects of biblical interpretation deserve renewed attention in Christian communities. See, for example, Steven Greenberg, *Wrestling with God and Men: Homosexuality in the Jewish Tradition* (Madison: University of Wisconsin Press, 2004); and Daniel Boyarin, *Carnal Israel: Reading Sex in Talmudic Culture* (Berkeley: University of California Press, 1995).

43 See Nissinen, *Homoeroticism in the Biblical World*, 37–56. Paul would likely have known the connection between the Levitical holiness code and idolatrous cults as well, which lends further support to interpreting the first chapter of Romans with reference to temple prostitution.

44 Jack Rogers, *Jesus, the Bible, and Homosexuality: Explode the Myths, Heal the Church*, revised edition (Louisville: Westminster John Knox Press, 2009), 68–69.

45 The treatment not only of women but also of children as property, as well as the practice of keeping concubines and slaves in ancient Mediterranean households, mark these differences even further. See Carol L. Meyers, "Everyday Life: Women in the Period of the Hebrew Bible," in *Women's Bible Commentary*, ed. Carol A. Newsom and Sharon H. Ringe, expanded edition (Louisville: Westminster John Knox Press, 1998), 251–59; Gale A. Yee, *Poor Banished Children of Eve: Woman as Evil in the Hebrew Bible* (Minneapolis: Fortress Press, 2003), 29–58; and Amy L. Wordelman, "Everyday Life: Women in the Period of the New Testament," in *Women's Bible Commentary*, 482–88.

gay or lesbian. These historical and cultural differences, however, do not render these biblical passages irrelevant: Scripture continues to bear witness to the primacy of covenantal relationship with the one true God of Israel, whom Christians believe and proclaim is revealed decisively in the life, death, and resurrection of Jesus Christ. Scripture would have us make that divine covenant primary in the ordering of our household relations in culturally appropriate ways.

In households formed by married different-sex couples and covenanted same-sex couples alike, the process of conforming to the likeness of Christ and striving toward holiness of life unfolds in deeply shared accountability. The couple continually attempts to place their desires within the vows and commitments they have made to each other. Living together in a household may provide the stability which makes possible the vulnerability necessary to self-giving and other-receiving.[46] In a household, the members of the couple become one another's nearest neighbor so that they may grow together in the love of God. The household shelters the daily practice, which Jesus urged, of finding one's life by giving it to another.

For same-sex couples as for married different-sex couples, households provide the structure for the daily life of covenanted closeness: laboring to provide for one another and to support family, organizing a household and its daily table, maintaining and sharing property, caring for another in sickness and at death.[47] Households may be schools for virtue and for penance and reconciliation, as well as habitations of mutual support and joy, places for glimpsing and also deepening our experience of the presence of God. People living alone, who are single, bereaved, or divorced, are also called to live out their baptismal vocation by the love, service, hospitality, and accountability of their relationships within the Church and in the communities of which they are a part, as well as through their service of prayer to others.

A household formed by a couple in a covenantal relationship can remind all of us of our incorporation into the paschal mystery through baptism, in which we are received into the household of God and encouraged to "confess the faith of Christ crucified, proclaim his resurrection, and share ... in his eternal priesthood."[48] In their household, a couple faces the many ways in which their faith forms

---

46 Rowan Williams, "The Body's Grace," in *Our Selves, Our Souls and Bodies: Sexuality and the Household of God,* ed. Charles Hefling (Cambridge, MA: Cowley Publications, 1996), 58–68.

47 See Deirdre J. Good, Willis J. Jenkins, Cynthia B. Kittredge, and Eugene F. Rogers, Jr., "A Theology of Marriage including Same-Sex Couples: A View from the Liberals," *Anglican Theological Review* 93:1 (Winter 2011): 63–64.

48 Holy Baptism, BCP, 308.

their daily lives. They offer themselves daily to each other in order to become part of the other's life, dying to sin and rising to a new life directed toward love of neighbor and love of God. In this giving of self and receiving of another, we see the gracious pattern of God's own triune life into which we are, more and more, caught up and transformed for mission.

In households we also see an image of the eucharist. The household tables around which couples in covenantal relationship gather evoke the eucharistic table around which we gather as the community of believers. In the household, as at the eucharist, couples take what is given to them and offer it to God. They are nourished and blessed by what they receive, and the Spirit then empowers them to be a blessing to others and to God. In a household, as at the eucharistic table, what God has joined together may become one body, and the Spirit may distribute a household's gifts to many. In households, same-sex as well as different-sex couples in covenantal relationships strive to imitate Jesus, who gave himself bodily for those he loved.

To give one's self over to love, care, and commitment in solidarity with another person, for better for worse, in sickness and in health, till death do us part, is daily and bodily to partake in the reconciling work of God in Christ. In the lives of intimate couples, sexual desire for one another can be forged into covenantal witness to the gospel.

Faithful Intimacy

The movement from sexual desire into faithful intimacy and covenantal commitment marks a particular kind of vocational path, which for Christians shapes the passion of *eros* into the affection of *agape* for the good of the Church and the world. Theological reflection on this path begins by affirming the goodness of sexual desire itself. Indeed, sexual desire is a metaphor for God's desire to be in relationship with us and the whole creation. Scripture and Christian tradition draw on sexually intimate relationships to point to the God who is Love and who stands in relationships of love with all creation. The long tradition of commentary on the biblical Song of Songs, for example, illustrates the spiritual significance of sexual relationships and the fruitfulness of reflecting theologically on the commitment of sexually intimate couples.[49] In such reflection, we can realize and

---

49 David M. Carr, *The Erotic Word: Sexuality, Spirituality, and the Bible* (Oxford: Oxford University Press, 2003). See also Douglas Burton-Christie, "Into the Body of Another: *Eros*, Embodiment and Intimacy with the Natural World," *Anglican Theological Review* 81:1 (Winter 1999): 13–37.

appreciate that "the whole story of creation, incarnation, and our incorporation into the fellowship of Christ's body tells us that God desires us." The good news of God's desire for us can then shape our intimate commitments and the life of the wider Christian community so that all of us may see ourselves as desired, as "the occasion of joy."[50]

The gift of human sexuality, established by God in creation, can be a source of sustaining joy, reminding us bodily of the abundance God intends for the whole creation. In the mutual self-offering of one to another in a sexual relationship of fidelity, we can catch a glimpse of the delight God exhibits for each of us. Yet sexual desire is also fraught with risk because it draws us into relationships of vulnerability, where not only the brightest and best dimensions of ourselves are offered to another but also where the painful aspects are exposed, the ones that we often prefer to keep hidden and that need healing. Sexual desire and intimacy make us vulnerable so that God can turn our limits to our good, showing us that we are not our own but belong to someone else.

Faithful relationships of sexual intimacy can also be an occasion to bear witness to God's love as they form the couples more fully in the image of Christ. In marriage, the Church blesses and celebrates these relationships as potential vehicles for God's grace. Many in the Episcopal Church today have come to believe that this is as true for same-sex couples as it is for different-sex couples.[51] Others, however, understand the doctrine of creation differently and believe that God's gift of human sexuality is intended only for different-sex couples. Even the language of "same-sex" and "different-sex" raises many complex questions, not only biologically, socially, and culturally, but also and especially biblically.

Genesis 1 and 2, for example, are often cited to support two interrelated convictions: first, that "gender complementarity" describes God's creation of human beings as male and female; and second, that such complementarity is best expressed in the procreation of children within monogamous marriage. The extensive biblical scholarship available on these passages—in both Jewish and Christian traditions—nuances those two convictions in some important ways.

In the first of the two creation accounts (Genesis 1:26–27), gender differentiation is attributed to the whole human species rather than to individuals, just as both male and female alike apply to God, in whose

---

50 Williams, "The Body's Grace," in *Our Selves, Our Souls and Bodies*, 59.
51 *To Set Our Hope on Christ*, 8–9, 24–25.

image humanity is made.[52] Similarly, the command to "be fruitful and multiply" (Genesis 1:28) is given to the human species, not to each individual. If this were not the case, people "who are single, celibate, or who for whatever reason do not have children—including Jesus of Nazareth"—would be viewed as "disobedient sinners."[53] Moreover, the generative aspects of a loving and faithful commitment can be seen in many different ways, not only in bearing and raising children. For same-sex couples, as one Episcopal bishop has pointed out, "the care and nurture of those already in the world may be a mission more excellently fulfilled by those who do not have the concerns of child-rearing."[54]

The second account in Genesis refers specifically to the creation of distinct individuals (Genesis 2:7–22), and introduces something that is *not* good in God's creation: "It is not good," God declares, "for the human being to be alone."[55] Here the story turns on the importance of companionship and not, as in the first account, on the procreation of children. Significantly, the companion God provides for the solitary human is not defined by "otherness" but by suitable similarity. In this passage, "there is no emphasis ... on 'difference' or 'complementarity' at all—in fact, just the opposite. When Adam sees Eve, he does not celebrate her otherness but her sameness: what strikes him is that she is 'bone of my bones, flesh of my flesh.'" Reducing this story to the fitness of particular anatomical parts misses the poignancy of this story: "God sees the plight of this first human being and steps in and does whatever it takes to provide him with a life-giving, life-sustaining companion."[56] Rather than focusing on marriage, these creation accounts affirm God as the creator of all things and "the priority of human companionship."[57]

Genesis 1 and 2 can and should continue to shape, inform, and energize the Church's faithful witness to the God revealed in Scripture. These passages can do so as the Church proclaims God as the creator and affirms the goodness of God's creation, which includes the dignity of every human being as created in God's image. This affirmation

---

52 Some ancient Talmudic commentaries suggest, for example, that the original human shared with God all of the possible gender characteristics, which were later divided between "male" and "female." This text, in other words, raises a host of questions which the text itself does not address concerning gender and sexuality in both humanity and God. See Howard Eilberg-Schwartz, ed., *People of the Body: Jews and Judaism from an Embodied Perspective* (Albany: State University of New York Press, 1992).
53 Johnson, *A Time to Embrace*, 115–16.
54 Marshall, *Same-Sex Unions*, 38.
55 Genesis 2:18 (for the significance of this translation of the verse, see Johnson, *A Time to Embrace*, 114–115, 117).
56 Johnson, *A Time to Embrace*, 120.
57 Johnson, *A Time to Embrace*, 114.

remains vital, not least for the sake of embracing the full humanity of women. The unqualified dignity with which the biblical writer treated both men and women in the account of their creation stands out as quite remarkable in the patriarchal culture in which it was written.[58]

Paul, furthermore, would urge Christians to read the Genesis accounts of creation through the lens of the *new* creation, which God has promised in Christ, the first fruits of which God has provided by raising Christ from the dead (1 Corinthians 15:20–25). Living into that promise and anticipating its fulfillment, Paul urged the Christians in Galatia to understand their baptism as erasing familiar social and cultural hierarchies: "As many of you as were baptized into Christ have clothed yourselves with Christ. There is no longer Jew or Greek, there is no longer slave or free, there is no longer male and female; for all of you are one in Christ Jesus" (Galatians 3:27–28).[59] Rather than emphasizing the significance of gender, the faithfulness of sexually intimate couples can contribute to the Church's witness to the new life God offers in Christ and through the Spirit, which the Church celebrates in the "sacraments of the new creation."[60] For both same-sex and different-sex couples, then, the theological and moral significance of their covenantal commitment is rooted in the paschal mystery.

As in baptism and eucharist, the covenantal commitments of sexually intimate couples sweep their bodies up into a grand and risky endeavor: to see if they can find their life in God by giving it to another. In these covenants, two people vow to give themselves bodily and wholeheartedly to each other. They do this, in part, to live out the promises of baptism while also living into the self-offering of Christ,

---

58 William Stacy Johnson notes, for example, that in ancient Mediterranean society, women were considered human beings but decidedly deficient ones and were therefore rightly subservient to men (*A Time to Embrace*, 275, n.16). Dale B. Martin likewise relates this ancient view of the inferiority of women—as "deficient men"—to the difficulties in translating, let alone interpreting, two Greek words in the New Testament that have been frequently cited regarding homosexuality. Those words appear in 1 Corinthians 6:9 and 1 Timothy 1:10. The words "sodomite" or "homosexual" have appeared in some English translations of those verses, but the meaning of the Greek in both cases is obscure and elusive. Martin believes it likely that these words referred to cultural practices involving sexual exploitation (perhaps including rape) and also effeminate behavior, which for men in that society triggered both alarm and disgust ("*Arsenokoitês* and *Malakos*: Meanings and Consequences," in *Biblical Ethics and Homosexuality: Listening to Scripture*, ed. Robert L. Brawley [Louisville: Westminster John Knox Press, 1996], 117–36).

59 See Dale B. Martin, *Sex and the Single Savior: Gender and Sexuality in Biblical Interpretation* (Louisville: Westminster John Knox Press, 2006), 77–90.

60 Among the many sources for this connection between the sacramental life of the Church and the divine promise of the new creation, see Herbert McCabe, *The New Creation* (London: Continuum, 2010), where he refers to the Church's sacraments as "mysteries of human unity" insofar as we are, through the sacraments, being incorporated into the new creation God is bringing about (xii).

as expressed at the eucharistic table: "This is my body, given for you." The lifelong commitment of covenanted couples can, by God's grace, testify to the love of God by signifying Christ and the Church. These commitments can thus evoke for the wider community the very promise of the paschal mystery enacted in baptism and eucharist: we are being drawn deeper into God's own life where we learn that God's love is stronger than death.

Sexually intimate couples can also testify to the love of neighbor by loving each other, a love that requires both time and the sustenance of God's grace. Covenantal couples can model this love, not as a static tableau but as an ongoing school for virtue in which the practices of neighbor-love are developed, reformed, and brought toward perfection. The moral significance of a covenantal relationship is its potential to bring each of the covenant partners up against their embodied limits as finite creatures and to become willing to be vulnerable to another. A covenantal commitment challenges and inspires each partner to self-offering as each lives out with the other the relation of Christ and the Church (Ephesians 5:21–33). Members of a couple urge each other forward in growth, which occurs through and with the creaturely limitations that Christ took on for our good: the limits of time and the body. Our desires, including our sexual desires, "can be an especially intense and unsettling reminder of our radical availability to the other. Like parental affection or simple compassion, sexual desire can cause our heart to 'belong' to another. ... This desire shatters any illusions we may have regarding our ability to choose when and if we shall be connected to others; indeed, it is itself a warrant for the claim that our fundamental relation to one another is one of connection."[61]

Giving ourselves to another, as Christ gave himself for the world, takes time and the willingness to risk the vulnerability inherent to the commitment of love. The movement of sexual desire toward intimacy and into commitment begins as we give ourselves over to another in faithful relation and continues toward the final moment of committal, surrendering our lives to God. This movement describes a lifelong, deliberate process that, with obedience and faithfulness, produces visible holiness and the fruits of the Spirit. Both for the good of the couple and for the good of the Church, God blesses this loving, intimate commitment. This blessing, in turn, empowers the couple for their ministry in the world and energizes the Church for mission.

---

61 Thomas Breidenthal, "Sanctifying Nearness," in *Theology and Sexuality: Classic and Contemporary Readings,* ed. Eugene F. Rogers, Jr. (Oxford: Blackwell, 2002), 345.

Mutual Blessing and Fruitfulness

As Christians, all of our relationships—as single people, in households, as intimate couples—are occasions to live more fully into our Baptismal Covenant and participate more deeply in the paschal mystery of Christ's death and resurrection enacted at the eucharistic table. The commitment we exhibit in our relationships—to love our neighbor as we love ourselves and as God loves each of us in Christ— thus becomes a source of blessing for the whole Church.

This broad framework of covenantal relationship for the Church's life offers a way to reflect on the significance of the many types of covenants with which the Church is blessed—in ordination, monastic vows, marriage, and also in same-sex relationships. The blessing of any relationship is a blessing not only for those in a relationship but also and equally for the wider community in which the relationship is lived. This mutual blessing is exhibited in many ways, not least by enabling those engaged in such relationships to manifest the fruits of the Spirit (Galatians 5:22–23), which they might not have done apart from the relationship. Discerning the gifts of the Spirit in a relationship is one reason a faith community blesses that relationship.

In addition, pronouncing a blessing can become an important occasion for deepening the process of sanctification. Many couples desire this—and they need it. God can use the vulnerability of intimacy and the giving of ourselves to another to expose our weaknesses, make us better, set us apart, and spur our moral growth. The Church in turn can witness to the sanctifying work of the Spirit as God transforms the energy of *eros* into the virtues of faith, hope, and love.

A blessing changes a couple as they become more aware of God's grace and are commissioned by the Church to bear witness to the paschal mystery. A blessing changes the Church as well: holiness of life is made more manifest, so the community becomes accountable for supporting the couple as they grow into the sanctifying work of the Spirit.

Entering into a covenant of faithfulness with another human being is one among many ways Christians live out their baptismal calling in the world. As covenantal households are shaped by lives given over to service, compassion, generosity, and hospitality, the grace encountered at the eucharistic table is further manifested in the world. Thus, the fruitfulness of covenantal relationships and the blessings they offer to the Church belong to the mission of the Church in its ongoing witness to the gospel of Jesus Christ and our hope of union with God. This is the very source of our desire for communion with another.

4. The Church's Challenge: Christian Unity and Biblical Interpretation

O God the Father of our Lord Jesus Christ, our only Savior,
the Prince of Peace: Give us grace seriously to lay to heart the
great dangers we are in by our unhappy divisions; take away
all hatred and prejudice, and whatever else may hinder us
from godly union and concord; that, as there is but one Body
and one Spirit, one hope of our calling, one Lord, one Faith,
one Baptism, one God and Father of us all, so we may be all
of one heart and of one soul, united in one holy bond of truth
and peace, of faith and charity, and may with one mind and
one mouth glorify thee; through Jesus Christ our Lord. *Amen.*
— "For the Unity of the Church," BCP, 818

Christian unity with God and one another in Christ is a precious gift;
likewise, our differences as believers are gifts to be honored because
these differences belong to God's created order. Through these gifts we
are equipped for "building up the body of Christ, until all of us come
to the unity of the faith and of the knowledge of the Son of God"
(Ephesians 4:12–13).

The Book of Common Prayer (1979) encourages Episcopalians
to pray for Christian unity by recalling the Pauline letter to the
Ephesians. This letter reminds us that our bonds of affection are
rooted not in our own efforts but in God's gracious gift in baptism.
There is but one Body and one Lord. There is but one baptism,
by which we are joined—heart, soul, and mind—to one another
(Ephesians 4:5). Most of all, as the prayer quoted above reminds us,
this baptismal unity serves the Christian call to praise and glorify God.

In baptism, God binds us to God's own self by binding us to others
who are different from us, linking our salvation inextricably to the

salvation of others. Furthermore, the divine gift of unity in no way relies on uniformity. We are not united, one to the other, because we agree but because God has joined us together.[62] The bond we share in baptism makes room for us to disagree with one another within the bonds of affection we share as members of God's own household of love and grace. We enact this unity by continuing "in the apostles' teaching and fellowship, in the breaking of bread, and in the prayers."[63] We cannot live into this gift on our own, but with "sighs too deep for words," the Spirit "helps us in our weakness" (Romans 8:26). The Spirit slowly takes, offers, and transforms all the prayers of those who disagree with one another to make them occasions to manifest the Body of Christ more visibly in the world and in the Church as well. In this ongoing process of sanctification, we proclaim that we are marked as Christ's own forever as members of the Body of Christ.[64] This foundational reality of our shared life sends us out to the world in witness to Christ's reconciling love.[65]

The challenges in making God's gift of unity more and more visible appear, for example, within the New Testament concerning the divisions in the Corinthian church (1 Corinthians 3:1–9), in Paul's reminder to the Romans that the body includes many diverse members (Romans 12:3–8), and perhaps most notably in Paul's baptism of non-Jews, which caused a debate with Peter over how to interpret their inherited Scriptures. Paul recounts this disagreement in his letter to the Galatians (2:2–21). Peter's vision (Acts 10:9–16) prior to encountering Cornelius, a Roman centurion, and interacting with other Gentiles, moved him to declare that no one should be called "profane or unclean" (Acts 10:28), and to urge his fellow apostles not to withhold the water of baptism from those who had received the Holy Spirit just as they had (Acts 10:47). The inclusion of Gentiles who did not observe dietary laws within the household of the God of Israel overturned centuries of biblical interpretation.

Throughout the Church's history, Christians have endeavored to follow that apostolic practice of prayerful deliberation in the light of Scripture and to discern the will of God—"what is good and

---

62 See Thomas E. Breidenthal, "Communion as Disagreement," in *Gays and the Future of Anglicanism: Responses to the Windsor Report*, ed. Andrew Linzey and Richard Kirker (Ropley, UK: O Books, 2005), 188–198.

63 "The Baptismal Covenant," BCP, 304.

64 The centrality of baptism in our common life has been championed by a series of Anglican leaders, starting with Thomas Cranmer and including F. D. Maurice and William Reed Huntington. As Paul Avis describes it, Anglican ecclesiology depends on the insistence that "what unites us to Christ [that is, baptism] is all that is necessary to unite us, sacramentally, to each other" (*The Identity of Anglicanism: Essentials of Anglican Ecclesiology* [London: T&T Clark, 2007], 111).

65 On baptismal ecclesiology, see Weil, *A Theology of Worship*, 22–28.

acceptable and perfect" (Romans 12:2)—in each new time and place. As the Body of Christ, our fundamental call is to live together not only when we agree in our discernment but also when the Spirit leads faithful Christians to hold more than one view. Different interpretations of Scripture are possible, provided they lead us to love God and one another.[66]

General Convention Resolution 2009–C056 acknowledges differences of opinion within the Episcopal Church concerning the interpretation of Scripture and same-sex relationships. This theological resource has presented interpretations of some of the most difficult of these biblical passages to support the covenants of same-sex couples while understanding that some members of the Episcopal Church continue to hear the word of the Lord differently in these passages. All of us have more to learn from Scripture and from each other. The Spirit baptizes us all in the name of Jesus, who is himself the Word of God and the Lord of Scripture. In faithfulness to Christ, we acknowledge and respect those differences among us in our fervent hope that disagreements over this biblical material need not divide the Church.[67] Anglican Christians, along with Christians in many other communions and historical eras, have discovered in ever new ways how the grace of God in Christ offers a path toward unity even in the midst of profound disagreement.[68]

Our disagreements today belong in the context of the agreement we do enjoy concerning biblical interpretation: the saving love and grace of God in Christ call us to be a holy people, living in faithfulness and treating the human body as the temple of the Holy Spirit as we endeavor, with God's help, to fulfill our baptismal vows to "seek and serve Christ in all persons," loving our neighbors as ourselves, to

---

66 Augustine of Hippo believed that the command in Genesis to "increase and multiply" (1:22, 28) applied not only to the procreation of children but also to the proliferation of textual meanings of Scripture. Augustine also believed that there were limits to multiple interpretations: no interpretation of Scripture could be considered ethically Christian if it violated the commandment to love God and one's neighbor. See Dale B. Martin, *Pedagogy of the Bible: An Analysis and Proposal* (Louisville: Westminster John Knox Press, 2008), 59, 83–84.

67 Rowan Williams has noted, for example, that writers in our shared Anglican history have often turned to "a theologically informed and spiritually sustained *patience*" as Anglican Christianity continues to grow and change. These writers, Williams says, "do not expect human words to solve their problems rapidly, they do not expect the Bible to yield up its treasures overnight. ... They know that as Christians they live among immensities of meaning, live in the wake of a divine action which defies summary explanation. They take it for granted that the believer is always learning (*Anglican Identities* [Cambridge, MA: Cowley Publications, 2003], 7).

68 While the Church's history is replete with many such examples, for illustrations from Anglican history, see William L. Sachs, *The Transformation of Anglicanism: From State Church to Global Communion* (Cambridge: Cambridge University Press, 1993), esp. chap. 4, "The Struggle to Define the Church and its Belief," 120–63.

"strive for justice and peace among all people," and to "respect the dignity of every human being."[69] In such agreement, the love with which we treat each other is to be modeled on the love of God for God's people, as well as on the life and ministry of Jesus himself.

Scripture offers little material that would address modern notions of sexual orientation, and biblical writers devoted relatively little attention to questions of same-sex relations. Biblical scholars are divided regarding the translation and interpretation of the texts most often cited on this question.[70] Some maintain that these texts unequivocally forbid same-sex relationships; others argue that these texts do not refer to same-sex relationships as we understand them today and that each text must be interpreted within its own historical and literary contexts.[71]

Similar disagreements over biblical interpretation have marked the Church's life throughout its history. Faithful Christians struggled for centuries to understand whether Scripture encouraged a view of vowed religious life as a higher calling than marriage. Churches have disagreed over the biblical condemnation of "usury," which originally meant charging interest on loaned money, and whether it applies to contemporary economic systems. Protestant reformers disagreed about biblical interpretations of the eucharist and even whether particular biblical books ought to remain in the canon of Scripture. English reformers wrestled with differing biblical views concerning liturgical vestments, Church music, the relationship between Church and state, sacramental theology, and the role of ordained ministers.[72]

The Episcopal Church has struggled with how to interpret Scripture amid cultural change, whether concerning economic reform, divorce and remarriage, or contraception.[73] The practice of slavery and the role of women are two areas in which major departures from the

---

69 "The Baptismal Covenant," BCP, 305.
70 Those texts are Genesis 1–2, Genesis 19, Leviticus 18:22 and 20:13, Romans 1, 1 Corinthians 6:9, 1 Timothy 1:10, and Jude 7.
71 An overview of these positions appears in an issue of the *Anglican Theological Review* devoted to same-sex marriage; it offers "two interpretations of doctrinal and scriptural faithfulness that fundamentally disagree" (Ellen T. Charry, "Preface," *Anglican Theological Review* 93:1 [Winter 2011]: xiv). The two major essays in this issue of the journal originated as a project commissioned in spring 2008 by the House of Bishops of the Episcopal Church, to be overseen by the Theology Committee of the House of Bishops.
72 For a history of the various ways the Church has read difficult biblical passages, see John L. Thompson, *Reading the Bible with the Dead: What You Can Learn from the History of Exegesis That You Can't Learn from Exegesis Alone* (Grand Rapids: Eerdmans Publishing Company, 2007).
73 For an overview of challenges in biblical interpretation for a wide range of ethical concerns in the Episcopal Church, see Robert E. Hood, *Social Teachings in the Episcopal Church* (Harrisburg: Morehouse Publishing, 1990).

biblical text have been especially controversial. Christians, including Episcopalians, in the nineteenth century used the Bible extensively to justify the institution of slavery, particularly in the United States.[74] In 1863, for example, Presiding Bishop John Henry Hopkins of Vermont published a paper called "Bible View of Slavery," which defended slavery as "fully authorized both in the Old and New Testament," defining it as "servitude for life, descending to the offspring."[75]

The struggle to ordain women in the Episcopal Church also involved deep conflicts over biblical interpretation. Supporters of women's ordination based their arguments on the gospel's promise of freedom and wholeness for all, while opponents believed that the maleness of the disciples named in the New Testament established an unalterable tradition of male priesthood.[76]

The Episcopal Church eventually changed its positions regarding slavery and the ordination of women. The diversity of approaches to Scripture in both cases made these decisions contentious. Serious questions continue to be posed about how we understand the authority of Scripture, not only concerning slavery and the status of women but also, now, same-sex relationships. All three of these issues have threatened to divide the Church. No one today would justify the institution of slavery, but the worldwide Anglican Communion continues to live with disagreement about ordaining women and blessing same-sex relationships. With previous generations of the faithful who struggled in similar ways, our present disagreements need not compromise our shared witness to the good news of God in Christ as we look toward that day when our partial knowledge will be complete (1 Corinthians 13:12) and when God will be "all in all" (1 Corinthians 15:28).

The hope we share for that day of final fulfillment in Christ does not thereby erase the challenge of living into God's gracious gift of unity today. For most Christians, this means noting carefully the limits of acceptable differences; beyond those limits, the claim to Christian unity would prove difficult if not impossible. The challenge, then, is not whether limits to our differences exist, but how to discern when we have crossed those limits, and over what kinds of questions

---

74 Stephen R. Haynes, *Noah's Curse: The Biblical Justification of American Slavery* (New York: Oxford University Press, 2002).

75 John Henry Hopkins, "Bible View of Slavery," *Papers from the Society for the Diffusion of Political Knowledge*, no. 8 (1863): 132, 117; see also John Henry Hopkins, *A Scriptural, Ecclesiastical, and Historical View of Slavery, From the Days of the Patriarch Abraham, to the Nineteenth Century* (New York: W. I. Pooley and Co., 1864), 6.

76 Pamela W. Darling, *New Wine: The Story of Women Transforming Leadership and Power in the Episcopal Church* (Cambridge, MA: Cowley Publications, 1994), 149.

(whether doctrinal, moral, or liturgical, for example) we may hold differing beliefs and still remain in communion.[77] In the debate over same-sex relationships and biblical interpretation, Anglican Christians have disagreed about this process of discernment. Some Episcopalians have concluded that blessing such relationships goes beyond the limits of acceptable difference, and, acting on their conscience, they have parted company with the Episcopal Church, while others who disagree have chosen to remain. Our Church will continue to live with varying approaches to Scripture on this question.

At a pivotal moment among early believers, recorded in Acts 15, the possibility of including Gentiles in the Christian family sparked considerable controversy. The importance of this historical moment today lies not in the first-century differences between Jews and Gentiles but in the process of prayerful deliberation those early believers adopted. Facing the real possibility of irreparable division, the apostles sought a way to honor the centrality of Scripture while also attending carefully to the ongoing movement of the Spirit in their midst.

The Acts of the Apostles recounts that certain believers from the sect of the Pharisees were insisting that men could not be saved unless they were circumcised and kept the law of Moses (Acts 15:5). As the apostles and elders in Jerusalem considered this question, Peter (who had been persuaded by Paul's point of view) confirmed the work of the Holy Spirit among the Gentiles: "God, who knows the human heart, testified to them by giving them the Holy Spirit, just as he did to us; and in cleansing their hearts by faith he has made no distinction between them and us" (Acts 15:8–9). James considered this testimony and concluded that the Spirit's work urged a reconsideration of Scripture and an expansion of the gospel's reach to include Gentiles (Acts 15:13–21).

Acts 15 stands among other key biblical moments in which God's people have found their vision broadened to see a new thing God is bringing about (Isaiah 43:18–21), their assumptions challenged by the outpouring of God's Spirit where they had not expected it (Numbers 11:26–29; Joel 2:28), and the startling first fruits of God's new creation in raising Jesus Christ from the dead (1 Corinthians 15:20–25). These biblical turning points, in themselves, will not settle today's disagreements, yet they urge the same apostolic process of prayerful deliberation: reliance on the centrality of Scripture while attending carefully to the Spirit's work in our midst.[78]

---

77 For observations concerning matters that are essential to Christian life and those over which we may have legitimate differences of opinion, see *To Set Our Hope on Christ*, 49–52.
78 See Stephen E. Fowl, "How the Spirit Reads and How to Read the Spirit," in *Engaging*

The Episcopal Church listened closely to the Spirit concerning slavery
and the ordination of women. We are summoned today to listen to
the narratives of sanctification and holiness within the relationships of
same-sex couples and to discern and testify to the work of God in their
lives. As we listen, we trust in that Spirit who, as Jesus promised, will
lead us further into truth (John 16:13), praying as Christ himself did
for our unity with each other in God (John 17:11) and blessing God
for God's abundant goodness in Christ so that, with Paul, we may
share more fully in the blessings of the gospel (1 Corinthians 9:23).

Scripture: A Model for Theological Interpretation (Malden, MA: Blackwell Publishing,
1998), 97–127; Jeffrey S. Siker, "How to Decide? Homosexual Christians, the Bible, and
Gentile Inclusion," *Theology Today* 51:2 (July 1994): 219–34; and Rogers, *Jesus, the
Bible, and Homosexuality*, 89–90.

Responses to "Faith, Hope, and Love"

The essays in this section represent the viewpoints of the individual authors rather than the consensus of the Standing Commission on Liturgy and Music.

a. Thomas E. Breidenthal

Thomas E. Breidenthal is the Bishop of the Episcopal Diocese of Southern Ohio.

In "Faith, Hope, and Love: Theological Resources for Blessing Same-Sex Relationships," the Standing Commission on Liturgy and Music offers a thoughtful reflection on what the Church is saying and doing when it blesses a same-sex union. The argument can be summarized as follows: (1) The Church blesses moral practices that make for holiness; (2) holiness is conformation to the mission of God; (3) the mission of God is reconciliation between God and us, and between us and one another; (4) this boils down to love of God and love of neighbor; (5) faithful, monogamous same-sex unions are good incubators of this love; (6) therefore in blessing these unions the Church sees and affirms a moral practice that makes for holiness. What we are *doing* is invoking God's favor to develop a couple's capacity for love of God and neighbor and to empower them for mission.

Commendably, the Standing Commission insists that blessed unions are not a private affair, but are accountable to the Christian community as a whole. The essay notes that this is true for "different-sex" couples as well, though they might "likewise find this to be a new way of thinking about their own marital vows" (III.3). Also, it invites us to approach same-sex unions in the wider context of Christian householding, thus reminding us that intentional communities (monastic and otherwise), as well as the single life, can form us for God's mission. That mission, defined as reconciliation, is firmly grounded both in the Trinity and in our own need and capacity for community, "created in the Trinitarian image of God, an image that is inherently relational" (III.3). That image is perfected in Jesus, in whom the self-giving and eternal love of the divine persons is played out in Christ's death and resurrection on our behalf. We are most in sync with God and with our God-given nature when we give our life for another, and we understand the paschal mystery—what Jesus' death and resurrection accomplished—when we give our life to another and receive it back restored and transformed. Finally, "Faith, Hope, and Love" makes clear connections between self-giving and the Church's two main sacraments. Baptism unites us with Christ in his death and resurrection, and the eucharist sustains our union with him through a lifetime of schooling in love.

Still, this essay raises several concerns. Most importantly, the underlying argument is obscured and sometimes contradicted by undue emphasis on the preexisting goodness of the unions that we bless. The essay rightly seeks to ground Christian householding in the eucharistic pattern of the Christian life, but in so doing seems at times to blur the distinction between this ground and the practices which it supports: "[The] eucharistic pattern—often described with the actions *take, bless, break,* and *give*—shapes all the relationships that we bring into our baptismal life with God. We *take* these relationships, *bless* God for their goodness, ask God to bless them and *break* them open further to divine grace, so that we may *give* them to the world as witnesses to the gospel of Jesus Christ" (III.3). This and other such statements are true taken on their own, but in combination with the claim that blessed unions are set apart just as the eucharistic bread is set apart, they convey a cumulative impression that these unions function primarily as vehicles of grace for a needy world. I do not dispute that this is a hoped-for by-product of all Christian householding, but I am not sure we should view it as its goal. As the essay itself says, the purpose of a covenanted relationship is to help two people learn how to love each other as Christ loves us. For most of us sinners, this is accomplishment enough, and it is for the grace to achieve such love for one person in one lifetime that couples come seeking a blessing from the Church. This is not to say that a sustained commitment to love another person completely does not mediate grace to onlookers. But it is a grace made perfect in weakness (2 Cor. 12:9). It is as sinners that we enter into sacred unions, and it is only in expectation of God's sanctifying grace that we dare to call them sacred.

There is no doubt that the authors of "Faith, Hope, and Love" agree with this, since they speak of the grace required to fulfill the purpose of a covenanted union: "The Church prays for the divine grace and favor the couple will need to live into their commitment to each other with love, fidelity, and holiness of life" (III.1). Yet, strikingly, help with temptation and sin is never included among the benefits of being blessed. Thus one comes across sentences like this: "Members of a couple urge each other forward in growth, which occurs through and with the creaturely limitations that Christ took on for our good: the limits of time and the body" (III.3). What is left out here is the condition of fallen humanity that Christ did *not* take on, namely our sinfulness. It is our sinfulness that makes us dangerous to one another, and renders every union risky. Surely it is with this riskiness in mind that same-sex couples come seeking God's aid and the Church's support. Although the Standing Commission's essay acknowledges that dynamic, it clearly takes a backseat to a different, problematic message: the Church's blessing is first and foremost the recognition of goodness already present. I understand that impulse. We want to right the balance and repent of our old derision—or at best, our toleration—of faithful same-sex couples in our midst. It is also probably the case that since most couples coming forward for a blessing have been together for a long time, the Church experiences its act of blessing as long-overdue recognition and approval. Most of the couples that now come seeking a blessing have a long history of faithful struggle together, and many have long been vehicles of grace to those around them. But this season will soon be past, and we will see increasing numbers of gay and lesbian couples, many of them young adults, who, like their heterosexual counterparts, really are just now making the move from trial or experiment to mutual commitment. As that reality is borne in upon us, we will need to reemphasize a major element of blessing that "Faith, Hope, and Love" downplays. In blessing any covenanted union, the Church invokes God's grace to bring to fruition a holy intention rendered fragile by inexperience and sin.

This leads me to a larger question about the Church's approach to sexual morality in general. The Standing Commission does not address this topic, nor was it asked to do so. Yet their discussion of same-sex blessings begs that question, since, as I have already noted, they refer to blessed unions as being set apart: "The blessing of the eucharistic table sets us apart as the Body of Christ in the world, called and empowered to proclaim the gospel, just as the blessing of a covenantal relationship sets that relationship apart as 'a sign of Christ's love to this sinful and broken world'" (III.2, with reference to BCP, 429). In so doing, the Commission intends to stress that covenanted relationships are ordered to a specific vocation, namely, to draw others to the saving work of Christ. I agree with that intention, but I do not think we should talk about these unions being set apart. Such language suggests that lifelong unions are not necessarily the norm for sexual partners, but a particular vocation taken on by a few. To be "set apart" implies being distinguished from a group that is both normative and entirely acceptable. The obvious analogy is to clergy, who are set apart for specific ministries within the Church. Here the laypersons comprise the normative group and clergy are the exception. Yet, though our expectations of the two groups may differ somewhat, the same Baptismal Covenant obligates both. A less obvious analogy, but one central to "Faith, Hope, and Love," is to the bread set apart for the eucharist. All bread is the good work of human hands, but we set some aside to become the Body of Christ. In each case, out of something of positive value—the people of God and the bread of human labor—a part is extracted for a particular purpose to serve the Church as a whole. "Faith, Hope, and Love" suggests that as the eucharistic bread is set apart and blessed, so a covenanting couple that is blessed is set apart. But set apart from whom? Clearly, from couples who have not committed to lifelong faithful monogamy. It is not so clear how we are to regard this other, supposedly larger and normative group. If we go with the relation of laity to clergy, or of ordinary to eucharistic bread, then we imply that there is nothing amiss with couples who do not intend to be faithful and monogamous. They are like good Catholics in the heyday of religious orders who chose marriage over celibacy. Do we intend to draw a similarly benign contrast between sexually involved couples who intend lifelong monogamous fidelity and those who do not? Have we abandoned the principle that sex should *ordinarily* go hand in hand with commitment to permanence, however much we may fall short of that ideal? If that is the case, we should admit it. If it is not the case, we need to say so.

Perhaps I am objecting to the language of this document because theological statements can and do generate ancillary questions. Here's one about the eucharist, which has a bearing on the discussion so far. Why does "Faith, Hope, and Love" refer constantly to the *blessing* of bread and wine in the eucharist, and not, as is more usual in our tradition, to their *consecration*? The essay repeatedly refers to the blessing of the eucharistic bread and wine, and, quoting 1 Corinthians 10:16, to "the cup of blessing that we bless" (see III.2 and III.3). It goes on to point out that the Great Thanksgiving is deeply rooted in the Jewish understanding of blessing. To bless something is to bless God who made it, and in so doing to reveal its essential goodness as coming from God's hands. All this is true, and its bearing on what it means to bless anything is obvious. But to restrict the eucharistic action to blessing diminishes it. We do not merely set the elements of bread and wine apart for a sacred purpose. Having thanked God, we invoke the Holy Spirit to make Christ present to us in them. "The cup of blessing that we bless, is it not" (to complete Paul's phrase) "a communion in the blood of Christ?" By the Spirit the elements are changed; they become Christ for us. By the same Spirit we are made Christ's body—the exodus body into which we are incorporated in baptism. There is a reason why the *Book of Common Prayer* refers to this transformation as consecration, not blessing (BCP, 408). To bless is, indeed, to acknowledge something good and to commend it to God's use. By contrast, to consecrate is to set something apart in the expectation that something essential about it will be changed. We believe that the elements of bread and wine become the body and the blood of Christ. As Anglicans, we refrain from explicating that change further (transubstantiation? consubstantiation? real presence?), but we do insist on the change. This is why the eucharistic action is not only *anamnesis* (a recalling of what God has done for us), but requires *epiclesis*, going beyond the Jewish prayer of blessing to ask the Father to send the Holy Spirit upon the bread and wine that they may become Christ for us.

I draw attention to this distinction between blessing and consecration, not only because it has a bearing on our understanding of the eucharist, but because it has a bearing on our understanding of the Church's blessing of sexual unions. We reserve the term "consecration" for change which effects union with Christ, whether of the eucharistic elements or the gathered Church, or, secondarily, as a synonym for ordination, understood as a setting apart to represent the Church as the Body of Christ. It is in union with Christ that the Church blesses. Christ's "This is my body" at the last supper, which anticipates his self-offering on the cross, also goes beyond the Jewish blessing. In addition to blessing his Father, and so acknowledging the bread and wine as coming from his hand, Jesus gives himself to us. In so doing he bestows life, healing, power, protection, comfort, and direction on us. This bestowal is the fullness of what Christians mean by a blessing. Christ's offering of himself cannot be understood apart from its Jewish ground—gratitude to God for gifts received in right relation to God—but it goes beyond this ground to stand in identification with God as God's Word, both to bestow the gifts of the Spirit and to cooperate with the Spirit in its work.

So blessing is, first and foremost, Christ's blessing. This is a blessing poured out on sinners from the cross. It is only in the acknowledgment of our sin that we can receive this blessing thankfully. But when we do receive it thankfully, we enter into communion with Christ, because we own his death for us and, in thankful response, are moved to spend the rest of our lives dying to sin. This is why Paul says that the cup of blessing is a communion in the blood of Christ. Our thanksgiving—that is, our blessing of God—comes at the price of repentance and loss. It is when our thanksgiving passes through that narrow door that our offering is accepted and returned to us as holy, bringing us into the presence of our risen Savior and transforming us into his Body. Here, and only here, can we speak properly of the Church as offering its own or God's blessing to anyone. The Church blesses as the Body of Christ, but does so as a Body redeemed from sin—a joyful Body, to be sure, but a chastened and humbled Body, too. We are always sinners blessing sinners.

This sensibility is discernible at various points in "Faith, Hope, and Love," but its various elements never quite coalesce. Once again, my hunch is that its authors were avoiding any suggestion that people in same-sex unions struggle with sin, lest they expose such unions once again to being singled out as especially sinful. I acknowledge the charity at play here. But in the long run we gain ground only if, for same-sex or heterosexual unions, a clear line is drawn from sin to repentance, from repentance to grace, from grace to thanksgiving.

b. John E. Goldingay

John E. Goldingay is the David Allan Hubbard Professor of Old Testament at Fuller Theological Seminary in Pasadena, California, and priest-in-charge of St. Barnabas Church, Pasadena.

When I lived in England, I knew quite well two women who had lived together for most of their adult lives. I have reason to think it was a celibate relationship, but I have no basis for knowing whether they felt any sexual attraction. I can imagine them giving each other a kiss or a hug before they went to bed each night in their separate bedrooms. I might call their relationship quasi-covenantal; in their latter years, one of them had a stroke, and the other looked after her and continued to make it possible for them to share a church involvement and to take holidays together. The one on whom fell the major responsibility for caring once commented wryly on the similarity of her situation and mine, because I had a similar responsibility for my disabled wife.

It has been instructive for me to reflect on the "faith, hope, and love" expressed in that relationship, and I could be glad to pray for God's blessing on it—indeed, I probably did so. I am sad that it is harder nowadays for such relationships to happen and to flourish without their being imagined to be something else.

Most of the essay on "Faith, Hope, and Love" comprises helpful reminders on the Church's mission, on blessing, on covenant, and on unity. But how far do these reminders apply to the blessing of same-sex relationships (with the connotations this phrase has in our culture)? The essay refers to the earlier study commissioned by the House of Bishops, which issued in a report outlining a "liberal" and a "traditionalist" position regarding same-sex relationships. I was a member of the traditionalist group within the task force that produced the study. "Faith, Hope, and Love" goes with the liberal position, as it must if it is to provide support for the development of resources for the blessings of same-sex relationships. My comments here, therefore, largely restate aspects of the traditionalist position.

First, the biblical arguments. To begin with, let us agree that Genesis 18–19 is irrelevant in light of the fact that no one is arguing for the kind of sexual relationships described there. On the other hand, one might note that Scripture does speak of same-sex relationships, such as those between Naomi and Ruth and between David and Jonathan, that offer models for thinking about relationships like that between my two friends. (It has of course been speculated that the two biblical relationships were same-sex relationships in our sense, but the stories offer no pointer to that possibility—and the Old Testament does not shy away from referring to sex when it is a significant aspect of a narrative; further, it is unlikely that the books describing these relationships would have envisaged that possibility, or that the books would have found acceptance into the canon of Scripture on that hypothesis.)

The arguments that Genesis 1–2 need not imply a validation of heterosexual relationships alone are not convincing. Genesis 1 talks about male and female in connection with the fulfillment of God s purpose in creation and the fruitfulness of humankind. Humanity's blessing and proliferation though heterosexual relationships is implied in the creation of male and female. The traditionalist document quotes Anglican biblical scholar Gordon Wenham, writing on Genesis: "Here then we have a clear statement of the divine purpose of marriage: positively, it is for the procreation of children; negatively, it is a rejection of the ancient oriental fertility cults."[79] Genesis 2:24 is explicitly about heterosexual marriage: "Therefore a man leaves his father and his mother and clings to his wife, and they become one flesh." While "one flesh" may suggest more than their sexual relationship, it hardly means less. Further, one reason why it is not good for the man to be alone is that he cannot generate children. He needs help if he is to do so. Procreation is integral to marriage's purpose, and is the reason why marriage involves a man and a woman. So the centerpiece in the vision of human marriage in Genesis is not intimacy, relationship, or romance, but family. The man and the woman will be the means and context in which the family will grow so as to serve God and the land. This point in itself does not exclude same-sex marriages, but it does not point to their being an equally valid option.

In Romans 1, sexual relationships between people of the same sex are an expression of human waywardness and of the rejection of the truth, and a result of God's wrath operating in the world. It is important to

---

79 Quoted in John E. Goldingay, Grant R. LeMarquand, George R. Sumner, and Daniel A. Westberg, "Same-Sex Marriage and Anglican Theology: A View from the Traditionalists," *Anglican Theological Review* 93:1 (Winter 2011): 24–25.

note that Paul sees such relationships as a *result* of God's wrath operating against sin in the world, not a *cause* of that wrath. Heterosexual people are as much implicated in this waywardness (not least in our sexual relationships) as people involved in same-sex relationships, which is reason for us to identify with our brothers and sisters involved in same-sex relationships, not to repudiate or shame them.

First Corinthians 6:9–11 and 1 Timothy 1:10 offer lists of people who will not inherit the kingdom of God, lists that include people involved in homosexual behavior and people who are greedy, rebellious, and guilty of certain other sins. The lists do not look as if they are intended to be comprehensive and do not imply that a distinctive shame attaches to that particular sin. Both passages use the term *arsenokoitai,* which denotes men who lie with another man as with a woman. It echoes the proscription in Leviticus, and thus suggests that the New Testament understands Leviticus to be proscribing a practice that was more than a matter of purity and impurity. First Corinthians 6:9 also uses the word *malakoi,* a term in Hellenistic Greek for someone who is the passive partner in a same-sex relationship. The use of both terms undermines the argument that these passages are especially concerned with pederasty.

On the basis of its study of such passages, the traditionalist argument in the report to the House of Bishops concluded, "The one-flesh pattern of heterosexual marriage in Genesis was the background for the descriptions of sinful behavior in the letters to Timothy, to the Corinthians, and to the Romans. Because homosexual behavior was more common in the Greco-Roman world, there was a need to update and expand the list of actions contrary to the Decalogue by including homosexual behavior along with theft, adultery, and so on."[80] It would be more realistic to infer that the Scriptures' perspective on this subject is limited than to infer that our culture enables us to clarify its meaning as being open to affirming same-sex relationships.

Second, the question of mission and context. In the world as it was designed "from the beginning," marriage involved the lifelong commitment of one man and one woman as the context for raising a family. At least four forms of relationship come one point short of that vision: polygamy; marriage that avoids having children; marriage in which one person has a still-living divorced partner; and same-sex relationships.

To express the matter thus is not to imply that all of these four forms of relationship have the same theological or ethical status, but I find

---

80 "A View from the Traditionalists," 27.

it helpful to see that there is a partial analogy between them. Within my own extended family and circle of friends are marriages that involve a partner whose former spouse is still living, a marriage where the couple has avoided having children, people who are in same-sex relationships, and someone who comes from a polygamous marriage. I would like to be able to seek God's blessing on such marriages and relationships, but I am unclear in what sense I can do so, as I could for the couple I described at the beginning of this response to the essay.

Two of those four forms of union appear in Scripture; two do not. I find it helpful to look at the two that do not appear in light of the way Scripture speaks of the two that do.

Jesus explicitly discusses divorce, and provides the helpful insight into the Torah that the Torah deals with both the ideal world (how things were from the beginning) and how things are in the world we know, where human hardness of heart is a reality. Deuteronomy's acceptance of divorce belongs in the latter category. Jesus does not bring a new standard of his own to the question, but affirms the visionary standard within the Torah. Elsewhere, he describes the entirety of the Torah and the Prophets as an outworking of love for God and love for one's neighbor, and one can see how this description applies to the Deuteronomic rule that presupposes divorce. Marriages do break down, and in a traditional society women may then be in an especially vulnerable position. The rule about giving a woman divorce papers is an expression of love that offers them some protection.

The Torah and the Prophets also acknowledge the practice of polygamy. They implicitly recognize problems polygamy can solve; they certainly portray problems it can generate. They do not explicitly say that it stands in tension with the creation vision for marriage, but this inference seems plausible. I can imagine Jesus taking a similar view of polygamy to the one he takes of divorce.

The Bible does not refer to the committed, covenantal same-sex relationships that are presupposed by our discussion of blessing such relationships, but I take them to have a similar status. They, too, do not correspond to the creation ideal but reflect the reality of human hardness of heart. Paul's comments in Romans encourage us to think not so much in terms of the individual hardness of heart of the people involved in these relationships, but of the hard-heartedness of humanity as a whole.

Considering these four issues together also helps us take into account the sociological and cultural factors involved in our thinking about these relationships, to which the essay refers in the section on mission. On the one hand, fifty years ago divorce was much less common than is now the case, and the Church did not marry divorced people. (As a newly-ordained priest in England, I recall initiating the arrangement for a couple's wedding before it transpired that the divorced man was describing himself as a bachelor on the basis that he was no longer married.) Twenty-five years ago, I blessed the marriage of a woman and a man who had been divorced; in England, I could not have done so in a church, but I could in our seminary chapel (the woman is now an archdeacon). In the twenty-first century, one of my own bishops has commented that she is hesitant about approving a marriage for someone who has been twice-divorced, but she sometimes does so. A big change in attitude and practice to divorce in the Church has come about not because we have studied Scripture and the Church's tradition more, but because of sociological and cultural factors. There are positive and negative aspects to this development.

With regard to same-sex relationships, there are parallel sociological and cultural considerations. One is the general sexualization of U.S. culture. Another is the collapse of the old family structures of which unattached people could be a part (the study's material on household is helpful in this connection). Related is the general assumption that people will be involved in sexual activity, and the apparent quaintness of the idea that it should not be so. Another is the ease with which people of same-sex attraction can engage in sexual activity without thereby earning public disapproval. Another is the increasing legal recognition of same-sex partnerships or marriage in Western countries. A further aspect of the cultural shift is the assumption that marrying someone of the same sex is simply a matter of proper freedom and choice. There is no moral difference between the two forms of relationship. That view also seems obvious to many Christians, who then add that neither is any theological difference involved.

Yet while same-sex relationships thus seem as "natural" to some people as heterosexual relationships seem, the jury is still out on the scientific questions on same-sex relationships, as is noted in the study of "Biological Mechanisms in Homosexuality: A Critical Review" in *The Anglican Communion and Homosexuality*.[81] The essay's section on mission notes these cultural circumstances in which we take part in God's mission, and in particular the "shift in cultural perspectives" on sexuality. It can be read as implying that we must go along with the cultural shift. Yet there surely can be cultural shifts

---

81 David de Pomerai, "Biological Mechanisms in Homosexuality: A Critical Review" in Philip Groves, ed., *The Anglican Communion and Homosexuality: A Resource to Enable Listening and Dialogue* (London: SPCK, 2008), 268–292.

that we do not go along with. The fact that there is a cultural shift
is a fact that we need to take into account, but our mission might be
to confront it, not baptize it. One way we might be able to get some
perspective on cultural shifts and on our relationship to them is by
looking at ourselves from the perspective of people in other cultures,
and particularly other churches. We might note the analogy between
the way many Western people are appalled by polygamy, while many
people in traditional societies are appalled by same-sex relationships
or serial monogamy. It is particularly unfortunate that we as a Church
do not seek to look at ourselves from other perspectives in this way
and can seem simply to assume that we are the enlightened.

Nor does acceptance of same-sex relationships parallel the abolition
of slavery, the proscribing of racism, the elimination of woman's
subordination, or the acceptance of women's ordination. In each of
these areas, there is material in Scripture that explicitly expresses what
I have called God's vision as well as material that makes allowance for
human hardness of heart. There is nothing in Scripture that expresses
a vision for same-sex relationships.

I close with a further adaptation of words from the traditionalist
submission to the House of Bishops. The lack of clarity concerning
same-sex attraction on the part of biological and social scientists, the
wounds in much of the rest of the Anglican Communion caused by
our unilateral action, and the apparent implications of Scripture and
the Church's tradition all make it hard to see how the essay's useful
material on blessing can be applied to same-sex relationships.

I appreciate the fact that the essay itself closes with a challenge
concerning Christian unity and biblical interpretation. I know priests
who are afraid that the time will come when a bishop will withhold
a license from them if they are not prepared to bless same-sex
relationships or (in due course) to conduct same-sex marriages. It will
be nice if the essay's closing challenge will mean that people who do
not accept the Church's new stance on same-sex relationships will not
be excluded from its ministry.

c. Deirdre Good

Deirdre Good is an independent scholar living and working in New York City.

I thank the Standing Commission on Liturgy and Music for their important reflections on the theological resources of the Episcopal Church for same-sex relationships. My invited response simply indicates that I have been, since my marriage to Julian Sheffield in 2008, in a different place. This description of our same-sex marriage service is offered as a contribution to the discussion, as our Church moves toward what I hope will be the recognition and use of a single marriage service for same-sex and different-sex couples.

When we planned our wedding in 2008, it proved strikingly easy to modify a few single words in the Book of Common Prayer's Celebration and Blessing of a Marriage so that two persons of the same sex could administer the sacrament to each other with integrity. Why this was the case is something that bears reflection.

First, the *words*.

The Book of Common Prayer has the celebrant declare at the outset, "Dearly beloved: We have come together in the presence of God to witness and bless the joining together of *this man and this woman* in Holy Matrimony." Our wedding service substituted: "Dearly beloved: We have come together in the presence of God to witness and bless the joining together of *these women* in Holy Matrimony."

The Declaration of Consent is repeated without a change in language: "N., will you have this woman to be your wife ... ?"

In the Ministry of the Word, the opening lines of the prayer change from "O gracious and everliving God, you have created us male and female in your image: Look mercifully *upon this man and this woman* who come to you seeking your blessing," to "O gracious and everliving God, you have created us in your image: Look mercifully

79

upon *these women* who come to you seeking your blessing." These
changes render without distortion the idea that humanity is created in
God's image and likeness (Genesis 1:26–27).

Following the vows, instead of the celebrant saying the words, "I now
pronounce that they are husband and wife," our priest presiding said,
"I now pronounce you married." In our case, in a state that legalized
same-sex marriage, this recognized our relationship in both legal and
religious spheres.

Second: the possible *reasons*.

Marriage realizes an order in creation. Here we join with those who
state that Christianity is a "deeply material religion," regarding the
"knowledge of God as mediated through ... creation."[82] The presence
of God in the world is made accessible in the central doctrine of the
Incarnation by means of which God is known not simply through
experience of the physical world but one in which God becomes part
of creation, being born as a human being. Thus God can be known
as a person directly. Christianity elevates the dignity of the human
person now made to be a participant with God in the safeguarding
of the cosmos and in recognition of finitude. As to the creation of
humanity and the institution of marriage, we disagree that experience
of male/female sexual relations best interprets that order; we think
instead that the order of creation is best known within the sanctifying
relation of Christ and the Church as *ekklesia* or community (Tyndale:
congregation). This is to say that we think the diversity of creation
is realized and perfected in the community of Christ. Thus our
minimalist modification of the BCP's Celebration and Blessing of
a Marriage deemphasizes the male–female or "complementarian"
element of the marriage typology while stressing and amplifying the
unitive and egalitarian dimension of the Christological analogy or
"mystery." This functions to enhance what we have come to recognize
and understand as the implicit unitive elements of the service.

We believe marriage is a discipline. The discipline of marriage relies
on the difficulty of living with another "in prosperity and adversity"
(BCP, 423), not to avoid our faults, but precisely to expose them—so
that they can be healed. Nor does the clause "when they hurt each
other" included in the prayers (BCP, 429) confine itself to minor
slights. Since hurt and acknowledgment—sin and confession—are
central to Christian growth and the sacraments, this prayer sets their
discipline in the theater of the whole fallen world. What matters
in a marriage is not whether the ministers of that marriage to each

82 Edward Norman, *An Anglican Catechism* (New York: Continuum, 2001), 15.

other are same- or differently-sexed; what matters is that they were
separate and they become united. The existing Prayer Book rite does
an extraordinarily good job of expressing that uniting for couples of
whatever sexual orientation, setting them on the path that will "make
their life together a sign of Christ's love to this sinful and broken
world, that unity may overcome estrangement, forgiveness heal guilt,
and joy conquer despair" (BCP, 429).

d. Dora Rudo Mbuwayesango

Dora Rudo Mbuwayesango is the Iris and George E. Battle Professor of Old Testament at Hood Theological Seminary in Salisbury, North Carolina.

I commend the members of the Standing Commission on Liturgy and Music for their dedication and good work in producing for the Church this much-needed resource for the blessing of same-sex relationships. Lesbians and gays have always been accepted by God as part of God's good creation and part of God's redeemed people, and I am glad that the Episcopal Church is now ready to recognize a dawning of the kingdom of God in our time. The essay lays out well why we should have a liturgy for blessing same-sex relationships. The following is my humble contribution to the furthering of the conversation that General Convention requested of the Standing Commission.

III. 1. The Church's Call: A Focus on Mission

The place of blessings in the mission of the Church is well put: "The public affirmation of the blessing of a covenantal relationship also sets that relationship apart for a sacred purpose: to bear witness to the creating, redeeming, and sustaining love of God." As "Faith, Hope, and Love" affirms in its preface, "Everything we do as Christians is meant to express the Church's call to participate in God's own mission in the world." The missional character of blessing lies in the truth that one is blessed in order to serve.

While it is true that this missional understanding of blessing is located in Scripture, the passages given from the Hebrew Bible do not seem to reflect that point. The witness from the book of Genesis seen in Abraham (12:2b) and Jacob (28:14b) would need to be read through Galatians 3:8, where Paul interprets it to include the extension of blessings to the Gentiles. In the context of Genesis there are two ways to understand these verses. In the first place those other nations' blessings were dependent on their treatment of either Abraham or Jacob. Secondly, Abraham's blessing extends beyond the individual in the sense of its extension to his direct descendants (Gen. 15:12–21; 17:1–8). But passages like Micah 4:1–4 and Isaiah 2:2–4 better demonstrate this missional understanding of blessing: God's grace in elevating Jerusalem/Zion will result in the revelation of God and in greater service to the other nations in the establishment of justice and peace among and within the nations.

Worship and Mission: An Eschatological Vision. Worship equips for mission in the realization of the just reign of God. Rites of blessing by the Church, of which the blessing of covenantal relationships is a part, equip couples with the grace necessary to "make their life together a sign of Christ's love to this sinful and broken world, that unity may overcome estrangement, forgiveness heal guilt, and joy conquer despair" (BCP 429). The Church's vocation is in bringing up the just reign of God. And the just reign of God does not participate in the unjust marginalization of segments of persons who are part of God's creation.

Same-Sex Relationships and the Church's Mission. It is a pity that the Church, in many ways, has been challenged by culture instead of challenging culture in recognizing the humanity of lesbian and gay persons. In fact, Christians have often stood, and in many ways continue to stand, in the way of granting human and civil rights to this important segment of humanity. But I am glad that the Episcopal Church is finally striving to do what the Spirit is leading it to do in affirming same-sex relationships. The many ways that same-sex relationships contribute to the mission of the Church are well presented in this section. But I would like to point to one aspect that has significance on the use of the marriage metaphor for the divine– human relationship. This metaphorical depiction of the divine–human relationship in the biblical texts (particularly in the prophets Hosea, Jeremiah, and Ezekiel) is characterized by an association of divine love, compassion, commitment, and reconciliation with divine wrath and punishment in the form of the rape and mutilation of women. Patriarchy's gender hierarchy and androcentric bias privileged male sexuality in a way that distorted human sexuality in general. And when that metaphor is used to depict the divine–human bond, the image of that bond is also distorted. Same-sex relationships have the potential to model mutuality in sexual relationships, which, in turn, redeems the metaphor of sexual bond for the divine–human covenant relationship: the Church can then celebrate and live up to its identity as the Bride of Christ.

The Challenge of God's Blessings for Mission. A large part of Christ's mission was to expand the horizon of the kingdom of God. The suffering, death, and resurrection of Christ broke geographical and

temporal boundaries. During his ministry, Jesus did not limit himself
to those who thought they belonged, but made it a point to reach out
to those whom *others* thought did not belong, and he was criticized
for it. Jesus went beyond the earlier, limited attempts to expand the
horizons: "To the eunuchs who keep my sabbaths, who choose the
things that please me and hold fast my covenant, I will give ... an
everlasting name that shall not be cut off. And the foreigners who
join themselves to the LORD, to minister to him, to love the name
of the LORD, and to be his servants ... —these I will bring to my
holy mountain, and make them joyful in my house of prayer; their
burnt offerings and their sacrifices will be accepted on my altar; for
my house shall be called a house of prayer for all peoples" (Isaiah
56:4–7). Unlike the prophet Isaiah, who advocated for those ready
on their own to come, Jesus went out seeking them. Acts 10 shows us
how the lessons from the past and the model of Jesus does not make
us immune to this shortcoming. But as history has shown us in the
development of the Church's traditions, we need the Holy Spirit to
continue to nudge us in the right direction every time God reveals a
segment of society overlooked and excluded from experiencing the
abundance of God's grace in the kingdom of God.

III. 2. The Church's Joy: A Theology of Blessing

Same-sex blessings are now part of communal worship—they are
outward and visible signs of God's grace. I would like to underscore
the fact that "the grace and blessing of God already discerned in
a couple's relationship does not thereby render a liturgical rite of
blessing redundant." As in the context of holiness depicted in the
Torah, God makes holy and the community enact holiness. In the case
of holiness, humans do rituals to enact the holiness established by
God. So God and people mutually construct holiness—God declares
and people enact it through rites.

The extension of the blessing to all nations becomes much more
evident in Christ. The references in the Old Testament are problematic
especially in Genesis 12:3 and much more limited in Isaiah 56 (see
my comment above). Paul's interpretation of Genesis 12:3 makes the
ultimate inclusion of all people that is evident in Jesus' ministry and
that of the early Church.

Indeed, "baptism and eucharist focus our attention on the particular
blessings of the paschal mystery of Christ's death and resurrection."
And these blessings then "encourage us to discern the many other
ways God's blessing is manifested in both creation and covenant."

We do not want to be blind to the potential vehicles for blessings, especially the love and faithfulness of covenantal relationship. As one-sided, abusive, and corrupt as marriage often was in ancient Israel, its focus on faithfulness nonetheless made it a suitable metaphor for the divine–human covenant. In the Old Testament, the wife was considered the property of the husband and thus the wife's faithfulness to her husband was absolute, while the same was not required of the husband. Faithfulness in love is what makes sexual bonds a vehicle for blessings.

I think one of the elements of God's blessings that bears emphasis is the abundance of God's blessing and grace. I am glad that this is very much emphasized in the essay. I think not realizing that abundance was one of the shortcomings of the religious leaders in Jesus' day continues to be manifested in our day. Jesus demonstrated the abundance of God's blessings in his teachings and actions. In some ways Jesus himself seems to have struggled with that reality, and it may have taken the Canaanite woman's challenge—"Yes, Lord, yet even the dogs eat the crumbs that fall from their masters' table" (Matt. 15:27)—for Jesus to acknowledge the abundance of God's blessings.

III. 3. The Church's Life: Covenantal Relationship

Creation, Baptism, and Eucharist. The prophets do use marriage as a metaphor for the bond between God and the people of Israel, but we should take note that most of those uses are tied to judgment. We should also take into consideration the patriarchal nature of marriage that put women in a disadvantaged and subordinate position to men, which is indicated in Ephesians 5:21–33. I believe that same-sex relationships help us to clearly see and demonstrate mutuality in committed sexual relationships because acts of love are not gendered and hierarchal.

Loving Our Neighbor as Ourselves. It is very important and insightful to recognize the concept of hospitality that governed the accounts in Genesis 19 and Judges 19, which is the focus of these stories. Also, the stories are about the gang rape of a male individual and not mutual sexual relationships between consenting individuals. The gang rape of women is not acceptable since Lot's daughters are divinely protected and the rape of the Levite's wife in Judges leads to civil war. Patriarchy and hetero-normativity govern how sexuality is depicted in these narratives and in the biblical narratives as a whole. Hospitality should not be extended only to some parts of humanity but to *all* humanity, whether female or male, heterosexual or homosexual, bisexual or transgender. The model of hospitality in these narratives should be critiqued as inadequate. Hospitality extended to all will result in the safety of all.

Called into Covenant. Covenants are lived in community and as Christians the Church is our community, and thus bears witness to individual and communal covenants. The Church then "rightly celebrates these moments of covenantal vocation" and calls us to live in households shaped by "deepening faithful intimacy."

The Vocation of Households. I am appreciative of the attempt to tackle biblical passages that are obscure and yet have been used to support heterosexuality, in opposition to same-sex sexuality. I would like to add that the Bible's construct of sexuality is limited by a concern for procreation and thus ignores all other sexual expressions, whether they are heterosexual or non-heterosexual. In other words, what we have in the Bible is not a definition of sexuality but procreation sexuality, and that makes it a very narrow and limited view of sexuality.

Faithful Intimacy. We need to acknowledge the problems that are found in the biblical use of sexual intimacy to reflect God's relationship with humanity. In the Hebrew Bible, in particular, the metaphor is mostly used by the prophets to depict Israel's unfaithfulness and God's judgment and punishment. God's desire and love are intricately tied to the "justified" abuse of the unfaithful wife. The sexual bond has to be untangled from its connection to sexual abuse before it should be readily accepted as a positive metaphor for God's love and desire for God's people. In the same way, the limitations of Genesis 1 and 2 have to be acknowledged when these are taken as defining sexuality. The broad framework of Genesis 1 and 2 has to be accepted, and when we see only the individuals in these texts we may be missing the point. Paul himself may be very wrong in seeing individuals as being in the image of God. I would suggest that humanity as a whole is in the image of God, and whatever our individual genders or sexualities, all of us together make the image of God. And together we are fruitful.

III. 4. The Church's Challenge: Christian Unity and Biblical Interpretation

When we recite the Nicene Creed and the Apostles' Creed in our liturgies we acknowledge the universal Church. There are many elements of the human experience that make us disagree in certain areas of faith, and while unity as a Church is of great value we should not hold on to that unity when it hinders the eschatological vision. The love of Christ compels us to seek justice for all humanity as we follow the model of Christ to love. I think the fact that the Gospel of John depicts Jesus praying for the unity of his disciples (John 17:20–24) reflects the difficulty of forging and maintaining that unity in an imperfect world. As we strive for that unity, we should not lose focus on God's mission and our mission in the world.

Concluding Wish

It is my hope that subsequent editions of the rites for the blessing of same-sex relationships will not seem to reflect that they are inferior to different-sex relationships. I also hope that our limited understanding of the blessedness of same-sex relationships will deepen and expand, and will no longer be as dependent on our understanding of different-sex or heterosexual marriage.

e. George R. Sumner

George R. Sumner was the Principal at Wycliffe College in Toronto. On May 16, 2015, he was elected Bishop of the Episcopal Diocese of Dallas.

I have been requested to respond to the document called "Faith, Hope, and Love: Theological Resources for Blessing Same-Sex Relationships." This is actually not the first time I have been asked by the Episcopal Church to weigh in on this subject. I was a traditionalist member of the House of Bishops' Theology Committee, which met over two years and at considerable expense to the Church, beginning in 2008. Our group was a congenial and generous-spirited one, and we presented both sides of the theology of marriage in relation to same-sex relations, along with rebuttals of the opposing team's claims. Our work was presented to the House of Bishops, and eventually published in the *Anglican Theological Review* in the Winter 2011 issue. Our document did not receive any mention in the introduction to "Faith, Hope, and Love," though it is cited in a footnote in the last section, on Christian unity. Apparently the Church has moved beyond the point where two points of view need to be represented in official reflection on this issue. I will not attempt to summarize all our points in this short piece, since anyone interested can find the complete essays at the *Anglican Theological Review* website. As for the more recent document, it is an articulate presentation of the progressive position, but does not break any new ground. It will reinforce the views of those who agree, but offers little of interest for those who do not.

As to the prior committee of which I was a part, after two years of work, it was clear to most of us that the matter came down to culture. The revisionist case cannot be made from the Bible, tradition, or science, and there were moments of candor on this score from the progressive side. Is the new trend a wind of the Spirit, or not? Can the stool in question stand on that one leg? I am by trade a missiologist, and so it was interesting for me to note how the tag *missio Dei* was deployed to bolster the progressive argument. It was claimed that what God is now doing in the world trumped all other evidence. But some historical study around the concept of the *missio* tag reveals the tendency we humans have to conflate the trajectory of God's work in the world with our own political predilections, when our perception is unaided by Scripture and tradition.

As to the politics of the moment, conservative Episcopalians are in an awkward position. Even as these resources for same-sex blessing rites are being appropriated by the Church, consideration of marriage itself has begun. There is a strong suggestion that a proposed change to the rite of marriage cannot be far behind. I believe that the move to bless same-sex unions was a mistake, but I also believe that proceeding on to marriage, and ensconcing the change in the Book of Common Prayer, would exacerbate the problem. That move would enflame the conflict further, especially in the Anglican Communion. It would threaten to move the new liturgical practice from option to coercion. It would put at risk the credibility of liberal leaders who told their flocks they only supported blessings. It would show a lack of the patience which is implied in the idea of doctrinal reception. It would fail to hear the voice of wisdom saying "enough is enough."

If the Church is not really interested in hearing from conservative theologians like me on this issue, what am I to do with the remainder of my airtime? The truly pressing issue before the Church is the following: Will room be found for the loyal opposition, for conservative Episcopalians? Is our Church to be truly liberal, and will it live up to the claim it makes about its own comprehensiveness? After all our talk about "the other" nowadays, what will liberal Episcopalians do with the fact that "the other" is in many cases a traditional Evangelical or Anglo-Catholic or charismatic? Years ago, at an event for Episcopal Foundation fellows, my friend Paul Zahl said that the great ethical challenge for those in power in the national Church now is how to deal with its relatively powerless conservative minority. This question is yet more urgent when that minority also happens to have the weight of the tradition and the strongest bonds of affection with the wider Communion on its side.

I was taught in my seminary days about F. D. Maurice's vision of a kind of liberal Anglicanism that needed all its parties, each one challenging the other like flint. I have my own issues with Maurice, but surely he was the forerunner of modern Anglicanism. Is there the will, not to mention the theological virtues of faith, hope, and love, on the part of the majority, to live out this vision? Will the Church encourage that freedom of theological expression which we are proud of in the breadth of our tradition? Do we mean it when we talk about the value of conscience in our Anglican tradition, especially for dioceses and parishes in the coming years? In this vein, is the Church willing to guarantee them access to the traditional rite of marriage, come what may, as a concrete step toward assuring a real comprehensiveness? I was, I assume, asked to respond to this document as a gesture of inclusion, and so it is the question of real and costly inclusion that I wish to bring before the Church.

f. Fredrica Harris Thompsett

*Fredrica Harris Thompsett is the Mary Wolfe Professor
Emerita of Historical Theology
at the Episcopal Divinity School, Cambridge, Massachusetts*

I do remember my baptism. I was an eight-year-old Episcopalian and fascinated by the strong promises made in my behalf. The minister used the office for children, yet we—my twin brother and I—kept adding in the "I will's" and "I do's." The promise that we might be granted the "power and strength" to "triumph against the devil, the world, and the flesh" (1928 BCP, 278) was, to say the least, unforgettable to my young mind. This was strong stuff, well worthy of the joyous family celebration that followed.

Recently the modern liturgical renewal movement has strengthened and brought Holy Baptism into greater visibility across many denominations. For Episcopalians these positive revisions in Holy Baptism are represented in the 1979 Book of Common Prayer. Today there are more occasions for congregations to celebrate Holy Baptism and together commit and recommit themselves to the challenges conveyed in the Baptismal Covenant. This liturgical shift has restored baptism's prominence in shaping our religious identity both as individuals and as worshiping communities. As a theologian and historian, I know that these changes in contemporary liturgies of baptism not only restore early Christian practices, they also align with distinct Anglican theological emphases.

Baptism is foundational. When I reflect theologically on how God is working today in our relationships and faithful living, I am drawn again and again to consider promises made and reaffirmed in baptism. Of particular importance in baptism and other sacraments is the generosity of God's covenantal love. Today's celebrations of baptism move us liturgically closer to glimpsing and understanding covenanting partnerships. Moreover, in our experience of promises publicly made in gathered community, we are affirming and welcoming individual lifetimes of godly living. We are moving away from worship patterns that unintentionally privatized and obscured the fact of God's great goodness in creation. In blessing lifelong relationships we are also, I believe, representing significant aspects of our Anglican heritage. Both in traditional marriage rites and in the proposed blessing of committed relationships of same-sex couples, the characteristics I first encountered as an eight-year-old child have been strengthened and extended.

For some Episcopalians the impetus to respond to our sisters and brothers who are gay and lesbian by providing ways to bless same-sex couples is primarily occasioned by secular cultural changes and has little to do with theological understandings. In this brief essay I wish to point to the theological continuity of our baptismal practices with the current call to reflect on how God is working today in committed same-sex relationships. In effect, the patterns of worship our Prayer Book prescribes have strengthened understanding of committed lifelong relationships. Three overlapping theological components are central both to baptism and to blessing same-sex unions. These are: (1) deepened insight into our covenantal relationship with God in Christ; (2) the public character and value of individuals and congregations sharing God's blessings; and (3) continuity with positive Anglican perspectives on committed intimate relationships.

Like most biblical covenants, the Baptismal Covenant is deeply grounded in the generosity of God's love. Our Hebraic ancestors, whether in the covenants of Noah, Abraham and Sarah, Moses, or Jeremiah, emphasized the steadfast loving-kindness of the Creator. The Hebrew word *hesed* is frequently used in these biblical texts. It is usually translated as "loving-kindness" and associated as a sure and steadfast foundation for covenantal living. There is nothing simple or short-lived about covenantal love. The foundation for covenantal theology is the expectant love and uncompromising faithfulness that God holds for God's people for generations to come. Our biblical ancestors emphasized the magnitude of God's empowering action, call, and summons into lifelong relationship. Biblical expressions of covenant thinking today are central for those of us who wish to be addressed by God and respond to God's presence in our lives.

Over the past thirty-five years, guided by the 1979 Book of Common Prayer, Episcopalians have become more familiar with the concept of covenantal relationships with God. This is underscored educationally in the Outline of the Faith, which describes a covenant as "a relationship initiated by God, to which a body of people responds in faith" (BCP, 846). It is underscored liturgically in the Baptismal Covenant (BCP, 304–305). Baptism is an expression of a sacramental

covenant in which we are adopted, that is chosen, as God's own
children and incorporated into full membership in Christ's Church.
In the Synoptic Gospels' telling of our Lord's baptism, Jesus is
proclaimed as God's "Son, the Beloved," with whom God is "well
pleased" (Matthew 3:17, Mark 1:11, Luke 3:22b). In our baptism we
too are adopted as God's "own children" and "marked as Christ's
own for ever" (BCP, 311, 308). Baptism reveals God's generosity
in creation, God's steadfast loving-kindness. God's gracious gift
of baptism incorporates and extends our lives into God's mission.
In contemporary worship experiences we have moved closer, as in
marriage and same-sex blessings, to glimpsing and proclaiming the
blessing of covenanting relationships.

Baptism is not simply or only an individual decision. As a covenant,
this sacrament is about God acting and the community of faith
responding. Therefore the service of Holy Baptism is more than a
private family matter, and it is designed for public occasions. Even as
baptism has been restored in the 1979 Book of Common Prayer to
a joyous place of graceful prominence in Episcopal worship, so too
blessing of same-sex relationships offers an opportunity for public
expression of God's abundant grace and goodness. Some same-sex
couples, their family, friends, and other community members may
experience restoration, healing, and forgiveness. Blessing services
signal acceptance, affirmation, commitment, and ongoing support
from God, from the Church, and from gathered family and friends.
For those whose intimate relationships may have in the past been
hidden, despised, shunned, ignored, or dismissed, the promise of
new life in Christ is liberating. I am reminded of the freedom from
cultural and social barriers promised by Paul in Galatians 3:27–28:
"As many of you as were baptized into Christ have clothed yourselves
with Christ. There is no longer Jew or Greek, there is now no longer
slave or free, there is no longer male and female; for all of you
are one in Christ Jesus." Paul envisioned baptism as overcoming
all that separates human beings from one another and from God.
God's promise of freedom and shared life in Christ replaces all prior
identities and divisions.

In my experience the public character of blessing same-sex unions
provides opportunities for pastoral witness and reconciliation. I
remember experiencing with joyful tears a blessing service held for
a couple who had been faithfully committed to one another for
more than fifty years. They were described by others as "pillars of
our congregation." Over the years their many gifts of service and
stewardship had been welcomed, yet their loving, lifelong, committed
relationship had not previously been even acknowledged, let alone

blessed. For my homosexual sisters and brothers the public assurance
of God's presence and affirmation of their most intimate relationships
has been a long time coming.

Anglican perspectives on committed intimate relationships have
traditionally emphasized the loving relational character of matrimony.
Early on in the Reformation our Episcopal ancestors were among
the first modern Christians to put a loving spin on marriage. Thomas
Cranmer, an Archbishop of Canterbury and the primary author of
the earliest editions of the English *Book of Common Prayer,* crafted
a liturgy which underscored marriage as a positive opportunity for
mutual enjoyment. Cranmer—himself a happily, if quietly, married
man with children—emphasized the benefit of marriage for England's
citizens. Marriage was, he said in the 1549 Form of the Solemnization
of Matrimony, for the "mutual society, help, and comfort, that the
one ought to have of the other, both in prosperity and adversity."
Perhaps with his own "dearly beloved Margaret Cranmer" in mind,
it was Cranmer who was the first to add to the official Church of
England marriage text the promise that each partner would "love and
cherish" the other. These words replaced the wife's required oath in
a late medieval service to be "buxom in bed and board." Archbishop
Cranmer's perspective on committed loving relationships benefited the
couple, the Church, and the wider society. In the shifting context of
the English Reformation, Cranmer seized opportunities for significant
liturgical, theological, and social change. These were expressed in
the new English *Book of Common Prayer.* In worship and common
prayer, cultural attitudes and expectations for married couples were
shaped anew.

What I suggest here is that liturgical resources for blessing same-
sex relationships have much in common with positive Anglican
perspectives on loving and faithful relationships. Archbishop Cranmer
recognized marriage as a vital social institution grounded in ideals
of mutuality, help, and comfort. The trajectory from a sixteenth-
century archbishop to an early twenty-first-century Chief Justice of
Massachusetts is slim at best. Yet it might be of interest to note that in
the 2003 ruling that allowed Massachusetts to become the first state
to issue marriage licenses to same-sex couples, Chief Justice Margaret
Marshall argued that neither Church nor society should hoard the
values bestowed in marriage or take their wider societal beneficial
intent for granted.[83] Marshall, herself a practicing Episcopalian,

---

83 The landmark ruling "Goodridge vs. the Department of Health," was decided by the State
   Appellate Court in November of 2003 and became law in May of 2004. It has withstood
   attempts to replace the word "marriage" with less embracing matrimonial terminology
   like "civil unions." In November of 2009, Episcopal Bishop M. Thomas Shaw, following

argued that this ruling affirmed "the dignity and equality of all individuals." Could it be that she was influenced by the Baptismal Covenant's promise to "respect the dignity of every human being" (BCP, 305)? Could it be that common prayer has had a steadily progressive impact influencing both individual hearts and societal laws?

I am on firmer, far less conjectural, theological ground in naming Incarnational theology as a central aspect of Anglican theology. In Anglican theology the legacy of the Incarnation has become a cherished focal point, a guiding principle shaping Anglican understandings of human and divinity alike. Michael Ramsey, who many may remember as one of the great Archbishops of Canterbury of the twentieth century, concluded that "the Incarnation meant not only that God took human flesh but that human nature was raised up to share in the life of God."[84] The redemptive work of the Incarnation provides the foundation for Anglican optimism about humanity. This God not only creates but also restores the dignity of human nature. This God in Christ partakes of the fullness of human life. This God bears the full range of love's power, including the capacity to instill and invite devotion, passion, affection, and sexuality expressed in our most intimate relationships. Biblical scholar and Anglican theologian L. William Countryman has noted that baptism interprets the goodness of the gifts bestowed by God in creation.[85] The blessing of covenanted couples, whether same-sex or different-sex partners, reminds us of the worth of intimate human relationships established by God in creation. In the blessing of covenanted couples and in marriage rites the goodness of faithful sexual intimacy is affirmed. Incarnational theology and baptismal theology alike proclaim that, in Jesus, God is with us in a new way. Similarly, in marriage, as in the blessing of covenanted couples, the newness of life in Christ is affirmed by both the couple and the wider community.

I have emphasized the theological grounding that the sacrament of Holy Baptism offers for other expressions of covenantal love. It might not be a stretch to recall and adapt a saying articulated forty years ago when the Episcopal Church was debating the ordination of women: "If you are not going to ordain women, stop baptizing them."

---

a permissive (though not obligatory) action of General Convention for bishops in states which legally allow same-sex marriage, permitted clergy in the Diocese of Massachusetts to officiate at same-sex weddings.

84 On the centrality of the Incarnation in Ramsey's theology see Kenneth Leech, "'The Real Archbishop': A Profile of Michael Ramsey," *The Christian Century* (March 12, 1986): 266–69.

85 See L. William Countryman, *Living on the Border of the Holy: Renewing the Priesthood of All* (Harrisburg: Morehouse Publishing), especially chapter 5, 81-110,

Anglican theologian Marilyn McCord Adams commends this saying as "forwarding a *strong doctrine of baptism*." She contends, as I do, that "the strong doctrine of baptism is radical and bears repeating."[86] When considering the opportunity to bless covenanted same-sex couples, a similar baptismally-grounded axiom might be: "If we are not open to blessing committed relationships of same-sex couples, we should stop baptizing them." The covenant of baptism offers a lifelong foundation for deepening other covenanted relationships of love and service to God's reconciling mission. Anglican Christians are known for finding integrity and coherence in the ways our patterns of worship shape our beliefs. As the theological resources in "I Will Bless You, and You Will Be a Blessing" indicate, promises affirmed by baptism shape an encouraging framework for blessing faithful relationships of covenanted love.

---

86 See Marilyn McCord Adams, "The Ordination of Women: Some Theological Implications," in *Looking Forward, Looking Backward: Forty Years of Women's Ordination*, ed. Fredrica Harris Thompsett (New York: Morehouse Publishing, 2014), 72–73.

IV. Hearing, Seeing, and Declaring New Things

Pastoral Resources for Preparing Couples for a Liturgy of Blessing or Marriage

Contents

Overview: Pastoral Care for Gender and
Sexual Minority Couples
  1. Available Resources: Materials for Pastoral Preparation
  2. Particular Issues Affecting Gender and
     Sexual Minority Couples
  3. Presenters
  4. Outline of Pre-Blessing Preparation for Gender and
     Sexual Minority Couples

Handouts
  1. *Theological Reflection on Covenantal Relationship:*
     Spiritual Practice for Gender and Sexual Minority Couples
  2. *Declaration of Intention for Marriage*
  3. *Declaration of Intention for Lifelong Covenant*
  4. *About Presenters—For the Couple*
  5. *Information for Presenters*
  6. *Model Congregational Guidelines*

Overview: Pastoral Care for Gender and Sexual Minority Couples

You have heard; now see all this; and will you not declare it?
From this time forward I make you hear new things, hidden
things that you have not known.

—Isaiah 48:6

I will give you as a light to the nations, that my salvation may
reach to the end of the earth.

—Isaiah 49:6

The pastoral resources in this essay are provided to assist clergy and
trained lay people who are preparing gender and sexual minority[87]
couples for marriage or a blessing of their relationship, using one
of the liturgies authorized by The Episcopal Church. For couples
preparing for a blessing, the expectation of such preparation is
equivalent to the canonical requirement that couples preparing for
marriage receive instruction "in the nature, purpose, and meaning,
as well as the rights, duties and responsibilities of marriage" (Canon
I.18.3[c]).

Preparation is similar for all couples, whether gender and sexual
minority or different-sex/gender. Most clergy and lay people who
currently offer premarital preparation to different-sex couples are more
than capable of working with gender and sexual minority couples.
However, understanding the differences is necessary—and helpful.

---

87 The term "gender and sexual minorities" (GSM) is increasingly used in academic study
of gender/sexual identity and/or orientation, recognizing the complexity of both human
biology and the social construction of gender and sexuality. This term is used in this
pastoral resource except when referring to marriage, since "same-sex marriage" is
commonly used in civil law.

The pastoral resources described in this essay address differences in the preparation of gender and sexual minority couples and different-sex couples and include some of the available resources for preparing gender and sexual minority couples for marriage or the blessing of their relationship.

Commonly Used Terms for Gender and/or Sexual Minorities

Because human sexuality exists on a spectrum, because the number of possible identities that communities or individuals may craft (consciously and unconsciously) defies limitation, and because language constantly evolves, terminology for gender and sexual minorities (GSM) sometimes proves elusive. As a general consideration, it is always best to refer to someone by name, not a category, and to ask people how they identify themselves or prefer to be called. It is not as important that the preparer fully understand the complexities of identity and/or orientation as that the couple themselves do; however, clergy and lay preparers are encouraged to read some of the excellent resources available about GSM experiences or to consult with a professional.

The Gay and Lesbian Alliance Against Defamation (GLAAD)—an organization that advises media and other organizations concerning the language and images they use to represent GSM people and issues—provides extensive, widely used, and highly readable reference guides for commonly used terminology. Some common terms are described below with reference to the glossary available at glaad. org. For a more comprehensive consideration, you may also wish to consult *An Ally's Guide to Terminology: Talking About LGBT People & Equality*, published by GLAAD.

Sex: The biological condition of being male or female is typically identified visually at birth based on visible anatomy of the newborn. However, for a variety of reasons the sex of a person cannot always be definitively determined from visual assessment. While sex differences are biological, biology is flexible, dynamic, and not unaffected by environment and culture. Furthermore, it is important to bear in mind that biology does not determine identity.

Gender Identity and Expression: Individuals usually have a stable, deep, and strongly felt sense of their own gender that manifests very early in childhood; that gender identity, however, may not always correspond to the person's sex. A person whose gender identity does not correspond with the sex assigned at birth may be called a transgender person (though individuals sometimes use or prefer other language). The GLAAD "Media Reference Guide—Transgender Issues" describes transgender as "an umbrella term for people whose gender identity and/ or gender expression differs from what is typically associated with the sex they were assigned at birth."[88] Transgender people who, through surgery and/or hormone treatment, alter their biological sex to align with their gender identity are sometimes called transsexual, though the term is not preferred by all. It should be noted, however, that not all transgender people are able or wish to medically alter their biological sex.

A person's internal gender identity may or may not be expressed to society. Gender expression refers to how an individual manifests gender to society, including "one's name, pronouns, clothing, haircut, behavior, voice, or body characteristics."[89] Societies typically associate these characteristics with masculinity and femininity; however, the associations vary from culture to culture. Transgender people often express the gender with which they internally identify in ways that their society will recognize; others, though, both transgender and cisgender (a term used to describe non-transgender people), develop expressions that are intentionally gender non-conforming.

While many people understand themselves as being a man or a woman, others identify themselves in ways that are not limited by this traditional binary. Sometimes those who resist or reject the traditional gender categories identify themselves as "genderqueer" (though this term is not universal).[90]

Sexual Orientation: Although they are often associated with each other, gender identity and sexual orientation do not have a direct correspondence. For instance, a transgender man[91] (someone who was assigned the female sex at birth, but identifies as a man) who is sexually drawn to women is considered "straight."

---

88 http://glaad.org/reference/transgender.

89 http://glaad.org/reference/transgender.

90 For stories of transgender Episcopalians, see "Voices of Witness: Out of the Box," http://www.youtube.com/watch?v=QzCANWGsEdc.

91 While some transgender people do describe themselves as a "transgender man/woman" others prefer the language man/woman without the modifier. Still others resist the gender binary altogether. Because individual perceptions and preferences vary, it is best not to assign a category (or a pronoun) to someone without asking how they understand and prefer to talk about their own gender identity.

Rather than "homosexual," which carries offensive, negative
connotations for many, the preferred term for someone
"whose enduring physical, romantic and/or emotional
attractions are to people of the same sex"[92] is "gay" or "gay
person." Some women prefer to use the term "lesbian"
while others prefer "gay woman." A person whose sexual
orientation encompasses people of both the same and different
sex are generally called "bisexual" or "bi." Despite common
assumptions to the contrary, "[b]isexual people need not have
had specific sexual experiences to be bisexual; in fact, they
need not have had any sexual experience at all to identify
as bisexual."[93] A significant number of gay, lesbian, and bi
people have adopted the formerly offensive term "queer" to
describe themselves or GSM people more generally; however,
the term continues to be offensive to others and should not
be used to describe someone unless they express an explicit
preference for it.

Contextual Competence

Clergy and qualified lay people preparing couples for marriages or
blessings need to be *contextually competent*, a concept derived from
cultural competence. In fields such as health care, social work, and
education, culturally competent professionals embody awareness,
a positive attitude, knowledge, and skills that enable them to work
effectively in cross-cultural situations.

Consider the different situations that one might encounter when
preparing a couple for a blessing or marriage:

- Preparing a couple in their seventies for a blessing of their
  relationship is very different from preparing a couple in their
  twenties.

- Preparing a couple entering a new relationship is different
  from preparing two people who have been living in a
  committed relationship for a long time.

- Preparing an interracial couple differs in some aspects from
  preparing a couple of the same race.

- Preparing a couple without children differs from preparing
  parents.

---

92 http://www.glaad.org/reference/lgb.
93 http://www.glaad.org/reference/lgb

Being "contextually competent" means understanding and appreciating these, and many more, differing situations. Clergy and trained lay preparers need to examine their own contextual competence as they consider working with GSM couples. If they cannot work with a GSM couple with appreciation and awareness, then the best practice is to refer the couple to another clergyperson or trained lay preparer, and seek further training for themselves.

The materials below will help clergy and trained lay preparers adapt their skills to work with GSM couples in a contextually competent manner.

1. Available Resources: Materials for Pastoral Preparation

In a 2010 churchwide survey regarding pastoral and teaching materials, the Standing Commission on Liturgy and Music found that the following resources are among those commonly used to prepare GSM couples for a blessing.

Prepare/Enrich (Life Innovations, Inc.)
https://www.prepare-enrich.com

- A relationship inventory that assesses couples' strengths and growth areas on topics such as finances, communication, conflict resolution, and sexuality. This assessment tool is by far the one used most frequently among respondents to the Commission's survey. "Facilitators" (the term that Prepare/Enrich employs) must be trained in its use; see website for cost of materials.

- *Positives*: recently revised (2008), customized version easily used with GSM couples; uses the language of "partner"; most comprehensive tool to address personality, conflict resolution, family, health, and financial and spiritual issues; assesses goals, strengths, and growth areas; large, national norm base (more than five hundred thousand couples).

- *Negatives*: currently, research results are standardized only for different-sex/gender couples, so there is no "norm" against which to compare a GSM couple's data.

Premarriage Awareness Inventory (Logos Productions)
http://www3.logosproductions.com

- Preferred by those not trained in *Prepare/Enrich*

- *Positives*: three customized formats, including inventories for those living together or previously married; thorough personality assessment; coverage of major areas, such as faith, finances, family of origin, children, power issues, life goals.

- *Negatives*: standardized for different-sex/gender couples only, but author indicates that he will be implementing a GSM version (no target date given).

The Marriage Journey: Preparation and Provisions for Life Together,
by Linda Grenz and Delbert Glover (Church Publishing, 2003)

- Recommended by those who find online inventories impersonal.

- *Positives*: Uses "partner" instead of specifying gender; includes material for couples living together and those with children; clear, direct language; ideal for the technologically challenged couple.

- *Negatives*: no personality assessment included.

The following books were published too recently to be cited by respondents to the 2010 survey. Because they specifically address pastoral needs of same-gender couples, we include them among available resources.

All Whom God Has Joined: Resources for Clergy and Same-Gender Loving Couples
by Leanne McCall Tigert and Maren C. Tirabassi (Pilgrim Press, 2010).

Premarital Counseling for Gays and Lesbians: Case Studies and Helpful Questions
by Pamela Milam (ASD Publishing, 2012).

2. Particular Issues Affecting Gender and Sexual Minority Couples

Issues or differences that are particular to gender and sexual minority (GSM) couples are not necessarily challenges in preparation. They are more often gifts, especially if the clergyperson or layperson preparing a couple understands variation as part of God's plan for the world and a sign of God's blessing. Contextual competence is important here, especially in a preparer's awareness of places where skills for preparing different-sex/gender couples do not transfer to GSM couples. In addition, preparers need to examine their own understanding of marrying or blessing a GSM couple, as well as the assumptions of the couple's faith and civil communities, including diocesan authority and various state laws.

GSM couples come to ask for marriage or a blessing with a variety of life backgrounds; thus provision for some variations and differences appear, for example, in the prayer choices in the liturgy. Other variations that clergy or lay preparers will meet in their work with GSM couples follow below.[94]

Same-Sex Marriages, Canon Law, and Diocesan Policies

Canon I.18.1 requires clergy to "conform to the laws of the State governing the creation of the civil status of marriage." With the U.S. Supreme Court ruling issued on June 26, 2015, GSM couples may be married in any U.S. jurisdiction. In dioceses outside the United States, civil law varies, and clergy must familiarize themselves with the law applicable in their context.

General Convention Resolution 2015-A054 authorizes "The Witnessing and Blessing of a Marriage" and "The Celebration and

---

94 This material is adapted from "Pastoral Resources for Province One Episcopal Clergy Ministering to Same-Gender Couples."

Blessing of a Marriage 2" for trial use, and Canon I.18.1 allows clergy to solemnize a marriage of a GSM couple, using either of these liturgical forms, provided that the marriage is permitted by civil law and that the clergyperson follows the provisions of Canons I.18 and I.19. The resolution stipulates that "bishops exercising ecclesiastical authority or, where appropriate, ecclesiastical supervision will make provision for all couples asking to be married in this Church to have access to these liturgies," while also requiring that the liturgies be used "under the direction and with the permission of the Diocesan Bishop." Clergy and couples seeking to be married must follow the policies of their diocese when preparing to use one of these trial-use liturgies for marriage.

General Convention Resolution 2015-A054 also authorizes "The Witnessing and Blessing of a Lifelong Covenant" for use "under the direction and with the permission of the bishop exercising ecclesiastical authority." This liturgy is intended for use with GSM couples in jurisdictions where same-sex marriage is not legal. Clergy and couples seeking a blessing must follow the policies or guidelines of their diocese.

Canon I.19.3 sets out requirements that must be followed in cases of remarriage after divorce or dissolution of a marriage. Because some dioceses require professional counseling for a couple if one member of the couple (or both) has been divorced more than once or has had more than one previous long-term relationship, clergy should check with the diocesan office for guidance on what is expected in such situations.

For clergy who feel they cannot solemnize a marriage or confer a liturgical blessing for any GSM couple, the best practice is to refer the couple to another clergyperson. Some of these clergy may also wish to provide an additional pastoral response to those couples, thereby affirming and supporting their desire for God's blessing upon their relationship.

Currently, very few denominations authorize their clergy to conduct same-sex blessings or marriages, so an Episcopal clergyperson may be approached by a couple seeking a blessing of their union simply because it is not an option for them within their own denomination. Episcopal clergy may expect that some of these couples from other denominations feel tender and vulnerable in their relationship to the wider Church and so may need particular nurture and support.

Possible Issues Arising from Sexual Orientation or Gender Identity

This section addresses some of the more common issues that may arise in the process of preparing a GSM couple for marriage or a blessing of their lifelong covenant.

"Late bloomers" who "come out" later in life: Some GSM people recognize their sexual orientation or gender identity from a very young age. Others may have a growing realization that does not become fully clear until much later in life; some may have understood their sexual orientation or gender identity for some time but are only recently "coming out" publicly. A "late bloomer" may need some time to begin to live into his/her truest life or explore with a counselor this core change in self-perception before entering into a lifelong commitment.

Previous relationships: Some individuals may have lived a heterosexual life to a point, perhaps inwardly questioning their sexual orientation or gender identity, before deciding that they felt more strongly toward people of the same sex or gender; others may have simply fallen in love with someone of the same sex or gender, perhaps by surprise. Still others may have accepted their own bisexuality and at one point decided to make a commitment to a person of a different sex/gender. These earlier relationships may have been more or less satisfactory depending on the extent to which familial, societal, and/or religious expectations played a part, and the compatibility between the partners. There are likely to be many important relationships from these earlier partnerships which will need to be honored and successfully incorporated into the life of the new couple.

Internalized homophobia: One or both members of a GSM couple may have been subjected to a continual societal onslaught of negative or stereotypical messages. These messages may have been internalized, possibly resulting in a person growing severely uncomfortable with his/her sexual orientation or gender identity. A clergyperson or trained lay preparer who perceives that a person has significant negative feelings or stigma about his/her orientation may appropriately refer the person for counseling with a therapist trained to handle this issue.

Biphobia: Bisexuality is sometimes unfairly and inaccurately associated with promiscuity and infidelity. This prejudice is found among people of varying sexual orientations, including other GSM people. Bi people are not more or less inclined to sexual license than any other people; clergy and lay preparers should guard against making assumptions about bisexuals.

Long-Term Relationships

Preparers may be working with people who have been together
for many years or have previously had long-term, monogamous
relationships. This means that preparers must be open to learning and
benefiting from the wisdom generated by a couple's long years together.

Particular Hurt

One or both members of a GSM couple may have been wounded by
exclusion or marginalization, that is, experiences and feelings of being
"other" or "less than." Certainly, GSM people are at risk of being
victims of abuse or exploitation, as well as self-hatred and fear of
rejection. Clergy and laypeople preparing GSM couples for marriage
or blessings need to be sensitive to these issues.

Very often, due to prior experiences with organized religions who
reject and do not approve of GSM people or relationships, these
individuals do not feel welcome in a house of worship. In addition,
one or both members of the couple may have a history of being
excluded from benefits that heterosexuals receive from the State. For
the couple, a clergyperson or layperson providing marriage or blessing
preparation represents the Church, so a preparer will need to build
a trusting relationship with the couple in order to support them in
dealing with the anger, hurt, or confusion that erupts from rejection.

In or Out?

Although a couple is seeking a public union, one or even both members
of the couple may need to remain "closeted" in some aspects of
their individual lives. For instance, one person may be employed in
a workplace or profession where being "out" could jeopardize the
ability to function there at top form or even to continue to work there.
Unfortunately, a prime example is the Church. For GSM clergy in many
denominations, "coming out," especially when in a relationship, can
result in being stripped of the ability to function as ordained clergy or
to hold any position of leadership in the Church. In secular places of
employment, where GSM people might be protected by law, their sexual
orientation or gender identity could affect their ability to be hired or
result in a tense and unfriendly work environment. Being "out" could
have a negative impact on seeking or maintaining a position in public
office. Lesbians and gays serving in the military no longer need to remain
closeted, but many who were in the military previous to this change might
need to talk about their pasts as closeted members of the armed services.

GSM couples take risks, even to their lives, when they display affection in public; when they cannot hold hands, they hold secrets. Because of this, there can be tension in a relationship when one person is fully "out" and comfortable with some public, visible displays of affection while the other is not. In some work situations, one person in the relationship may need to be careful when calling a partner at the workplace or taking messages at home.

Couples need to discuss when, where, and with whom it is safe to be open about their relationship in general. Specifically, as part of their preparation, they need to discuss each other's comfort levels and needs regarding making their relationship known in a public ceremony.

Relational History and Resolution of Previous Relationships

All couples have to deal with what went before. GSM couples may not be going through legal divorces, but as with any relationship, they will still likely need to process issues related to their previous relationships on an emotional and practical level. Couples will be freer to proceed into a new lifelong committed relationship when they have processed what one or the other has learned from earlier relationships and when they have resolved matters of finance, property, child custody, and responsibility to former spouses or partners.

Families of Origin

Most clergy and trained laypersons inquire about each individual's family of origin when preparing different-sex/gender couples for marriage. The answers can give the couple insights regarding a number of issues, including their understanding of what a healthy or unhealthy relationship looks like and their attitudes toward finances and parenting practices; the responses may also enable couples to identify unresolved issues that could affect the relationship.

One area which may be unique to GSM couples is their families' responses to their orientation, their public lives as GSM people, and their life together as a couple. Couples will benefit from exploring questions such as: Have the individuals "come out" to their own families? If so, what was the response? Has either member of a couple told his/her family about the intended marriage or blessing liturgy? Is the family supportive, hostile, or grieving, or simply absent? How will each family respond to the individual's partner: will the family define a partner as a spouse and therefore part of the family, or will they treat one's partner as a friend or roommate? In other words, has the couple discussed what they anticipate their relationship with the in-laws will be as they enter into a lifelong, committed relationship? Likewise, is the couple able to engage a network of support, individually and as a couple, and do they perceive how it will become a part of their new life together?

Legal Matters

For different-sex/gender couples, marriage automatically comes with legal protections and obligations (above and beyond the legality of the union itself). In civil jurisdictions outside the United States where no civil union or same-sex marriage is allowed, it is critical that GSM couples pursue private legal protections that substitute for some of the legal protections flowing from civil marriage (though private measures cannot cover all of the legal attributes of civil marriage). The couple should consider arranging for medical and financial durable powers-of-attorney, wills, and living wills, and may need to seek professional advice regarding financial and property matters. In addition, couples should consider soliciting legal advice on their rights and risks, especially regarding issues of tax, Social Security, or other state and federal legal matters.

Children

As with any different-sex/gender, childless couple preparing for marriage, GSM couples should also discuss with each other whether one or the other wants children. This discussion might include topics such as when and how to have children, the impact of children on finances and employment, and matters of parenting, such as childcare and discipline. Couples entering the relationship with children should discuss how to help the children adjust and integrate into the new family constellation. GSM couples, especially those blessed with children from a previous relationship, also need to support their children through various stages of development, particularly as the children relate to their peers, who may have no understanding of, or possibly even a hostile reaction to, a friend with GSM parents. For example, if a parent becomes involved with a GSM partner, it may be controversial and require some adjustment in their child's social circle.

GSM couples should be aware of the legal ambiguity pertaining to custodial cases and may want to seek counsel to protect themselves and their children.

3. Presenters

Presenters are people chosen by the couple to support and present them to the presider and the assembly during the marriage or blessing liturgy. The liturgies include the option of presenters, just as some congregations offer to different-sex/gender couples. This option gives a voice to important people in the life of the couple during the liturgy and enriches the experience for all present. Presenters can also serve an important role in supporting the couple before and after the blessing liturgy. The selection of a couple mature in their relationship can be particularly helpful to a couple starting life together. The couple, together with the clergy or lay preparer, should talk as soon as possible about selecting presenters, so that the prayerful work of the presenters can begin early on.

Two short handouts provided in this pastoral resource (one for the couple and one for presenters) detail the role of presenters and are intended for use at the conclusion of the initial preparation session. They are designed for use with "The Witnessing and Blessing of a Lifelong Covenant" and "The Witnessing and Blessing of a Marriage." Congregations offering presenters for "The Celebration and Blessing of a Marriage 2" can use these handouts by substituting the text of the presentation from the Additional Directions on pages 186-87.

4. Outline of Pre-Blessing / Marriage Preparation for Gender and Sexual Minority Couples

Below is a guideline for a five-session, pre-blessing/marriage preparation that may be used along with the materials described above. In a 2010 churchwide survey regarding pastoral and teaching materials, the Standing Commission on Liturgy and Music found that a large number of trained lay preparers and clergy want a very specific template; however, those with experience preparing couples may choose to adapt, combine, or reorder this outline. Ideally, sessions last 60 to 90 minutes each, and both partners should be present for all sessions (although the preparer may decide to meet with one of the individuals to address specific issues).

Goal

Pre-blessing/marriage preparation sets as its goal the strengthening of a lifelong, monogamous partnership rooted in Christ. General Convention Resolution 2000–D039 addresses the hope—the Church's and the couple's—for an enduring relationship:

> *Resolved,* That we expect such relationships will be characterized by fidelity, monogamy, mutual affection and respect, careful, honest communication, and the holy love which enables those in such relationships to see in each other the image of God; and be it further
>
> *Resolved,* That we denounce promiscuity, exploitation, and abusiveness in the relationships of any of our members; and be it further
>
> *Resolved,* That this Church intends to hold all its members accountable to these values, and will provide for them the prayerful support, encouragement, and pastoral care necessary to live faithfully by them.

Expectations

Realities:

- Clergy and lay people are trained in many different ways to conduct premarital preparation.

- Clergy and trained lay people apply a wide variety of methods for pre-blessing/marriage preparation.

Assumptions:

- The priest or bishop is prepared to preside at the blessing.

- The clergyperson or trained layperson is experienced in preparing couples before marriages and / or blessings.

- The clergyperson or trained layperson is willing to refer the couple to a professional therapist should circumstances warrant.

Truth:

- Each couple is unique, requiring adaptations as appropriate.

Preparing Gender and Sexual Minority Couples in Long-term Relationships

When preparing people who have been together for many years, the session structure may need to be changed, and fewer sessions may be needed. One suggestion is to adapt the first session to get to know the couple, introduce the liturgy, and so on. The second session could employ the following questions or discussion topics, which respect the length of the couple's relationship and invite them to discuss their understanding of the Church.

- What does it mean to you to have your relationship blessed by the Church after all these years?

- How will having the Church's blessing and making a commitment in public, even if you have done so privately or in a non-Church setting, affect you or your relationship?

- What can your relationship teach the Church?

Finally, the third session could be adapted from the current fifth session: wrapping up, clarifying the liturgy, and fielding any other questions that may have arisen.

Session One: Getting To Know You and an Overview

This session focuses on getting to know one another. It also starts to address the details of the rite, offering the couple and the clergyperson an opportunity to study the rites together, looking at their meaning and choices and affirming that the blessing, grounded in God, is given through the Church. Some clergy, however, may prefer to do a very general overview of the rites in this session, then study them more intensely later in the process.

Addressing the practical issues of the blessing or marriage at the outset helps to build trust and allows the couple to open themselves to the substance of the next four sessions. By providing even a general overview of the rites, the preparer can address questions and alleviate anxieties about the actual day. For a marriage, the couple and clergyperson officiating will need to decide, either in this session or later in the preparation, which rite to use.

Session One includes a great deal of material, some of which may be moved to another session. Handouts for this session include:

- The liturgy "The Witnessing and Blessing of a Lifelong Covenant"; for a marriage, the preparer may have all of the rites available to review with the couple.

- 1. *Theological Reflection on Covenantal Relationship: Spiritual Practice for Gender and Sexual Minority Couples* (found at the end of this outline).

- 2. *Declaration of Intention for Marriage* OR 3. *Declaration of Intention for Lifelong Covenant* (found at the end of this outline).

- 4. *About Presenters—For the Couple* (found at the end of this outline).

- 5. *Information for Presenters* (found at the end of this outline).

Outline of Session One

- Pray together.

- Get to know one another (varies as to how well the preparer knows the couple).

- Explore the couples' religious backgrounds, their experiences with the church(es), and their reasons for being in this congregation.

- Reflect on the theological significance of the couple's relationship. The handout *Theological Reflection on Covenantal Relationship: Spiritual Practice for Gender and Sexual Minority Couples* may be useful in this discussion. (This reflection might be moved to a later session.)

- Review and ask the couple to sign the *Declaration of Intention for Marriage or Declaration of Intention for Lifelong Covenant.*

- Walk through the blessing rite or marriage rites, raising theological issues and naming liturgical choices:

  - Discuss the eucharist as normative in the service. However, including a celebration of the eucharist may not be appropriate if only one member of the couple is Christian.

  - Emphasize the difference between a civil service and an ecclesial blessing.

  - Answer general questions regarding details of the service and the Church's practice.

  - Introduce the possibility of presenters.

At the end of the session, provide written handouts and suggest "homework" topics for the couple to think about for Sessions Two and Three:

- Families of origin and growing up in them
  - What worked and didn't work so well in their families of origin (this topic may also influence work in Session Four)
  - Family Church/religious history as well as each individual's history—positive and negative—with the Church/religion

- Marriages of family members, particularly parents
  - Parents' ways of dealing with conflict
  - Parents' styles of child-rearing
  - Family tolerance of children's sexual orientation.

Session Two: Learning from the Past, Part 1

This session provides a time for one member of the couple to speak and for the other to listen. Session Two opens with prayer, then looks back to focus upon the relationship of one partner with his/her family of origin, including exploring the marriage(s) of his/her parents and siblings and, if possible, grandparents and close friends. This discussion includes what the individual would or would not replicate from the past in his/her own ongoing and future relationships, particularly the relationship that is to be blessed. In addition, the individual can look at levels of acceptance of his/her relationship by his/her family and at other issues from family of origin and childhood.

The guiding assumption underlying this analysis is that certain issues are replicated from generation to generation, and that, once the issues are identified, individuals can choose to continue those patterns or deliberately alter them. This session works most effectively if the conversation flows naturally, rather than following a rigid interview, and if it includes the following important areas:

- Family: number and birth order of siblings
- Money: its role and influence in the family
- Sex: attitudes in family of origin about monogamy, fidelity, and the role of sex in relationship
- Alcohol and drugs: their places within the family as children grew
- In-laws: relationship with in-laws and greater family
- Children:
  - agreement or disagreement between parents about child-rearing
  - the individual's feelings about being a child in his/her family
- Conflict: parents' methods of arguing and disagreeing.

As the conversation concludes, the preparer invites the individual to identify what he/she would or would not replicate in his/her own adult relationship with the life partner. Following that, the silent partner is given the floor to comment on what he/she has heard and learned, especially any surprises.

Session Three: Learning from the Past, Part 2

This session continues the look back by extending the chance for the other member of the couple to speak about his/her family of origin. Both members of the couple need the opportunity to explore the topics and to hear each other's stories so that each can learn and appreciate more deeply what the other brings to their relationship.

Session Three, which also begins with prayer, duplicates with the second person the process with the first from Session Two. If time permits at the end, the couple might discuss the impact of family history on their own relationship.

Session Four: Looking to the Future

This session, an opportunity to look at the relationship today and into the future, invites the couple to name areas in the relationship that appear strong and supportive while also opening a space to identify and address areas that may be problematic. Thoughts, questions, and new information from previous sessions may help determine where the couple is today and where their relationship and household may need attention in the future.

After opening with prayer, this session should include discussion of:

The couple's relationship in general: in-depth exploration of where they have been and where they are now.

- The role of sex and intimacy in the relationship (for example, potential changes of sexual behavior as a result of committing to a monogamous relationship).
- The role of alcohol and drugs in the relationship.
- Money (for example, household finances and financial planning).
- Legal protections (for example, medical and financial durable powers-of-attorney, wills, living wills, and insurance).
- Household roles (for example, who takes out the trash, who keeps the social calendar).
- Communication:
  - How the couple talks things through.
  - What happens when they disagree.
- Concerns for the future.
- Decision-making as a couple.
- Dealing with families as individuals (one's own as well as one's partner's) and as a couple.
- Support networks, now and in the future.

Session Four concludes with a discussion of the need for boundaries between generations so that the couples' life as a unit may be seen as distinct from older and younger generations.

Session Five: Liturgical Decisions and Wrap-up

Session Five, focused on the marriage or blessing service itself, is an opportunity to make choices for the liturgy, based on the *Theological Reflection on Covenantal Relationship* handed out (and discussed) at the first session. The depth of this discussion will be determined by what was or was not addressed in Session One. In addition, as the final session, Session Five serves as a time to consider questions that may have arisen from previous sessions.

Outline of Session Five

- Pray together.

- Address questions and concerns regarding previous sessions and other issues that have arisen.

- Review theological reflections in light of previous sessions and what is to come. The preparer can help the couple connect the spiritual practices of their life as a couple and the "staging" of the service. For example, will they process into the service together or separately, or will they be already in the worship space as the liturgy begins? Will they sit together during the Ministry of the Word or across the aisle from one another?

- Discuss details of the service itself:
  - Scripture (which passages speak particularly to the couple's life together?) and whether non-biblical readings may be included
  - Will the liturgy take place at the congregation's principal weekly celebration? Is celebration of the eucharist to be omitted for pastoral cause?
  - Other liturgical choices, especially:

    Which collect will be used?

    Which of the two vows will be used?

    Will rings be exchanged, or, if rings have already been worn, are they to be blessed?

    What music, if any, will be included? (The couple should consult with the congregation's musician.)

• Discuss presenters and their roles in supporting the couple in
  the service and in their ongoing life.

In closing, the preparer can assure the couple that they have done hard
and important work together, work that is a gift both to the preparer
and to the couple. The preparer can express his/her eager anticipation
of the couple's marriage/blessing and of meeting their close and
extended families, seeing them with their friends, and celebrating their
relationship in the sight of God.

Handouts for "Hearing, Seeing, and Declaring New Things"

Contents

The *Declaration of Intention* requires the replacement of *N.N.* and *N. N.* in the first sentence with the couple's names.

Handouts 4 and 5 are designed for use with the liturgies "The Witnessing and Blessing of a Lifelong Covenant" and "The Witnessing and Blessing of a Marriage." The preparer should insert the correct title of the rite. These handouts may be modified if one of the other marriage liturgies is to be used.

Handouts 4 through 6 are samples that may be adapted for the use of a specific congregation. In these, "N. Episcopal Church" should be replaced with the congregation's name, and a similar change made for "Episcopal Diocese of X."

Theological Reflection on Covenantal Relationship: Spiritual Practice for Gender and Sexual Minority Couples

Christian Life and Covenants

All Christians are called to bear witness to the good news of God's love and grace in Jesus Christ, through the power of the Holy Spirit. We are empowered for such witness by our covenantal relationship with God.

Baptism initiates us into that covenant, making us Christ's own forever and members of Christ's Body, the Church. The eucharist sustains us in that covenantal life and strengthens us to be Christ's witnesses in the world.

Our covenantal life with God is expressed in relationships of commitment and faithfulness, including those of gender and sexual minority couples. It is the Church's joy to celebrate these relationships as signs of God's love, to pray for God's grace to support couples in their life together, and to join with these couples in our shared witness to the gospel in the world.

Themes for Theological Reflection and Spiritual Practice

A sacramental framework for covenantal relationships offers a way to reflect on the grace of Christ and the fruit of the Spirit in the lives of faithful, committed couples. Several theological themes can assist couples as they consider their covenantal vows as a form of spiritual practice:

- *Vocation*: God calls people into various kinds of relationship, whether as single people, in monastic communities, or as intimate couples. These vocational callings can empower our witness to the gospel. The

decision to enter into a marriage or covenantal union
is a vocation marked by these characteristics: "fidelity,
monogamy, mutual affection and respect, careful, honest
communication, and the holy love which enables those in
such relationships to see in each other the image of God."

- *Households*: Covenantal relationships are often lived in
  households in which we practice daily the giving of ourselves
  for the good of another. While households take many
  different forms, they create a space of mutual trust and
  accountability. The joy, intimacy, and shared vulnerability
  of households can thus help us learn the spiritual disciplines
  of compassion, forgiveness, and reconciliation in lives of
  committed monogamy and fidelity.

- *Fruitfulness*: The divine grace that sustains a covenantal
  relationship bears fruit in countless ways, not only for the
  couple but for the wider community as well. Covenanted
  couples manifest this grace in their shared gifts for ministry
  and in lives of service, generosity, and hospitality.

- *Mutual Blessing*: A blessed relationship is set apart for a
  divine purpose: to bear witness to the creating, redeeming,
  and sanctifying love of God in the world. As the Spirit
  empowers the couple for this witness, the Church is likewise
  blessed and strengthened for its mission and ministry.

In all of these ways and more, the blessing of a relationship invites
the couple and the whole Church to renew our commitment to the
Baptismal Covenant. That commitment is expressed by *faith* in the
good news of Jesus Christ, in the *hope* for union with God that Christ
promised, and with the *love* that knits us together as the Body of
Christ. As the apostle Paul says, we live our life together as God's
people with faith, hope, and love. And the greatest of these is love (1
Corinthians 13:13).

Declaration of Intention for Marriage

NOTE: Canon I.18.4 requires couples to sign this Declaration of Intention prior to the solemnization of their marriage.

We understand the teaching of the Church that God's purpose for our marriage is for our mutual joy, for the help and comfort we will give to each other in prosperity and adversity, and, when it is God's will, for the gift and heritage of children and their nurture in the knowledge and love of God. We also understand that our marriage is to be unconditional, mutual, exclusive, faithful, and lifelong; and we engage to make the utmost effort to accept these gifts and fulfill these duties, with the help of God and the support of our community.

_____   _____
SIGNATURE   SIGNATURE

_____
DATE

Declaration of Intention for Lifelong Covenant

NOTE: This template is presented for use with gender and sexual minority couples preparing for The Witnessing and Blessing of a Lifelong Covenant, since a similar declaration is required by the Canons of the Episcopal Church (Canon I.18.4) prior to the solemnization of a marriage.

In the Name of the Father, and of the Son, and of the Holy Spirit. Amen.

We, N.N. and N.N., desiring to receive the blessing of a Lifelong Covenant, do solemnly declare that we hold this covenant to be our lifelong commitment as provided by The Episcopal Church gathered in General Convention.

We believe that our covenant is intended by God for our mutual joy, for the encouragement and support given one another in daily life and changing circumstances, for bringing God's grace to our community, for the deepening of faith as we experience God's love in our love for one another, and (if it may be) for the physical and spiritual nurture of children. This covenant shall be nurtured and characterized by fidelity, monogamy, mutual affection and respect, careful, honest communication, and the holy love which shall enable us to see in each other the image of God.

And we do engage ourselves, so far as in us lies, to make our utmost effort to establish this covenant and to seek God's help hereto.

SIGNATURE   SIGNATURE

DATE

SAMPLE HANDOUT 4

About Presenters—For the Couple

At N. Episcopal Church, we consider "The Witnessing and Blessing of a Lifelong Covenant" ["The Witnessing and Blessing of a Marriage"] to be a celebration supported by the congregation, much as candidates for baptism are supported by all the members of the Church. Just as those who are baptized are initiated into the full life of the Church, those who receive the Church's blessing upon their relationship are embraced in a new way in the faith community.

The Blessing Liturgy [The Marriage]

The presentation takes place immediately after the sermon, as follows:

The couple comes before the assembly. If there is to be a presentation, the presenters stand with the couple, and the Presider says to them

Presider   Who presents N. and N., who seek the blessing of God and the Church on their love and life together?

Presenters   We do.

Presider   Will you love, respect, and pray for N. and N., and do all in your power to stand with them in the life they will share?

Presenters   We will.

Choosing Presenters

There are a variety of possibilities for choosing presenters who will
stand with you and present you at the liturgy. It can be helpful to
choose at least one member of this faith community to walk with you
through this process. If you are new to the congregation, the priest
(or other person designated) can help you discern whom you might
consider. The selection of a couple mature in their relationship can be
particularly helpful if you are just beginning your life together. Often,
couples will choose their own parents, children, or other supportive
family members to be their presenters.

Presenters can pray for you during the period of preparation before
your blessing [marriage], keep you connected to the congregation, and
continue to support you in your ongoing covenanted life together.

Finally, in choosing, remember that these people will stand with you
during the liturgy and present you at this rite. Also remember that,
immediately after you are presented, the entire congregation will vow
to support you as you, in turn, become a blessing and bear grace to
the entire congregation.

Because presenters serve an important role before and after the
blessing [marriage], you and your clergyperson should talk early about
selecting presenters, so that your prayerful partnership may begin as
soon as possible.

Information for Presenters

At N. Episcopal Church, we consider "The Witnessing and Blessing of a Lifelong Covenant" ["The Witnessing and Blessing of a Marriage"] to be a celebration supported by the congregation, much as candidates for baptism are supported by all the members of the Church. Just as those who are baptized are initiated into the full life of the Church, those who receive the Church's blessing upon their relationship are embraced in a new way in the faith community.

At the blessing service [marriage], you present the couple to the presider and to the assembly, as follows:

The couple comes before the assembly. If there is to be a presentation, the presenters stand with the couple, and the Presider says to them

Presider	Who presents N. and N., as they seek the blessing of God and the Church on their love and life together?
Presenters	We do.
Presider	Will you love, respect, and pray for N. and N., and do all in your power to stand with them in the life they will share?
Presenters	We will.

As a presenter, your role begins even before the blessing [marriage]. We encourage you to pray for the couple both privately and in the Prayers of the People at Sunday services during their period of preparation. You can continue to support their ongoing life by acknowledging the anniversary of their blessing [marriage] and offering your presence whenever their household experiences times of difficulty or celebrates occasions of joy. If you are a member of the congregation, you also have a role in keeping them connected to others in the congregation.

As a presenter, you promise to support the couple as they become a blessing and bear grace to their families and friends, the Church, and the world. In this role, then, you are a witness to the blessing given and received in the liturgy and carried forth by the couple into the world.

SAMPLE HANDOUT 6

Model Congregational Guidelines

NOTE: Most congregations adopt some form of marriage
policy expressing norms and guidelines for different-sex/gender
couples preparing for marriage. All congregations may engage
in a helpful and fruitful exercise to develop guidelines that
reflect the Christian community in which they worship; the
guidelines that are developed should apply to both different-
sex/gender couples and gender and sexual minority couples.
Obviously, such a policy is optional at the discretion of the
clergy in consultation with the vestry or bishop's committee.
As always with liturgical matters, final decisions are the
responsibility of the clergy. Following is a model of a guideline
that applies for all couples preparing for marriage or a blessing.
It may be modified to meet specific situations and needs.

Information for All Couples Seeking the Church's Blessing at N. Episcopal Church

A. Introduction

The Christian community at N. Episcopal Church understands that
relationships are complex and that making a lifelong commitment
to a relationship through a marriage or blessing is a significant,
exciting, and wonder-filled event in people's lives. We also believe that
a Christian community that agrees to bless such a relationship needs
to be intentional about supporting the couple as they prepare for the
blessing and as they live out their lives.

We understand that committed, lifelong relationships, whether for
gender and sexual minority couples or different-sex/gender couples,
are to be outward and visible signs of an inward, spiritual, and God-
given love. In this context, N. Episcopal Church seeks to support all

couples in their commitment to one another and to help make the love of God more visible for the whole community.

B. Guidelines

The following guidelines have been adopted by the lay and ordained leaders of N. Episcopal Church:

1. As required for different-sex/gender couples seeking marriage according to the *Book of Common Prayer*, at least one member of a gender and sexual minority couple must be baptized.

2. It is desirable that at least one member of the couple be an active member of this, or some other, Christian community. We hope this membership might include giving serious, prayerful consideration to supporting the congregation through time, talent, and/or treasure.

3. Approximately six months' notice should be given to allow for planning and pastoral preparation.

4. If the couple has no connection with N. Episcopal Church but wishes to have the marriage or blessing at N. Episcopal Church or to use the services of N. Episcopal Church's priest:

   • They should be able to show that at least one of the couple has active membership in another Episcopal or Christian congregation.

   • They need to complete marriage or blessing preparation with their own or other clergyperson or a qualified lay preparer.

   • They might consider making a financial contribution to N. Episcopal Church in thanksgiving for their marriage or blessing and for the ongoing support of the Church, its ministry and mission. A creative formula to calculate this contribution might be to consider a tithe (10 percent) of the budget for the entire celebration. (Clergy have discretion here, as resources vary greatly from couple to couple. Also, if a couple is returning to Church for the first time, an unconditional welcome may be the best pastoral response.)

In all cases, it is important that all concerned comply with the laws of the State, the Canons of the Episcopal Church, and the canons and policies of the Episcopal Diocese of X, as well as the directives of the diocesan bishop, including compliance with diocesan policies for cases in which the relationship is not the first marriage or committed relationship for one or both people.

V. Liturgical Resources

Contents

1. The Witnessing and Blessing of a Lifelong Covenant

Concerning the Service

This rite is appropriately celebrated in the context of the Holy Eucharist and may take place at the principal Sunday Liturgy. This rite then replaces the Ministry of the Word. A bishop or priest normally presides. Parallel texts from *Enriching Our Worship 1* are included as options for elements of this rite.

At least one of the couple must be a baptized Christian.

Two or more presenters, who may be friends, parents, family members, or drawn from the local assembly, may present the couple to the presider and the assembly.

As indicated in the opening address, the consent, and the blessing of the rings, the rite may be modified for use with a couple who have previously made a lifelong commitment to one another.

The Witnessing and Blessing of a Lifelong Covenant

The Word of God

Gathering

The couple to be blessed joins the assembly.

A hymn of praise, psalm, or anthem may be sung, or instrumental music may be played.

The Presider says the following, the People standing

Presider	Blessed be God: Father, Son, and Holy Spirit.
People	Blessed be God, now and for ever. Amen.

In place of the above may be said

Presider	Blessed be the one, holy, and living God.
People	Glory to God for ever and ever.

From Easter Day through the Day of Pentecost

Presider	Alleluia. Christ is risen.
People	The Lord is risen indeed. Alleluia.

In place of the above may be said

Presider	Alleluia. Christ is risen.
People	Christ is risen indeed. Alleluia.

Then may be said

Presider	Beloved, let us love one another,
People	For love is of God.

Presider   Whoever does not love does not know God,
People   For God is love.

Presider   Since God so loves us,
People   Let us love one another.

The Presider may address the assembly in these words

> Dear friends in Christ [*or* Dearly beloved,]
> in the name of God and the Church
> we have come together today with N.N. and N.N.,
> to witness the vows they make,
> committing themselves to one another.
> Forsaking all others,
> they will bind themselves to one another
> in a covenant of mutual fidelity and steadfast love,
> remaining true to one another in heart, body, and mind,
> as long as they both shall live.
>
> Such a lifelong commitment
> is not to be entered into lightly or thoughtlessly,
> but responsibly and with reverence.
> Let us pray, then, that God will give them the strength
> to remain steadfast in what they vow this day.
> Let us also pray for the generosity to support them
> in the commitment they undertake,
> and for the wisdom to see God at work
> in their life together.

Or this, for those who have previously made a lifelong commitment to one another

> Dear friends in Christ [*or* Dearly beloved],
> in the name of God and the Church,
> we have come together with N.N. and N.N.,
> to witness the sacred vows they make
> as they solemnize [*or* reaffirm] their commitment to
>   one another.
> Today they renew their covenant of mutual fidelity
>   and steadfast love,
> forsaking all others and remaining true to one another
>   in heart, body, and mind,
> as long as they both shall live.
>
> Let us pray, then, that God will give them the strength
> to remain steadfast in what they vow this day.

Let us also pray for the generosity
to support them in the commitment they undertake,
and for the wisdom to see God at work
      in their life together.

The Collect of the Day

Presider   The Lord be with you.   *or*   God be with you.

People   And also with you.

Presider   Let us pray.

The Presider says one of the following Collects

God of abundance:
assist by your grace N. and N.,
whose covenant of love and fidelity we witness this day.
Grant them your protection, that with firm resolve
they may honor and keep the vows they make;
through Jesus Christ our Savior,
who lives and reigns with you
      in the unity of the Holy Spirit,
one God, for ever and ever. *Amen.*

or this

Almighty and everliving God:
look tenderly upon N. and N.,
who stand before you in the company of your Church.
Let their life together bring them great joy.
Grant them so to love selflessly and live humbly,
that they may be to one another and to the world
a witness and a sign of your never-failing love and care;
through Jesus Christ your Son our Lord,
who lives and reigns with you and the Holy Spirit,
one God, to the ages of ages. *Amen.*

or this

O God, faithful and true,
whose steadfast love endures for ever:
we give you thanks for sustaining N. and N.
      in the life they share
and for bringing them to this day.
Nurture them and fill them with joy in their life together,
continuing the good work you have begun in them;

and grant us, with them, a dwelling place
    eternal in the heavens
where all your people will share the joy of perfect love,
and where you, with the Son and the Holy Spirit,
    live and reign,
one God, now and for ever. *Amen.*

or this, for those who bring children

Holy Trinity, one God,
three Persons perfect in unity and equal in majesty:
Draw together with bonds of love and affection
N. and N., who with *their families*
seek to live in harmony and forbearance all their days,
that their joining together will be to us
a reflection of that perfect communion
which is your very essence and life,
O Father, Son, and Holy Spirit,
who live and reign in glory everlasting. *Amen.*

The Lessons

The people sit. Then one or more of the following passages of Scripture is read. If the Holy Communion is to be celebrated, a passage from the Gospels always concludes the Readings. When the blessing is celebrated in the context of the Sunday Eucharist, the Readings of the Sunday are used, except with the permission of the Bishop.

Ruth 1:16-17
1 Samuel 18:1b, 3, 20:16-17, 42a;
    or 1 Samuel 18:1-4
Ecclesiastes 4:9-12
Song of Solomon 2:10-13, 8:6-7
Micah 4:1-4

Romans 12:9-18
1 Corinthians 12:31b-13:13
2 Corinthians 5:17-20
Galatians 5:14, 22-26
Ephesians 3:14-21
Colossians 3:12-17
1 John 3:18-24
1 John 4:7-16, 21

When a biblical passage other than one from the Gospels is to be read, the Reader announces it with these words

Reader   A Reading from _____.

After the Reading, the Reader may say
              The Word of the Lord.

or

              Hear what the Spirit is saying to God's people.

or

              Hear what the Spirit is saying to the Churches.

People   Thanks be to God.

Between the Readings, a Psalm, hymn, or anthem may be sung or said. Appropriate Psalms are
              Psalm 65
              Psalm 67
              Psalm 85:7-13
              Psalm 98
              Psalm 100
              Psalm 126
              Psalm 127
              Psalm 133
              Psalm 148
              Psalm 149:1-5

Appropriate passages from the Gospels are
              Matthew 5:1-16
              Mark 12:28-34
              Luke 6:32-38
              John 15:9-17
              John 17:1-2, 18-26

All standing, the Deacon or Priest reads the Gospel, first saying
              The Holy Gospel of our Lord Jesus Christ according to
              _____.

or

              The Holy Gospel of our Savior Jesus Christ according to
              _____.

People   Glory to you, Lord Christ.

After the Gospel, the Reader says
>The Gospel of the Lord.

People   Praise to you, Lord Christ.

The Sermon

The Witnessing of the Vows and the Blessing of the Covenant

The couple comes before the assembly. If there is to be a presentation, the presenters stand with the couple, and the Presider says to them

Presider   Who presents N. and N., as they seek the blessing of God
and the Church on their love and life together?

Presenters We do.

Presider   Will you love, respect, and pray for N. and N., and do
all in your power to stand with them in the life they will
share?

Presenters We will.

The Presider then addresses the couple, saying

>N. and N., you have come before God and the Church to
exchange [*and renew*] solemn vows with one another and
to ask God's blessing.

The Presider addresses one member of the couple

Presider   N., do you freely and unreservedly offer yourself to N.?

Answer   I do.

Presider   Will you [*continue to*] live together in faithfulness and
holiness of life as long as you both shall live?

Answer   I will, with God's help.

The Presider addresses the other member of the couple

Presider   N., do you freely and unreservedly offer yourself to N.?

Answer   I do.

Presider   Will you [*continue to*] live together in faithfulness and
holiness of life as long as you both shall live?

Answer   I will, with God's help.

The assembly stands, the couple faces the People, and the Presider addresses them, saying

Presider	Will all of you gathered to witness these vows do all in your power to uphold and honor this couple in the covenant they make?
People	We will.

Presider	Will you pray for them, especially in times of trouble, and celebrate with them in times of joy?
People	We will.

The Prayers

The Presider then introduces the prayers

Presider	Then let us pray for N. and N. in their life together and for the concerns of this community.

A Deacon or another leader bids prayers for the couple.

Prayers for the Church and for the world, for the concerns of the local community, for those who suffer or face trouble, and for the departed are also appropriate. If the rite takes place in the principal Sunday worship of the congregation, the rubric concerning the Prayers of the People on page 359 of the Book of Common Prayer is followed.

Adaptations or insertions may be made to the form that follows.

A bar in the margin indicates a bidding that may be omitted.

Leader	For N. and N., seeking your blessing and the blessing of your holy people; Loving God, *or* Lord, in your mercy,
People	Hear our prayer.

Leader	For a spirit of loving-kindness to shelter them all their days; Loving God, *or* Lord, in your mercy,
People	Hear our prayer.

Leader	For friends to support them and communities to enfold them; Loving God, *or* Lord, in your mercy,
People	Hear our prayer.

Leader	For peace in their home and love in their family; Loving God, *or* Lord, in your mercy,
People	Hear our prayer.
Leader	For the grace and wisdom to care for the children you entrust to them [*or* may entrust to them]; Loving God, *or* Lord, in your mercy,
People	Hear our prayer.
Leader	For the honesty to acknowledge when they hurt each other, and the humility to seek each other's forgiveness and yours; Loving God, *or* Lord, in your mercy,
People	Hear our prayer.
Leader	For the outpouring of your love through their work and witness; Loving God, *or* Lord, in your mercy,
People	Hear our prayer.
Leader	For the strength to keep the vows each of us has made; Loving God, *or* Lord, in your mercy,
People	Hear our prayer.

The leader may add one or more of the following biddings

Leader	For all who have been reborn and made new in the waters of Baptism; Loving God, *or* Lord, in your mercy,
People	Hear our prayer.
Leader	For those who lead and serve in communities of faith; Loving God, *or* Lord, in your mercy,
People	Hear our prayer.
Leader	For those who seek justice, peace, and concord among nations; Loving God, *or* Lord, in your mercy,
People	Hear our prayer.
Leader	For those who are sick or suffering, homeless or poor; Loving God, *or* Lord, in your mercy,
People	Hear our prayer.

Leader	For victims of violence and those who inflict it; Loving God, *or* Lord, in your mercy,
People	Hear our prayer.
Leader	For communion with all who have died, [especially those whom we remember this day: _____]; Loving God, *or* Lord, in your mercy,
People	Hear our prayer.

*The Presider concludes the Prayers with the following or another
appropriate Collect*

> Giver of every gift, source of all goodness,
> hear the prayers we bring before you for N. and N.,
> who seek your blessing this day.
> Strengthen them as they share in the saving work of Jesus,
> and bring about for them and for all you have created
> the fullness of life he promised,
> who now lives and reigns for ever and ever. *Amen.*

If the Eucharist is to follow, the Lord's Prayer is omitted here.

Leader	*Leader*
As our Savior Christ has taught us, we now pray,	And now, as our Savior Christ has taught us, we are bold to say,
People and Leader	*People and Leader*

Our Father in heaven,
    hallowed be your Name,
    your kingdom come,
    your will be done,
    on earth as in heaven.
Give us today our daily bread.
Forgive us our sins
    as we forgive those
    who sin against us.
Save us from the time of trial,
    and deliver us from evil.
For the kingdom, the power,
    and the glory are yours,
    now and for ever. Amen.
	Our Father, who art in heaven,
	    hallowed be thy Name,
	    thy kingdom come,
	    thy will be done,
	    on earth as it is in heaven.
	Give us this day our daily bread.
	And forgive us our trespasses,
	    as we forgive those
	    who trespass against us.
	And lead us not into temptation,
	    but deliver us from evil.
	For thine is the kingdom,
	    and the power, and the glory,
	    for ever and ever. Amen.

Commitment

The people sit. The couple stands, facing the Presider.

Presider   N. and N., I invite you now, illumined by the Word of God
             and strengthened by the prayer of this community, to make
             your covenant before God and the Church.

Each member of the couple, in turn, takes the hand of the other and says

In the name of God,
I, N., give myself to you, N., and take you to myself
I will support and care for you by the grace of God:
in times of sickness, in times of health.
I will hold and cherish you in the love of Christ:
in times of plenty, in times of want.
I will honor and keep you with the Spirit's help:
in times of anguish, in times of joy,
forsaking all others, as long as we both shall live.
This is my solemn vow.

or this

In the name of God,
I, N., give myself to you, N., and take you to myself
I will support and care for you:
in times of sickness, in times of health.
I will hold and cherish you:
in times of plenty, in times of want.
I will honor and love you:
in times of anguish, in times of joy,
forsaking all others, as long as we both shall live.
This is my solemn vow.

*If rings are to be exchanged, they are brought before the Presider, who
prays using the following words*

Let us pray.

Bless, O God, these rings
as signs of the enduring covenant
N. and N. have made with each other,
through Jesus Christ our Lord. *Amen.*

The two people place the rings on the fingers of one another, first the one, then the other, saying

> N., I give you this ring as a symbol of my vow,
> and with all that I am, and all that I have, I honor you,
> in the name of God.   *or*   in the name of the Father,
>   and of the Son,
>   and of the Holy Spirit.

If the two have previously given and worn rings as a symbol of their commitment, the rings may be blessed on the hands of the couple, the Presider saying

> Let us pray.
> By the rings which they have worn, faithful God,
> N. and N. have shown to one another and the world
> their love and faithfulness.
> Bless now these rings,
> that from this day forward
> they may be signs of the vows N. and N. have exchanged
> in your presence and in the communion of your Church,
> through Christ our Lord. *Amen.*

Pronouncement

The Presider joins the right hands and says

> Now that N. and N. have exchanged vows of love and fidelity
> in the presence of God and the Church,
> I now pronounce that they are bound to one another
> as long as they both shall live. *Amen.*

Blessing of the Couple

As the couple stands or kneels, the Presider invokes God's blessing
upon them, saying

Let us pray.

Most gracious God,
we praise you for the tender mercy and unfailing care
revealed to us in Jesus the Christ
and for the great joy and comfort bestowed upon us
in the gift of human love.
We give you thanks for N. and N.,
and the covenant of faithfulness they have made.
Pour out the abundance of your Holy Spirit upon them.
Keep them in your steadfast love;
protect them from all danger;
fill them with your wisdom and peace;
lead them in holy service to each other and the world.

The Presider continues with one of the following

God the Father,
God the Son,
God the Holy Spirit,
bless, preserve, and keep you,
and mercifully grant you rich and boundless grace,
that you may please God in body and soul.
God make you a sign of the loving-kindness and
        steadfast fidelity
manifest in the life, death, and resurrection of our Savior,
and bring you at last to the delight of the
        heavenly banquet,
where he lives and reigns for ever and ever. *Amen.*

or this

God, the holy and undivided Trinity,
bless, preserve, and keep you,
and mercifully grant you rich and boundless grace,
that you may please God in body and soul.
God make you a sign of the loving-kindness and
        steadfast fidelity
manifest in the life, death, and resurrection of our Savior,
and bring you at last to the delight of the
        heavenly banquet,
where he lives and reigns for ever and ever. *Amen.*

The Peace

The Presider bids the Peace.

Presider   The peace of the Lord be always with you.
People   And also with you.

In place of the above may be said

Presider   The peace of Christ be always with you.
People   And also with you.

The liturgy continues with the Holy Communion. When the Eucharist is not celebrated, the Presider blesses the people. The Deacon, or in the absence of a Deacon, the Priest, dismisses them.

At the Eucharist

The liturgy continues with the Offertory, at which the couple may present the offerings of bread and wine.

The following proper preface may be said.

> Because in the giving of two people to each other in
>   faithful love
> you reveal the joy and abundant life you share
> with your Son Jesus Christ and the Holy Spirit.

The following postcommunion prayer may be said.

> God our strength and joy,
> we thank you for the communion of our life together,
> for the example of holy love that you give us in N. and N.,
> and for the Sacrament of the Body and Blood
> of our Savior Jesus Christ.
> Grant that it may renew our hope
> and nourish us for the work you set before us
> to witness to the presence of Christ in the world,
> through the power of your Spirit,
> and to the glory of your Name. Amen.

2. The Witnessing and Blessing of a Marriage

Concerning the Service

This rite is appropriately celebrated in the context of the Holy Eucharist and may take place at the principal Sunday Liturgy. This rite then replaces the Ministry of the Word. A bishop or priest normally presides. Parallel texts from *Enriching Our Worship 1* are included as options for elements of this rite.

At least one of the couple must be a baptized Christian, and the marriage shall conform to the laws of the state and canons of this church.

Two or more presenters, who may be friends, parents, family members, or drawn from the local assembly, may present the couple to the presider and the assembly.

As indicated in the opening address, the consent, and the blessing of the rings, the rite may be modified for use with a couple who have previously made a lifelong commitment to one another.

The Witnessing and Blessing of a Marriage

The Word of God

Gathering

The couple joins the assembly.
A hymn of praise, psalm, or anthem may be sung, or instrumental music may be played.

The Presider says the following, the People standing

Presider   Blessed be God: Father, Son, and Holy Spirit.
People   Blessed be God, now and for ever. Amen.

In place of the above may be said

Presider   Blessed be the one, holy, and living God.
People   Glory to God for ever and ever.

From Easter Day through the Day of Pentecost

Presider   Alleluia. Christ is risen.
People   The Lord is risen indeed. Alleluia.

In place of the above may be said

Presider   Alleluia. Christ is risen.
People   Christ is risen indeed. Alleluia.

Then may be said

Presider   Beloved, let us love one another,
People   For love is of God.

Presider   Whoever does not love does not know God,
People   For God is love.

Presider   Since God so loves us,
People   Let us love one another.

The Presider may address the assembly in these words

> Dear friends in Christ [*or* Dearly beloved],
> in the name of God and the Church
> we have come together today with N.N. and N.N.,
> to witness the vows they make,
> committing themselves to one another
> in marriage [according to the laws of the state *or* civil
> jurisdiction of X.]
> Forsaking all others,
> they will bind themselves to one another
> in a covenant of mutual fidelity and steadfast love,
> remaining true to one another in heart, body, and mind,
> as long as they both shall live.
>
> The lifelong commitment of marriage
> is not to be entered into lightly or thoughtlessly,
> but responsibly and with reverence.
> Let us pray, then, that God will give them the strength
> to remain steadfast in what they vow this day.
> Let us also pray for the generosity
> to support them in the commitment they undertake
> and for the wisdom to see God at work
> in their life together.

Or this, for those who have previously made a lifelong commitment to one another

> Dear friends in Christ [*or* Dearly beloved],
> in the name of God and the Church
> we have come together today with N.N. and N.N.
> to witness the sacred vows they make this day
> as they are married
> [according to the laws of the state *or* civil jurisdiction of X.],
> and reaffirm their commitment to one another.
> Forsaking all others,
> they will renew their covenant of mutual fidelity and
> steadfast love,
> remaining true to one another in heart, body, and mind,
> as long as they both shall live.

Let us pray, then, that God will give them the strength
to remain steadfast in what they vow this day.
Let us also pray for the generosity
to support them in the commitment they undertake,
and for the wisdom to see God at work in their life together.

The Collect of the Day

Presider   The Lord be with you.   *or*   God be with you.
People   And also with you.
Presider   Let us pray.

The Presider says one of the following Collects

God of abundance:
assist by your grace N. and N.,
whose covenant of love and fidelity we witness this day.
Grant them your protection, that with firm resolve
they may honor and keep the vows they make;
through Jesus Christ our Savior,
who lives and reigns with you in the unity of the Holy Spirit,
one God, for ever and ever. *Amen.*

or this

Almighty and everliving God:
look tenderly upon N. and N.,
who stand before you in the company of your Church.
Let their life together bring them great joy.
Grant them so to love selflessly and live humbly,
that they may be to one another and to the world
a witness and a sign of your never-failing love and care;
through Jesus Christ your Son our Lord,
who lives and reigns with you and the Holy Spirit,
one God, to the ages of ages. *Amen.*

or this

O God, faithful and true,
whose steadfast love endures for ever:
we give you thanks for sustaining N. and N.
    in the life they share
and for bringing them to this day.
Nurture them and fill them with joy in their life together,

continuing the good work you have begun in them;
and grant us, with them, a dwelling place
        eternal in the heavens
where all your people will share the joy of perfect love,
and where you, with the Son and the Holy Spirit,
        live and reign,
one God, now and for ever. *Amen.*

or this, for those who bring children

Holy Trinity, one God,
three Persons perfect in unity and equal in majesty:
Draw together with bonds of love and affection
N. and N., who with *their families*
seek to live in harmony and forbearance all their days,
that their joining together will be to us
a reflection of that perfect communion
which is your very essence and life,
O Father, Son, and Holy Spirit,
who live and reign in glory everlasting. *Amen.*

The Lessons

*The people sit. Then one or more of the following passages of Scripture
is read. If the Holy Communion is to be celebrated, a passage from the
Gospels always concludes the Readings. When the blessing is celebrated
in the context of the Sunday Eucharist, the Readings of the Sunday are
used, except with the permission of the Bishop.*

Ruth 1:16-17
1 Samuel 18:1b, 3, 20:16-17, 42a;
        or 1 Samuel 18:1-4
Ecclesiastes 4:9-12
Song of Solomon 2:10-13, 8:6-7
Micah 4:1-4

Romans 12:9-18
1 Corinthians 12:31b-13:13
2 Corinthians 5:17-20
Galatians 5:14, 22-26
Ephesians 3:14-21
Colossians 3:12-17
1 John 3:18-24
1 John 4:7-16, 21

When a biblical passage other than one from the Gospels is to be read, the Reader announces it with these words

Reader   A Reading from _____.

After the Reading, the Reader may say
          The Word of the Lord.

or
          Hear what the Spirit is saying to God's people.

or
          Hear what the Spirit is saying to the Churches.

People   Thanks be to God.

Between the Readings, a psalm, hymn, or anthem may be sung or said. Appropriate Psalms are
          Psalm 65
          Psalm 67
          Psalm 85:7-13
          Psalm 98
          Psalm 100
          Psalm 126
          Psalm 127
          Psalm 133
          Psalm 148
          Psalm 149:1-5

Appropriate passages from the Gospels are
          Matthew 5:1-16
          Mark 12:28-34
          Luke 6:32-38
          John 15:9-17
          John 17:1-2, 18-26

All standing, the Deacon or Priest reads the Gospel, first saying
          The Holy Gospel of our Lord Jesus Christ according to
          _____.

or
          The Holy Gospel of our Savior Jesus Christ according to
          _____.

People   Glory to you, Lord Christ.

After the Gospel, the Reader says
            The Gospel of the Lord.
People   Praise to you, Lord Christ.

The Sermon

The Witnessing of the Vows and the Blessing of the Covenant

The couple comes before the assembly. If there is to be a presentation, the presenters stand with the couple, and the Presider says to them

Presider   Who presents N. and N., as they seek the blessing of God and the Church on their love and life together?
Presenters We do.

Presider   Will you love, respect, and pray for N. and N., and do all in your power to stand with them in the life they will share?
Presenters We will.

The Presider then addresses the couple, saying

            N. and N., you have come before God and the Church to exchange [*and renew*] solemn vows with one another and to ask God's blessing.

The Presider addresses one member of the couple, saying

Presider   N., do you freely and unreservedly offer yourself to N.?
Answer   I do.

Presider   Will you [*continue to*] live together in faithfulness and holiness of life as long as you both shall live?
Answer   I will, with God's help.

The Presider addresses the other member of the couple, saying

Presider   N., do you freely and unreservedly offer yourself to N.?
Answer   I do.

Presider   Will you [*continue to*] live together in faithfulness and holiness of life as long as you both shall live?
Answer   I will, with God's help.

The assembly stands, the couple faces the People, and the Presider addresses them, saying

Presider	Will all of you gathered to witness these vows do all in your power to uphold and honor this couple in the covenant they make?
People	We will.
Presider	Will you pray for them, especially in times of trouble, and celebrate with them in times of joy?
People	We will.

The Prayers

The Presider then introduces the prayers

Presider	Then let us pray for N. and N. in their life together and for the concerns of this community.

A Deacon or another leader bids prayers for the couple.

Prayers for the Church and for the world, for the concerns of the local community, for those who suffer or face trouble, and for the departed are also appropriate. If the rite takes place in the principal Sunday worship of the congregation, the rubric concerning the Prayers of the People on page 359 of the Book of Common Prayer is followed.

Adaptations or insertions may be made to the form that follows.

A bar in the margin indicates a bidding that may be omitted.

Leader	For N. and N., seeking your blessing and the blessing of your holy people; Loving God, *or* Lord, in your mercy,
People	Hear our prayer.
Leader	For a spirit of loving-kindness to shelter them all their days; Loving God, *or* Lord, in your mercy,
People	Hear our prayer.
Leader	For friends to support them and communities to enfold them; Loving God, *or* Lord, in your mercy,
People	Hear our prayer.

Leader   For peace in their home and love in their family;
              Loving God,   *or*   Lord, in your mercy,

People   Hear our prayer.

Leader   For the grace and wisdom to care for the children you
              entrust to them [*or* may entrust to them];
              Loving God,   *or*   Lord, in your mercy,

People   Hear our prayer.

Leader   For the honesty to acknowledge when they hurt each other,
              and the humility to seek each other's forgiveness and yours;
              Loving God,   *or*   Lord, in your mercy,

People   Hear our prayer.

Leader   For the outpouring of your love through their work and
              witness;
              Loving God,   *or*   Lord, in your mercy,

People   Hear our prayer.

Leader   For the strength to keep the vows each of us has made;
              Loving God,   *or*   Lord, in your mercy,

People   Hear our prayer.

The leader may add one or more of the following biddings

Leader   For all who have been reborn and made new in the waters
              of Baptism;
              Loving God,   *or*   Lord, in your mercy,

People   Hear our prayer.

Leader   For those who lead and serve in communities of faith;
              Loving God,   *or*   Lord, in your mercy,

People   Hear our prayer.

Leader   For those who seek justice, peace, and concord among
              nations;
              Loving God,   *or*   Lord, in your mercy,

People   Hear our prayer.

Leader   For those who are sick or suffering, homeless or poor;
              Loving God,   *or*   Lord, in your mercy,

People   Hear our prayer.

Leader   For victims of violence and those who inflict it;
              Loving God,   *or*   Lord, in your mercy,

People   Hear our prayer.

Leader   For communion with all who have died [especially those
              whom we remember this day: _____];
              Loving God,   *or*   Lord, in your mercy,

People   Hear our prayer.

The Presider concludes the Prayers with the following or another appropriate Collect

> Giver of every gift, source of all goodness,
> hear the prayers we bring before you for N. and N.,
> who seek your blessing this day.
> Strengthen them as they share in the saving work of Jesus,
> and bring about for them and for all you have created
> the fullness of life he promised,
> who now lives and reigns for ever and ever. *Amen.*

If the Eucharist is to follow, the Lord's Prayer is omitted here.

Leader	*Leader*
As our Savior Christ has taught us, we now pray,	And now, as our Savior Christ has taught us, we are bold to say,
People and Leader	*People and Leader*

Our Father in heaven,
   hallowed be your Name,
   your kingdom come,
   your will be done,
   on earth as in heaven.
Give us today our daily bread.
Forgive us our sins
   as we forgive those
   who sin against us.
Save us from the time of trial,
   and deliver us from evil.
For the kingdom, the power,
   and the glory are yours,
   now and for ever. Amen.
	Our Father, who art in heaven,
	   hallowed be thy Name,
	   thy kingdom come,
	   thy will be done,
	   on earth as it is in heaven.
	Give us this day our daily bread.
	And forgive us our trespasses,
	   as we forgive those
	   who trespass against us.
	And lead us not into temptation,
	   but deliver us from evil.
	For thine is the kingdom,
	   and the power, and the glory,
	   for ever and ever. Amen.

The Marriage

The people sit. The couple stands, facing the Presider.

Presider　　N. and N., I invite you now, illumined by the Word of God
　　　　　　and strengthened by the prayer of this community,
　　　　　　to make your covenant before God and the Church.

Each member of the couple, in turn, takes the hand of the other and says

　　　　　　In the name of God,
　　　　　　I, N., give myself to you, N., and take you to myself.
　　　　　　I will support and care for you by the grace of God:
　　　　　　in times of sickness, in times of health.
　　　　　　I will hold and cherish you in the love of Christ:
　　　　　　in times of plenty, in times of want.
　　　　　　I will honor and love you with the Spirit's help:
　　　　　　in times of anguish, in times of joy,
　　　　　　forsaking all others, as long as we both shall live.
　　　　　　This is my solemn vow.

or this

　　　　　　In the name of God,
　　　　　　I, N., give myself to you, N., and take you to myself.
　　　　　　I will support and care for you:
　　　　　　in times of sickness, in times of health.
　　　　　　I will hold and cherish you:
　　　　　　in times of plenty, in times of want.
　　　　　　I will honor and love you:
　　　　　　in times of anguish, in times of joy,
　　　　　　forsaking all others, as long as we both shall live.
　　　　　　This is my solemn vow.

If rings are to be exchanged, they are brought before the Presider, who prays using the following words

　　　　　　Let us pray.

　　　　　　Bless, O God, these rings
　　　　　　as signs of the enduring covenant
　　　　　　N. and N. have made with each other,
　　　　　　through Jesus Christ our Lord. *Amen.*

The two people place the rings on the fingers of one another, first the one, then the other, saying

> N., I give you this ring as a symbol of my vow,
> and with all that I am, and all that I have, I honor you,
> in the name of God.   *or*   in the name of the Father,
>   and of the Son,
>   and of the Holy Spirit.

If the two have previously given and worn rings as a symbol of their commitment, the rings may be blessed on the hands of the couple, the Presider saying

> Let us pray.

> By the rings which they have worn, faithful God,
> N. and N. have shown to one another and the world
> their love and faithfulness.
> Bless now these rings,
> that from this day forward
> they may be signs of the vows N. and N. have exchanged
> in your presence and in the communion of your Church,
> through Christ our Lord. *Amen.*

Pronouncement

The Presider joins the right hands of the couple and says

> Now that N. and N. have exchanged vows of love and fidelity
> in the presence of God and the Church,
> I pronounce that they are
> married [according to the laws of the state *or* civil
> jurisdiction of X.]
> and bound to one another
> as long as they both shall live. *Amen.*

Blessing of the Couple

As the couple stands or kneels, the Presider invokes God's blessing upon them, saying

> Let us pray.

> Most gracious God,
> we praise you for the tender mercy and unfailing care
> revealed to us in Jesus the Christ

and for the great joy and comfort bestowed upon us
in the gift of human love.
We give you thanks for N. and N.,
and the covenant of faithfulness they have made.
Pour out the abundance of your Holy Spirit upon them.
Keep them in your steadfast love;
protect them from all danger;
fill them with your wisdom and peace;
lead them in holy service to each other and the world.

The Presider continues with one of the following

God the Father,
God the Son,
God the Holy Spirit,
bless, preserve, and keep you,
and mercifully grant you rich and boundless grace,
that you may please God in body and soul.
God make you a sign of the loving-kindness and
        steadfast fidelity
manifest in the life, death, and resurrection of our Savior,
and bring you at last to the delight of the heavenly banquet,
where he lives and reigns for ever and ever. *Amen.*

or this

God, the holy and undivided Trinity,
bless, preserve, and keep you,
and mercifully grant you rich and boundless grace,
that you may please God in body and soul.
God make you a sign of the loving-kindness and
        steadfast fidelity
manifest in the life, death, and resurrection of our Savior,
and bring you at last to the delight of the
        heavenly banquet,
where he lives and reigns for ever and ever. *Amen.*

The Peace

The Presider bids the Peace.

Presider	The peace of the Lord be always with you.
People	And also with you.

In place of the above may be said

Presider	The peace of Christ be always with you.
People	And also with you.

The liturgy continues with the Holy Communion. When the Eucharist is not celebrated, the Presider blesses the people. The Deacon, or in the absence of a Deacon, the Priest, dismisses them.

At the Eucharist

The liturgy continues with the Offertory, at which the couple may present the offerings of bread and wine.

The following proper preface may be said

> Because in the giving of two people to each other in
>   faithful love
> you reveal the joy and abundant life you share
> with your Son Jesus Christ and the Holy Spirit.

The following postcommunion prayer may be said

> God our strength and joy,
> we thank you for the communion of our life together,
> for the example of holy love that you give us in N. and N.,
> and for the Sacrament of the Body and Blood
> of our Savior Jesus Christ.
> Grant that it may renew our hope
> and nourish us for the work you set before us
> to witness to the presence of Christ in the world,
> through the power of your Spirit,
> and to the glory of your Name. Amen.

3. The Celebration and Blessing of a Marriage 2

Concerning the Service

At least one of the parties must be a baptized Christian; the ceremony must be attested by at least two witnesses; and the marriage must conform to the laws of the State.

A priest or a bishop normally presides at the Celebration and Blessing of a Marriage, because such ministers alone have the function of pronouncing the nuptial blessing, and of celebrating the Holy Eucharist.

When both a bishop and a priest are present and officiating, the bishop should pronounce the blessing and preside at the Eucharist.

A deacon, or an assisting priest, may deliver the charge, ask for the Declaration of Consent, read the Gospel, and perform other assisting functions at the Eucharist.

Where it is permitted by civil law that deacons may perform marriages, and no priest or bishop is available, a deacon may use the service which follows, omitting the nuptial blessing which follows The Prayers.

It is desirable that the Lessons from the Old Testament and the Epistles be read by lay persons.

In the opening exhortation (at the symbol of N.N.), the full names of the persons to be married are declared. Subsequently, only their Christian names are used.

Additional Directions are on pages 186-87.

The Celebration and Blessing of a Marriage 2

At the time appointed, the persons to be married, with their witnesses, assemble in the church or some other appropriate place.

During their entrance, a hymn, psalm, or anthem may be sung, or instrumental music may be played.

Then the Celebrant, facing the people and the persons to be married, addresses the congregation and says

Dearly beloved: We have come together in the presence of God to witness and bless the joining together of N. and N. in Holy Matrimony. The joining of two people in a life of mutual fidelity signifies to us the mystery of the union between Christ and his Church, and so it is worthy of being honored among all people.

The union of two people in heart, body, and mind is intended by God for their mutual joy; for the help and comfort given one another in prosperity and adversity; and, when it is God's will, for the gift of children and their nurture in the knowledge and love of the Lord. Therefore marriage is not to be entered into unadvisedly or lightly, but reverently, deliberately, and in accordance with the purposes for which it was instituted by God.

Into this holy union N.N. and N.N. now come to be joined.

If any of you can show just cause why they may not lawfully be married, speak now; or else for ever hold your peace.

Then the Celebrant says to the persons to be married

I require and charge you both, here in the presence of God,
that if either of you know any reason why you may not be
united in marriage lawfully, and in accordance with God's
Word, you do now confess it.

The Declaration of Consent

The Celebrant says to one member of the couple, then to the other

N., will you have this *woman/man/person* to be your *wife/
husband/spouse*; to live together in the covenant of marriage?
Will you love *her/him*, comfort *her/him*, honor and keep *her/
him*, in sickness and in health; and, forsaking all others, be
faithful to *her/him* as long as you both shall live?

Answer   I will.

The Celebrant then addresses the congregation, saying

Will all of you witnessing these promises do all in your
power to uphold these two persons in their marriage?

People   We will.

*If there is to be a presentation or a giving in marriage, it takes place at
this time.*

See Additional Directions, pages 186-87.

A hymn, psalm, or anthem may follow.

The Ministry of the Word

The Celebrant then says to the people

The Lord be with you.

People   And also with you.

Celebrant Let us pray.

O gracious and everliving God, you have created
humankind in your image: Look mercifully upon N. and
N. who come to you seeking your blessing, and assist them
with your grace, that with true fidelity and steadfast love
they may honor and keep the promises and vows they
make; through Jesus Christ our Savior, who lives and reigns

with you in the unity of the Holy Spirit, one God, for ever and ever. *Amen.*

Then one or more of the following passages from Holy Scripture is read. Other readings from Scripture suitable for the occasion may be used. If there is to be a Communion, a passage from the Gospel always concludes the Readings.

> Genesis 1:26–28 *(Male and female he created them)*
> Song of Solomon 2:10–13; 8:6–7
>   *(Many waters cannot quench love)*
> Tobit 8:5b–8 *(New English Bible)*
>   *(That she and I may grow old together)*
> 1 Corinthians 13:1–13 *(Love is patient and kind)*
> Ephesians 3:14–19
>   *(The Father from whom every family is named)*
> Ephesians 5:1–2 *(Walk in love, as Christ loved us)*
> Colossians 3:12–17
>   *(Love which binds everything together in harmony)*
> 1 John 4:7–16 *(Let us love one another, for love is of God)*

Between the Readings, a psalm, hymn, or anthem may be sung or said. Appropriate psalms are

> Psalm 67
> Psalm 127
> Psalm 128.

When a passage from the Gospel is to be read, all stand, and the Deacon or Minister appointed says

> The Holy Gospel of our Lord Jesus Christ according to
> _____.

People   Glory to you, Lord Christ.

> Matthew 5:1–10 *(The Beatitudes)*
> Matthew 5:13–16 *(You are the light ...*
>   *Let your light so shine)*
> Matthew 7:21, 24–29 *(Like a wise man who built*
>   *his house upon the rock)*
> John 15:9–12 *(Love one another as I have loved you)*

After the Gospel, the Reader says

> The Gospel of the Lord.

People   Praise to you, Lord Christ.

A homily or other response to the Readings may follow.

The Marriage

Each member of the couple, in turn, takes the right hand of the other and says

> In the Name of God, I, N., take you, N., to be my *wife/ husband/spouse,*
> to have and to hold from this day forward,
> for better for worse, for richer for poorer,
> in sickness and in health, to love and to cherish,
> until we are parted by death.
> This is my solemn vow.

The Priest may ask God's blessing on rings as follows

> Bless, O Lord, these rings to be signs of the vows
> by which N. and N. have bound themselves to each other;
> through Jesus Christ our Lord. *Amen.*

The giver places the ring on the ring finger of the other's hand and says

> N., I give you this ring as a symbol of my vow,
> and with all that I am, and all that I have, I honor you,
> in the Name of the Father, and of the Son,
> and of the Holy Spirit [*or* in the Name of God].

Then the Celebrant joins the right hands of the couple and says

> Now that N. and N. have given themselves to each other
>   by solemn vows,
> with the joining of hands and the giving and receiving
>   of rings,
> I pronounce that they are wed to one another,
> in the Name of the Father, and of the Son, and of the
>   Holy Spirit.
> Those whom God has joined together let no one put
>   asunder.

People   Amen.

The Prayers

All standing, the Celebrant says

> Let us pray together in the words our Savior taught us.

People and Celebrant

Our Father in heaven,	Our Father, who art in heaven,
hallowed be your Name,	hallowed be thy Name,
your kingdom come,	thy kingdom come,
your will be done,	thy will be done,
on earth as in heaven.	on earth as it is in heaven.
Give us today our daily bread.	Give us this day our daily bread.
Forgive us our sins	And forgive us our trespasses,
as we forgive those	as we forgive those
who sin against us.	who trespass against us.
Save us from the time of trial,	And lead us not into temptation,
and deliver us from evil.	but deliver us from evil.
For the kingdom, the power,	For thine is the kingdom,
and the glory are yours,	and the power, and the glory,
now and for ever. Amen.	for ever and ever. Amen.

If Communion is to follow, the Lord's Prayer may be omitted here.

The Deacon or other person appointed reads the following prayers, to which the People respond, saying, Amen.

If there is not to be a Communion, one or more of the prayers may be omitted.

Leader   Let us pray.

Eternal God, creator and preserver of all life, author of salvation, and giver of all grace: Look with favor upon the world you have made, and for which your Son gave his life, and especially upon N. and N. whom you make one flesh in Holy Matrimony. *Amen.*

Give them wisdom and devotion in the ordering of their common life, that each may be to the other a strength in need, a counselor in perplexity, a comfort in sorrow, and a companion in joy. *Amen.*

Grant that their wills may be so knit together in your will, and their spirits in your Spirit, that they may grow in love and peace with you and one another all the days of their life. *Amen.*

Give them grace, when they hurt each other, to recognize and acknowledge their fault, and to seek each other's forgiveness and yours. *Amen.*

Make their life together a sign of Christ's love to this sinful
and broken world, that unity may overcome estrangement,
forgiveness heal guilt, and joy conquer despair. *Amen.*

Bestow on them, if it is your will, the gift and heritage of
children, and the grace to bring them up to know you, to
love you, and to serve you. *Amen.*

Give them such fulfillment of their mutual affection that
they may reach out in love and concern for others. *Amen.*

Grant that all married persons who have witnessed these
vows may find their lives strengthened and their loyalties
confirmed. *Amen.*

Grant that the bonds of our common humanity, by which
all your children are united one to another, and the living
to the dead, may be so transformed by your grace, that
your will may be done on earth as it is in heaven; where,
O Father, with your Son and the Holy Spirit, you live and
reign in perfect unity, now and for ever. *Amen.*

The Blessing of the Marriage

*The People remain standing. The couple kneel, and the Priest says one
of the following prayers*

Most gracious God, we give you thanks for your tender
love in sending Jesus Christ to come among us, to be born
of a human mother, and to make the way of the cross to
be the way of life. We thank you, also, for consecrating the
union of two people in his Name. By the power of your
Holy Spirit, pour out the abundance of your blessing upon
N. and N. Defend them from every enemy. Lead them
into all peace. Let their love for each other be a seal upon
their hearts, a mantle about their shoulders, and a crown
upon their foreheads. Bless them in their work and in their
companionship; in their sleeping and in their waking; in
their joys and in their sorrows; in their life and in their
death. Finally, in your mercy, bring them to that table
where your saints feast for ever in your heavenly home;
through Jesus Christ our Lord, who with you and the Holy
Spirit lives and reigns, one God, for ever and ever. *Amen.*

or this

> O God, you have so consecrated the covenant of marriage
> that in it is represented the spiritual unity between Christ
> and his Church: Send therefore your blessing upon these
> your servants, that they may so love, honor, and cherish
> each other in faithfulness and patience, in wisdom and true
> godliness, that their home may be a haven of blessing and
> peace; through Jesus Christ our Lord, who lives and reigns
> with you and the Holy Spirit, one God, now and for ever.
> *Amen.*

The couple still kneeling, the Priest adds this blessing

> God the Father, God the Son, God the Holy Spirit, bless,
> preserve, and keep you; the Lord mercifully with his favor
> look upon you, and fill you with all spiritual benediction
> and grace; that you may faithfully live together in this life,
> and in the age to come have life everlasting. *Amen.*

The Peace

The Celebrant may say to the People

> The peace of the Lord be always with you.

People   And also with you.

*The newly married couple then greet each other, after which greetings
may be exchanged throughout the congregation.*

*When Communion is not to follow, the wedding party leaves the
church. A hymn, psalm, or anthem may be sung, or instrumental
music may be played*

At the Eucharist

*The liturgy continues with the Offertory, at which the newly married
couple may present the offerings of bread and wine.*

Preface of the Season

At the Communion, it is appropriate that the newly married couple
receive Communion first, after the ministers.

In place of the usual postcommunion prayer, the following is said

> O God, the giver of all that is true and lovely and gracious:
> We give you thanks for binding us together
> in these holy mysteries of the Body and Blood
> of your Son Jesus Christ.
> Grant that by your Holy Spirit,
> N. and N., now joined in Holy Matrimony,
> may become one in heart and soul,
> live in fidelity and peace,
> and obtain those eternal joys prepared for all who love you;
> for the sake of Jesus Christ our Lord. *Amen.*

As the wedding party leaves the church, a hymn, psalm, or anthem
may be sung, or instrumental music may be played.

a. The Blessing of a Civil Marriage

The rite begins as prescribed for celebrations of the Holy Eucharist, using the Collect and Lessons appointed in the Marriage service.

After the Gospel (and homily), the couple stand before the Celebrant, who addresses them in these or similar words

> N. and N., you have come here today to seek the blessing of God and of his Church upon your marriage. I require, therefore, that you promise, with the help of God, to fulfill the obligations which Christian Marriage demands.

The Celebrant then addresses one member of the couple, then the other, saying

> N., you have taken N. to be your *wife/husband/spouse*. Do you promise to love *her/him*, comfort *her/him*, honor and keep *her/him*, in sickness and in health, and, forsaking all others, to be faithful to *her/him* as long as you both shall live?

Answer   I do.

The Celebrant then addresses the congregation, saying

> Will you who have witnessed these promises do all in your power to uphold these two persons in their marriage?

People   We will.

If rings are to be blessed, the members of the couple extend their hands toward the Priest [or Bishop], who says

> Bless, O Lord, these rings to be signs of the vows by which N. and N. have bound themselves to each other; through Jesus Christ our Lord. *Amen.*

The Celebrant joins the right hands of the couple and says
> Those whom God has joined together let no one put
> asunder.

People   Amen.

The service continues with The Prayers on pages 179-80.

b. An Order for Marriage

If it is desired to celebrate a marriage otherwise than as provided on pages 157-82 above, this Order is used.

Normally, the celebrant is a priest or bishop. Where permitted by civil law, and when no priest or bishop is available, a deacon may function as celebrant, but does not pronounce a nuptial blessing.

The laws of the State having been complied with, the couple, together with their witnesses, families, and friends assemble in the church or in some other convenient place.

1. The teaching of the Church concerning Holy Matrimony, as it is declared in the formularies, is briefly stated.

2. The intention of the two to enter the state of matrimony, and their free consent, is publicly ascertained.

3. One or more Readings, one of which is always from Holy Scripture, may precede the exchange of vows. If there is to be a Communion, a Reading from the Gospel is always included.

4. The vows are exchanged, using the following form

> In the Name of God,
> I, N., take you, N., to be my *wife/husband/spouse*,
> to have and to hold from this day forward,
> for better for worse, for richer for poorer,
> in sickness and in health, to love and to cherish,
> until we are parted by death.
> This is my solemn vow.

or this

> I, *N.*, take thee *N.*, to my wedded *wife/husband/spouse*,
> to have and to hold from this day forward,
> for better for worse, for richer for poorer,
> in sickness and in health, to love and to cherish,
> till death us do part, according to God's holy ordinance;
> and thereto I plight [*or* give] thee my troth.

5. The Celebrant declares the union of the couple, in the Name of the Father, and of the Son, and of the Holy Spirit.

6. Prayers are offered for the couple, for their life together, for the Christian community, and for the world.

7. A priest or bishop pronounces a solemn blessing upon the couple.

8. If there is no Communion, the service concludes with the Peace, the couple first greeting each other. The Peace may be exchanged throughout the assembly.

9. If there is to be a Communion, the service continues with the Peace and the Offertory. The Holy Eucharist may be celebrated either according to Rite One or Rite Two, or according to the Order on page 401 of the *Book of Common Prayer* 1979.

Additional Directions

If Banns are to be published, the following form is used

> I publish the Banns of Marriage between *N. N.* of
> _____ and *N. N.* of _____.
> If any of you know just cause why they may not be joined together in Holy Matrimony, you are bidden to declare it. This is the first [*or* second, *or* third] time of asking.

The Celebration and Blessing of a Marriage may be used with any authorized liturgy for the Holy Eucharist. This service then replaces the Ministry of the Word, and the Eucharist begins with the Offertory.

After the Declaration of Consent, if there is to be a giving in marriage, or presentation, the Celebrant asks,

> Who presents [gives] these two people to be married to each other?

The appropriate answer is, "I do." If more than one person responds, they do so together.

For the Ministry of the Word it is fitting that the couple to be married remain where they may conveniently hear the reading of Scripture. They may approach the Altar, either for the exchange of vows, or for the Blessing of the Marriage.

It is appropriate that all remain standing until the conclusion of the Collect. Seating may be provided for the wedding party, so that all may be seated for the Lessons and the homily.

The Apostles' Creed may be recited after the Lessons, or after the homily, if there is one.

When desired, some other suitable symbol of the vows may be used in place of the ring.

At the Offertory, it is desirable that the bread and wine be presented to the ministers by the newly married persons. They may then remain before the Lord's Table and receive Holy Communion before other members of the congregation.

VI. Discussion Guide to

*"I Will Bless You
and You Will Be a Blessing"*
(revised and expanded edition)

Contents

Introduction to the Discussion Guide

This discussion guide invites the people of the Episcopal Church into a process of thoughtful consideration of the liturgical and theological resources for blessing same-sex relationships. Each of the five modules contains introductory teaching material and questions for group discussion; the first three also have handouts. The questions are shaped to equip individuals and groups to explore the materials in this collection in a reflective Christian manner.

These materials encourage participants to approach the discussion of resources for blessing same-sex relationships with respect for one another and for the various perspectives that individuals will bring to the conversation.

Because the same ideas will not inspire or challenge all groups, each area of study is wide-ranging and could span more than one session. Many congregations currently gather for Bible study and adult formation or education, and leaders can adapt these materials for such forums. Congregations may choose to engage in this process over an extended period of time or plan a one- to two-day retreat in order to enter more deeply into conversation and study. The amount of time suggested for particular discussions may be adjusted to meet the needs of a group. We strongly encourage that each session include time for Bible study related to the topic.

Encouraging time for participants to speak from their own experiences is essential when people engage in theological reflection on any topic. Significant factors in the conversation will include the cultural context of individuals and the makeup of the community. Each session's opening gives participants an opportunity to introduce themselves.

Ideally, the facilitator of these conversations will be someone who is respected by the community and who is respectful of, and familiar with, the group. Facilitators should read the entire resource "I Will Bless You, and You Will Be a Blessing" in preparation for leading discussion; they should also be familiar with local civil law and diocesan policies.

Establishing Group Norms for Conversations

Prayers and practices that make for good conversations

Parishioners enter the conversation about blessing same-sex relationships from many different starting points. Some congregations and individuals do not understand why any Episcopal church would bless same-sex relationships; others do not understand why the blessing of same-sex relationships continues to be controversial. Recognizing these differences, facilitators should begin these conversations with agreement for respectful conversation; a *Covenant for Discussion* is included among the handouts found at the end of this discussion guide. Beginning and ending each session with prayers of thanksgiving for the opportunity for dialogue can underscore the value of respectful discussion.

The idea that the Church is a safe place to disagree is attractive, but living it out is difficult. Doing so requires that we expand our boundaries to accept those we do not understand or with whom we do not agree on matters of great importance. We do this because, more than anything, Christians do agree on matters of the *greatest* importance—the love and salvation offered by Jesus Christ. While we may disagree over the definition of marriage and how we understand biblical texts about divorce and sexuality, we can agree on our shared participation in Christ's mission to restore all people to unity with God and each other in Christ.

The goal of dialogue is not to win the day for one's own point of view, but for all participants to grow in understanding of both themselves and others. If participants come to this conversation with open hearts and minds, it is possible to honor both the integrity and holiness of gay and lesbian couples and their families, and the deep traditions of the Church.

Recommended Background Materials

To Set Our Hope on Christ (2005)[95] was prepared as a response
to the request by the *Windsor Report* (2004) that the Episcopal
Church explain how "a person living in a same gender union may
be considered eligible to lead the flock of Christ." This document
provides an overview as to how and why the Episcopal Church has
moved toward the fuller inclusion of gay and lesbian people in the life
of the Church. The appendix comprises a historical summary of beliefs
and policies concerning sexuality in the Episcopal Church.

The June 2009 *Report of the Task Force on Holiness in Relationships
and the Blessing of Same-Sex Relationships*, from the Episcopal
Diocese of San Diego,[96] presents different points of view in an even-
handed manner. The report considers the interpretation of Holy
Scripture; marriage and holiness in Scripture; biblical texts that may
condemn same-sex relationships and those that may portray positive
roles of gays and lesbians; Church history and tradition; practical,
pastoral and sacramental theology; and the movement of the Holy
Spirit.

The 2015 *Report of the Task Force on the Study of Marriage*[97] is
the final report of the task force established by the 2012 General
Convention in Resolution 2012-A050. It considers marriage from
biblical, theological, historical, and liturgical perspectives. While
the work of the task force was not limited to consideration of the
marriage of same-sex couples, the essays may be useful in light of the
2015 General Convention decision to permit same-sex marriage.

---

95 *To Set Our Hope in Christ: A Response to the* Invitation *of* Windsor Report *¶135* is
    available on the website of the Episcopal Church: http://www.episcopalchurch.org/
    documents/ToSetOurHope_eng.pdf.
96 *Report of the Task Force on Holiness in Relationships and the Blessing of Same-Sex
    Relationships* is available on the website of the Episcopal Diocese of San Diego: http://
    www.edsd.org/mediafiles/holiness-in-relationships-task-force-report.pdf.
97 *Report of the Task Force on the Study of Marriage* is available on the website of the
    General Convention: http://extranet.generalconvention.org/staff/files/download/12485.pdf.

1. Study Area One

History: Reviewing the history of the Episcopal Church's decisions regarding same-sex relationships and reflecting on the current context

A. Preparing for the Session

Have the following handouts ready (included at the end of this Discussion Guide, unless otherwise noted):

- A. *Covenant for Discussion*
- B. *Understanding the History*
- C. *An Introduction to General Convention*
- *A Review of General Convention Legislation* (Appendix 3)
- D. *Relationships and Blessing: Reflection Questions*

Prepare for the Bible study to be offered in this session by choosing the passage to be read and deciding on the method of study.

B. Gathering

- Welcome participants and make any announcements necessary regarding hospitality (restrooms, coffee) and scheduling.
- Continue with a prayer of thanksgiving for the opportunity to have this conversation.
- Go around the room to have each person introduce herself or himself and share what he/she is most looking forward to in these conversations.
- Establish group norms for engaging in respectful conversation. Facilitators may distribute and review the *Covenant for Discussion* provided in the handouts, or choose a set of norms from their own resources.
- Introduce the Bible study prepared for this session.

C. Introducing the Topic

Distribute the worksheet *Understanding the History* and give
participants about 10 minutes to complete it.

After everyone has had time to write something, ask everyone to
share their answers to "A" (how long the Episcopal Church has been
talking about same-sex relationships and its gay, lesbian, bisexual,
and transgender members). Continue by inviting participants to share
whatever is comfortable from "B" for each decade. Listen to see
whether there is a thread or theme that runs through the memories.

D. General Convention Legislation

Give a very brief description of what General Convention is, who
attends, and what it does, using the handout *An Introduction to
General Convention.*

Distribute *A Review of General Convention Legislation*, and discuss
it in light of responses to the worksheet. Here—and throughout the
balance of the sessions—clearly distinguish when you are expressing
an idea or opinion based on your own experience and when you are
communicating official Church stances.

E. The Blessings of Relationships

Ask the group to call to mind at least three committed relationships
they are familiar with: for example, relationships of family members,
friends at work or school, or couples in your congregation; or their
own committed relationship. Remind them that they may know people
in committed relationships who are not married for one reason or
another.

Divide into groups of threes, and distribute the handout *Relationships
and Blessing: Reflection Questions*. Instruct the group to reflect for
15 or 20 minutes on the questions in the handout, which explore the
nature of committed relationships. Afterward, have them reflect back
to the larger group by asking these questions:

- What was especially illuminating or challenging in your
  conversations?
- Regarding the complexities of the relationships you
  discussed, were there any surprises?

- Based on your conversations, why do you think the Church blesses any committed relationships at all?

F. Conclusion

Thank the participants for coming, remind them of the next meeting date and time, and close with a prayer of thanksgiving.

2. Study Area Two

Theology and the Bible: Examining our understanding of God's blessing through the lens of theology and Scripture

A. Preparing for the Session

Have the following handouts ready (included at the end of this discussion guide):

- A. *Covenant for Discussion* (or other norm for discussion)
- E. *Theological Reflection on Same-Sex Relationships: A Summary of "Faith, Hope, and Love"*

Prepare for the Bible study to be offered in this session by choosing the passage to be read and deciding on the method of study.

B. Gathering

- Welcome participants and make any announcements necessary regarding hospitality (restrooms, coffee) and scheduling.

- Continue with a prayer of thanksgiving for the opportunity to have this conversation.

- Review group norms for engaging in respectful conversation, using the *Covenant for Discussion* or other set of norms established in the first session.

- Invite participants who attended the previous session to share illuminations and challenges that occurred to them regarding the history of the Episcopal Church, rites of blessing same-sex relationships, and their own experience of blessings revealed in committed relationships.

- Introduce the Bible study prepared for this session.

C. Introducing the Topic

Introduce the theological principles with these or similar words:

> In the Episcopal Church, we develop our theology, or the
> way we think about God, through Scripture, tradition, and
> reason. Consider, for example, the concept of "hospitality."
> Numerous examples in Scripture tell of God's hospitality
> toward God's people and of the people of God issuing or
> withholding God's hospitality from others. Although some
> of the stories seem to show behavior that conflicts with the
> ways God might have us respond to outsiders today, these
> biblical stories still help guide us. Other theological principles,
> like eschatology (beliefs about final events in the history of
> the world) and the triune nature of God, take a little more
> exploration from Scripture to interpret in light of Christian
> experience and understanding over the millennia since biblical
> times. We believe that God continues to reveal God's self
> to the world. We experience this revelation in many ways,
> including faithful, lifelong, committed relationships.

Distribute *Theological Reflection on Same-Sex Relationships* and ask
participants to read and reflect on this summary of the essay "Faith,
Hope, and Love." Describing relationships as "covenantal," this
document identifies four themes for theological reflection: vocation,
households, fruitfulness, and mutual blessing. Invite the group to
discuss some or all of these principles, using the introductions and
discussion questions that follow.

D. Covenant

Introduce the concept of "covenant" with these or similar words:

> Covenants are made and held in relationships not only
> between the individual and God but within a community,
> which is also held accountable. The Baptismal Covenant
> is an example that will be familiar to Episcopalians, where
> commitments are made by (or for) the individual being
> baptized as well as by the sponsors and the gathered
> community.
>
> Covenants take many forms in Scripture. They typically, but
> not always, contain a solemn agreement in which all parties
> pledge themselves to the others, outlining mutual obligations
> and responsibilities. Scripture tells about covenants

concerning marriage, water rights, tribal relationships, protection, and faithfulness; the covenants include rituals involving animals, exchanges, and other gestures of the now-sealed relationship. The book of Genesis contains a series of covenants God made. For example, after making a covenant with Noah (Genesis 6:18) to protect his family from the impending flood, God makes a covenant with creation: "I establish my covenant with you, that never again shall all flesh be cut off by the waters of a flood, and never again shall there be a flood to destroy the earth" (Genesis 9:11).

Relational commitment can lead a couple to enter into a lifelong covenant in which their love and faithfulness participate in and reflect God's own gracious covenant with us in Christ.

Discussion Questions to Further Reflection and Understanding

- One description of the difference between a contract and a covenant reads: *"A contract is an agreement made in suspicion. A covenant is an agreement made in trust."* What are some examples of contracts and covenants in your own life?

- Where have you seen God's graciousness evidenced in committed relationships of couples you have known?

E. Vocation

Introduce the theme of "vocation" with these or similar words:

Some people are called into long-term committed relationships as a vocation, defined here as a responsibility or way of life to which one is called by God. In Scripture, we find an example of this kind of relationship in Abraham and Sarah, who are vocationally linked to God and to one another. They are sent on a journey together that changes not just their names but the world (Genesis 11:27–25:11). Many other examples of committed relationships in the Bible—for example, Ruth and Naomi (Ruth 1), Eli and Samuel (1 Samuel 3), Jesus and his disciples—might be considered vocational, that is, carrying a function called by God. These partnerships defined not only the individuals but also the work they had to do together as a function of God's life in the world.

Discussion Questions to Further Reflection and Understanding

- Have you been in, witnessed, or read about relationships you could consider "vocational"? If so, what makes them so?

- In the Bible we are told that Paul, when counseling early Christians about the complexities and persecutions Christians were facing at the time, suggested that remaining single is a way to serve God, a vocation to "promote good order and unhindered devotion to the Lord" (1 Corinthians 7:35). Not everyone is called into long-term committed relationships; being single may be a vocation for some. Have you experienced, or do you know other people who have experienced, singleness as a vocation?

F. Households

Introduce the theme of "households" with these or similar words:

Households take many different forms. Consider the story of the prodigal son, in which obligations of loyalty and love were made, broken, and reconciled. Families of origin come with implicit household covenants. When individuals join together to create new households, they have the opportunity to bind themselves to one another in new ways. In these newly created households, the covenanted relationships within allow for holy love, care, risk-taking, and sacrifice on behalf of the other. People have reflected that, in such relationships, they begin to understand God's unconditional love of, and faithfulness to, us. They experience many of the gifts that such a household can bring, including mutual joy, companionship, faithfulness, compromise, charity, grace, and forgiveness.

Discussion Questions to Further Reflection and Understanding

- The *Theological Reflection on Same-Sex Relationships* handout states: "While households take many different forms, they create a space of mutual trust and accountability" where we can "learn the spiritual disciplines of compassion, forgiveness, and reconciliation." Have you known or experienced households that provide that "sacred space"? How does thinking about households as a theological concept resonate with your experience?

- In the story of the prodigal son (Luke 15:11–32), the household celebrates when the father welcomes the younger son with compassion, despite the son's disregard for their family agreements. What similar responses have you seen in households you have known, and what do such responses reveal about the nature of households?

- In the same story, the elder brother resents the prodigal. What do you think gets in the way of healing the break in mutual trust and accountability between these two members of the same household?

G. Mutual Blessing and Fruitfulness

Introduce the themes of "mutual blessing" and "fruitfulness" with these or similar words:

> Former Archbishop of Canterbury Donald Coggan summed up the essence of the apostle Paul's message to the world in three words: grace, love, and fellowship: "These are the key words of what has become the second-best-known prayer in the Christian Church: 'The grace of the Lord Jesus Christ, and the love of God, and the fellowship of the Holy Spirit, be with you all.'"[98] Grace. Love. Fellowship. These blessings are abundant in Christian relationships and in Christian communities.

> The apostle Paul tells us, "the fruit of the Spirit is love, joy, peace, patience, kindness, generosity, faithfulness, gentleness, and self-control" (Galatians 5:22). Just as Abraham was blessed by God in order to be a blessing (Genesis 12:2), the commitment exhibited in covenantal relationships becomes a source of blessing for the whole Church. When divine grace sustains a covenantal relationship it bears fruit in countless ways, not only for the couple but for the wider community as well.

> When we are present in any public naming of graces or gifts, be it baptism or graduation or the giving of an award, we are often reminded that the individual or group upon which the recognition is bestowed is expected to return that value back to society. At a liturgy of blessing, we are reminded of the value of the individuals entering into a covenant with one another—of their love, faith, loyalty, and devotion to each other and to God. As we bless their relationship we expect in return that this naming and strengthening of the couple will bless the congregation.

---

98 Donald Coggan, *Meet Paul: An Encounter with the Apostle* (London: SPCK, 1998), 73–75.

Discussion Questions to Further Reflection and Understanding

- In your experience, how have you seen covenantal relationships that are blessed in the Church become in turn a blessing for the Church?

- In your experience, how have you seen covenantal relationships bear fruit?

- How can the blessing of a same-sex relationship sustain and enable a couple to embody service, generosity, and hospitality beyond their household?

H. Conclusion

Thank the participants for coming, remind them of the next meeting date and time, and close with a prayer of thanksgiving.

3. Study Area Three

Liturgy: Discussing liturgy in general and the liturgical resources developed for the blessing of same-sex relationships

A. Preparing for the Session

Have the following handouts ready (included at the end of this discussion guide, unless otherwise noted):

- A. *Covenant for Discussion* (or other norm for discussion)
- F. *Principles for Evaluating Liturgical Materials*
- Liturgy: "The Witnessing and Blessing of a Lifelong Covenant" or "The Witnessing and Blessing of a Marriage"
- Liturgy: "The Celebration of a Marriage 2" (optional)

Prior to the session, solicit volunteers to walk through the liturgy (ending with the greeting of the Peace) during the session. Ask them to be respectful of the process and to recognize that even when role-playing the words and actions in a liturgy can have an impact on the people saying and doing them.

Prepare for the Bible study to be offered in this session by choosing the passage to be read and deciding on the method of study.

B. Gathering

- Welcome participants and make any announcements necessary regarding hospitality (restrooms, coffee) and scheduling.
- Continue with a prayer of thanksgiving for the opportunity to have this conversation.
- Review group norms for engaging in respectful conversation, using the *Covenant for Discussion* or other set of norms established in the first session.

- Invite participants who attended the previous session to share illuminations and challenges that have occurred to them regarding the interaction of the Bible and theology with the blessing of same-sex relationships.

- Introduce the Bible study prepared for this session.

C. Introducing the Topic

Introduce a discussion of the meaning and purpose of liturgy with these or similar words:

> Christians over the centuries have found ways to ritualize our story as a people of God, our place in God's life today, and our hope for an eternity with Christ. Liturgy, as an event, retells salvation history in word and sacrament: by the proclamation of Scripture, through preaching and prayer, and in the liturgy of the table. Each time we celebrate liturgy, we become active participants in re-presenting this history— life with God, from creation and fall through covenant, redemption, and fulfillment—and in bringing it into the present. When we consecrate water during baptism, we go back to the waters of creation at the beginning of our story. We are buried with Christ in this water and brought forth into a new life in Christ, a new future. Scripture calls us to keep rituals when we are told to "make this day holy" or to "remember this place" or to "do this" from this day forward in order to keep our inherited faith as present as it ever was.
>
> Liturgy can be understood as an exchange between heaven and earth. All that we have comes from God, and that is what we return. In our prayers, we as a community breathe in and out our petitions, thanksgivings, sorrows, hopes, and praises.
>
> Celebrating important moments in the lives of individual Christians and in the community often happens in the context of liturgy. In the liturgies of baptism, confirmation, marriage, and ordination, we join together to enact and celebrate our commitment to a vocation with Christ and with one another.

D. Qualities of Anglican Liturgy

Distribute the handout *Principles for Evaluating Liturgical Materials*, and introduce the principles with these or similar words:

In Resolution 2009–C056, the General Convention directed the Standing Commission on Liturgy and Music to "collect and develop theological and liturgical resources" for the blessing of same-sex relationships. The Commission discovered a vast array of unofficial liturgies, some dating back to the 1970s, and, more recently, rites of blessing commended for use in dioceses in the Episcopal Church and the Anglican Church of Canada. These liturgies were created in response to the pastoral needs of same-sex couples in various local jurisdictions. The Commission found strong similarities in the rites; many used The Celebration and Blessing of a Marriage from the *Book of Common Prayer* as a template.

This research led the Commission to develop liturgical principles to assess the resources it had collected and as the basis for creating a new liturgical resource to present to General Convention in 2012. Consistency with Anglican theological tradition and the liturgical style of the 1979 *Book of Common Prayer* was essential in developing these materials. Keeping proposed rites as an expression of the whole Church, not only the two people seeking a blessing, was also important. A full list of those qualities is in the handout.

These qualities can be gathered into two general categories: words and actions. In liturgy, words and actions together express and shape what we believe. In "The Witnessing and Blessing of a Lifelong Covenant," this combination of words and actions expresses what we understand and hope about blessing, households, and the revelation of God's love in the world through these committed relationships.

E. Exploring the Liturgy for Blessing Same-Sex Relationships

Distribute copies of the liturgy or liturgies you have decided to use ("The Witnessing and Blessing of a Lifelong Covenant" or "The Witnessing and Blessing of a Marriage"; "The Celebration and Blessing of a Marriage 2") and invite participants to keep in mind the principles outlined in the handout for evaluating liturgical materials as they role-play the liturgy.

Before reading through the liturgy with the volunteers selected in advance of the session, explain that it is not the intention of this "couple" to receive this blessing. Acknowledge that there may be anxiety when role-playing the rite, and invite participants to engage the experience prayerfully. When finished, remind the "couple," the "presider," and the "assembly" that the role-play is not binding, and thank the volunteers for their help.

Discussion Questions to Further Reflection and Understanding

- What did you hear?
- What did you see?
- What did you feel?
- How does this liturgy hold to the liturgical principles set forth in the handout?
- What words, symbols, and actions in this liturgy stand out for you and draw you into reflection on your own experience of covenantal relationship?
- What do the words, symbols, and actions call forth, challenge, or offer to the couple who experience them in the context of a blessing of their relationship?
- In your experience, which elements seem to have the most meaning when a community gathers to receive God's blessing?

F. Conclusion

Thank the participants for coming, remind them of the next meeting date and time, and close with a prayer of thanksgiving.

4. Study Area Four

Civil and Canon Law: Exploring legal, canonical, and spiritual issues that arise as the Church considers blessing same-sex couples

A. Preparing for the Session

Have the following handout ready:

- A. *Covenant for Discussion* (or other norm for discussion)

Set up two pages of newsprint, each with two columns:

One page of newsprint:

MARRIAGE

Secular Benefits/Obligations   Sacred Benefits/Obligations

The other page of newsprint:

BLESSING

Secular Benefits/Obligations   Sacred Benefits/Obligations

Prepare for the Bible study to be offered in this session by choosing the passage to be read and deciding on the method of study.

B. Gathering

- Welcome participants and make any announcements necessary regarding hospitality (restrooms, coffee) and scheduling.

- Continue with a prayer of thanksgiving for the opportunity to have this conversation.

- Review group norms for engaging in respectful conversation, using the *Covenant for Discussion* or other set of norms established in the first session.

- Invite participants who attended the previous session to share illuminations and challenges that have occurred to them regarding the liturgy for the blessing of same-sex relationships.

- Introduce the Bible study prepared for this session.

C. Introducing the Topic

Introduce the discussion of civil and canon law with these or similar words:

Resolution 2009–C056 directed the Standing Commission on Liturgy and Music to develop resources for blessing same-gender relationships. As the Commission went about its work, Episcopalians asked about the relationship between these blessings and marriage. Following the direction of General Convention, the Commission developed a resource for blessing relationships, not marriage. In 2015 the General Convention authorized two marriage liturgies for trial use and also authorized a liturgy for blessing same-sex relationships.

In June 2015, the Supreme Court of the United States issued a ruling that permits marriage of same-sex couples throughout the United States. In the years prior to this decision, several states permitted civil unions of same-sex couples but not marriage. Some dioceses of the Episcopal Church outside of the United States are in civil jurisdictions that do not permit same-sex marriage.

The Book of Common Prayer (p. 422) and Canon I.18.1 require Episcopal clergy to conform to the laws of their state governing the creation of a civil marriage.

D. Exploring the Benefits and Obligations of Marriage and Blessing

Invite people to brainstorm about the secular benefits and obligations of marriage, and note their answers in that column of the newsprint page headed "Marriage." Then ask about the sacred benefits and obligations of marriage and note their answers. Now, do the same on the page with the heading "Blessing" (that is, blessing a lifelong, committed relationship)—secular benefits and obligations first, then sacred benefits and obligations. Step back and ask people what they notice about the four lists. Have a conversation.

The following is a list of responses people might give:

Marriage: Secular Benefits/Obligation

- Legal status given by the state: global for different-sex couple; country-specific for same-sex couple

- Part of the institution of marriage and its social benefits

- Potential financial benefits—joint tax returns, automatic joint ownership, etc.—global for different-sex couple; only in certain countries for same-sex couple

- Clarity about the relationship—fits a known model, people know what you are talking about if you say you are married; clarity about monogamy and faithfulness

- Legal responsibilities shared by the couple

- Social status

- Usually, acceptance of parents, family, and friends of the relationship

Marriage: Sacred Benefits/Obligations

- God's blessing proclaimed by the Church

- Recognition of spiritual nature of relationship

- Public religious and spiritual commitment of love

- Call to constant reconciliation and assurance of forgiveness

- Spiritual preparation and counseling prior to ceremony

- "Church wedding" and social recognition and support of religious community

- Exchange and blessing of symbols of relationship—ring(s)

- Done as part of the Prayer Book and Episcopal Church norms

Blessing: Secular Benefits/Obligations

- Possible gained clarity about the relationship; commitment statements made to one another

- Possible social status

- Possible acceptance/recognition of parents, family, and friends

Blessing: Sacred Benefits/Obligations

- God's blessing proclaimed by the Church

- Recognition of spiritual nature of relationship; clarity about monogamy and faithfulness

- Public religious and spiritual commitment of love

- Call to constant reconciliation and assurance of forgiveness

- Spiritual preparation and counseling prior to ceremony

- "Church wedding" and social recognition and support of religious community

- Exchange and blessing of symbols of relationship— ring(s)

- Falls within Episcopal Church norms

Invite the group to draw conclusions from the lists and their discussion of them. They might discover that when the Church blesses same-sex couples such blessings seem to carry most but not all of the "sacred benefit" that one finds in marriage, and when the Church blesses same-sex couples such blessings seem to carry much less of the "secular benefit" that one finds in marriage.

E. Conclusion

Thank the participants for coming, remind them of the next meeting date and time, and close with a prayer of thanksgiving.

5. Study Area Five

Mission: Exploring the blessing of same-sex relationships as part of the Church's mission and God's reconciling work in the world

A. Preparing for the Session

Have the following handout ready:

- A. *Covenant for Discussion* (or other norm for discussion)

Prepare for the Bible study to be offered in this session by choosing the passage to be read and deciding on the method of study.

B. Gathering

- Welcome participants and make any announcements necessary regarding hospitality (restrooms, coffee) and scheduling.

- Continue with a prayer of thanksgiving for the opportunity to have this conversation.

- Review group norms for engaging in respectful conversation, using the *Covenant for Discussion* or other set of norms established in the first session.

- Invite participants who attended the previous session to share illuminations and challenges that have occurred to them regarding the comparison of marriage and blessings.

- Introduce the Bible study prepared for this session.

C. Introducing the Topic

Introduce this final session by reminding participants that we are a part of a larger story, using these or similar words:

> Using the "three-legged stool" of Anglicanism, we have explored Scripture, tradition, and reason relating to the development of rites for blessing same-sex relationships in the Episcopal Church. We have explored God's call to us to live in relationship to God and to one another. We may have disagreed, misunderstood, or challenged one another, but we have been reminded at each turn that our life together, centered in baptism and the eucharist, is central to being people of faith in this time and in this Church.

> The essay "Faith, Hope, and Love" has this to say about the significance for mission of blessing same-sex relationships:

> > This missional character of covenantal blessing, reflected in both Scripture and the historical traditions of the Church, deserves renewed attention today. The 2000 General Convention contributed to this renewal when it passed Resolution D039, which identified monogamy, fidelity, holy love, and other characteristics of lifelong, committed relationships. Significantly, that resolution was framed as a way to enable the Church to engage more effectively in its mission. Many in the Episcopal Church have witnessed these characteristics in the committed relationships of same-sex couples. That recognition can, and in many places already has, broadened the understanding of the Church's mission of participating in God's reconciling work in the world.

> Our willingness to continue to receive a new thing while remaining in communion and in love with one another models a gift we have to offer the world.

> We began our study by exploring the Episcopal Church's recent history regarding same-sex couples seeking acceptance and blessing of their relationships in the Church, and by reflecting on our own experiences of lifelong, committed relationships. We continued with a study of the theological and liturgical resources that the Standing Commission on Liturgy and Music developed. Finally, we compared the benefits and obligations of marriage and blessing same-sex relationships.

Discussion Questions to Further Reflection and Understanding

- Over the past few weeks, how have our conversations emerged in the course of your daily lives? Have you found yourselves talking (or e-mailing or Facebook-ing) with colleagues, friends, or family regarding the willingness of the Episcopal Church to provide these blessings?

- This discussion guide was designed to equip participants to understand the presence of rites of blessing same-sex relationships in our common life in the Episcopal Church. Did it fulfill that purpose for you? Why or why not?

- If your community is not considering offering these rites to same-sex couples seeking marriage or a blessing of their relationship, are you able to explain why other parishes or dioceses in the Episcopal Church are? If yes, where would you begin that explanation? If no, what more information or background would be helpful?

D. Conclusion

Thank everyone for participating, for their hard work and dedication, and for loving the Church and those who come through the doors enough to have these conversations together.

Close with a prayer of thanksgiving.

Covenant for Discussion

As we gather in the name of Christ to share our thoughts, feelings, and ideas, we accept this covenant to guide our conversation along God's path of love.

- I recognize that everyone comes to this experience with very different backgrounds, experiences, and views. I will respectfully seek clarification of other perspectives to add to my understanding.

- If I choose to disagree with a perspective different from mine, I will do this in a loving and respectful way.

I will:

- Speak only for myself (using "I" statements).

- Take responsibility for my own thoughts and feelings.

- Remember my baptismal promise to "respect the dignity of every human being."

- Seek and acknowledge common ground.

- Honor confidentiality unless permission to share is explicitly given.

- Practice "sacred listening" by:

  – Listening for God in the experiences of others.

  – Accepting those experiences as valid for the speakers.

  – Searching for strengths in the other's position.

  – Avoiding interruptions and argument.

  – Avoiding applause or other reactions to speakers.

  – Allowing each person to speak before I speak again.

If a particular group or person is going to be discussed, some of them should be present.

Adapted from *Our Covenant for Conversation*, the Episcopal Diocese of Vermont; *Good News: A Congregational Resource for Reconciliation*, by the Right Reverend Steven Charleston (2003); and *Intimate Human Relationships: Resources for Conversation in the Congregations and Deaneries of the Episcopal Diocese of Vermont*, edited by Anne Clarke Brown (2004).

Understanding the History

Please use this worksheet to record your memories and thoughts about discussion of same-sex relationships over the past few decades.

A . The Episcopal Church has formally been talking about same-sex relationships and its gay, lesbian, bisexual, and transgender members for how many years? _____

B. Under each decade list briefly—using just key words—what you remember about:

1. What was going on in your own life

2. What was going on in the world and/or the Church

3. What was going on with issues of same-sex relationships.

	1970s	1980s	1990s	2000s	2010s
What I remember in my own life					
What I remember happening in the world and/or the Church					
What I remember about issues of same-sex relationships					

An Introduction to General Convention

With few precedents for a republican form of Church governance, the first General Convention met in 1785 in Philadelphia. That convention began work on a constitution and a revision of the *Book of Common Prayer*, the Church's book of worship. Within ten years the General Convention had agreed on its form of governance and its pattern of worship, both of which endure to the present day.

Uniquely for its time, the first General Conventions determined on a bicameral house in which elected (rather than royally appointed) bishops would make up one house, and lay and ordained deputies (equally represented) would make up the other house.

All bishops of the Episcopal Church, active and retired, are entitled to seat, voice, and vote in the House of Bishops (unless deprived of the privilege). Each of the Episcopal Church's dioceses (and the Convocation of Churches in Europe and the Navajoland Area Mission) is entitled to elect eight deputies, four laypersons and four priests and/or deacons, to the House of Deputies. (The diocesan electors of deputies are themselves elected representatives from local parishes.) Deputies are not delegates; that is, they are not elected to represent the electing dioceses.

Deputies vote their conscience for the good of the Church. They cannot be instructed to vote one way or another, for to do so would preclude godly debate and preempt the work of the Holy Spirit. Deputies are expected to serve on committees, if appointed, to attend forums and hearings, to read the reports to the Church from its commissions, committees, agencies, and boards, to listen to, and if so moved, to respond to resolutions on the floor of the house.

The House of Bishops and House of Deputies meet, deliberate, and vote separately. To be enacted, resolutions must pass both houses in the same language. Both houses have the right to amend legislation, but the amendment must be accepted by the other house. Resolutions presented to Convention come from four sources: committees, commissions, agencies, and boards of the Church; bishops; dioceses and provinces; and deputies.

The House of Bishops is chaired by the Presiding Bishop, and the House of Deputies is chaired by an elected President of the House. In the absence of the presiding officer, a Vice Chair (in the House of Bishops) or Vice President (in the House of Deputies) chairs. In each house, a secretary and parliamentarian assist the presiding officer.

General Convention meets prayerfully. Each day, bishops, deputies, registered alternates, and delegates to the ECW Triennial Meeting gather for Bible study and the Holy Eucharist. Both the House of Deputies and the House of Bishops have chaplains, who lead their houses in regular prayer at the beginning and end of sessions and daily at noon. Chaplains are also asked to pray before the enactment of important legislation. Organizations within the Church sponsor additional worship services, while volunteers staff a prayer room in which there is continual intercession for the work of Convention.

Much of the work of Convention is carried out by legislative committees. The Presiding Bishop and the President of the House of Deputies determine the number of persons who serve on committees and their membership. In their appointments, the presiding officers consider previous experience, expertise, and interest, ensuring the committees represent diverse points of view, geographic, ethnic and gender diversity, and participation by younger deputies.

Resolutions proposed for discussion at Convention are referred to legislative committees, which consider, amalgamate, and perfect them before presenting them on the floor of Convention. Legislative committees hold hearings on legislation at which the following can speak: bishop, deputy, registered alternate deputy, or registered visitor.

Debate on the floor is governed by the Constitution and Canons of the Church, Rules of Order for each house, Joint Rules of Order (that apply to both houses) and Roberts' Rules of Order. Deputies are expected to listen respectfully to the views of others and to adhere to the rules, which require, for example, that persons of different points of view alternate at microphones.

Convention is more than legislation. One of the most interesting parts of Convention is the Exhibit Hall, a marketplace of goods and ideas in which the organizations and interest groups within the Church present their wares, recruit members, and do their best to influence legislation.

Many Church-related organizations hold meetings in conjunction with Convention, and there are lunches and dinners hosted by seminaries, provinces, societies, boards and staff offices of the Church.

The Episcopal Church Women (ECW) holds its triennial meeting simultaneously with the General Convention. The ECW meeting has changed over the past several decades; today it focuses on the mission and service of the Church, and many of the Church's most distinguished members are invited to address this body.

General Convention is a combination of legislative assembly, bazaar of goods and services, and family reunion. It is one of the most exciting and, truth be told, one of the most awe-inspiring gatherings in the world.

Adapted from an introduction to the 2009 General Convention prepared by the Reverend Dr. Gregory S. Straub, Executive Officer and Secretary of General Convention

Relationships and Blessing: Reflection Questions

I invite you to reflect on the committed relationships of couples you know (friends, colleagues, family members, and so on), whether same-sex or not, including your own, if you are in such a relationship.

Consider questions such as these:

- How is each relationship named or described: marriage? covenant? union? some other way? Are those involved in the relationship considered husband and wife? partners? lovers? Does the term vary depending on circumstances? How important (or not) is the terminology used for your understanding and experience of the relationship?

- As you reflect on these relationships, what about them (their qualities, gifts, character) would make them appropriate for a liturgical blessing? Or, to put this in another way, why do we "bless" committed relationships in a Church at all?

For those who are in a committed relationship:

- Have you discerned any spiritual gifts that have emerged from your commitment that you may not have recognized apart from that commitment?

- What role does your faith community play in your ongoing commitment? Does the community offer something you find important in your relationship?

- What role (if any) did your Christian faith play in the early and now ongoing development of your relationship and in discerning your commitment to each other?

- Would you consider your committed relationship as part of your Christian calling and vocation to ministry? If so, how and in what ways?

For those who are reflecting on another couple's relationship:

- Have you discerned any spiritual gifts emerging from their relationship that benefit the wider community or perhaps yourself?

- Have you discerned what you or your faith community contributes to their relationship?

- How would you name the primary "blessing" of that relationship in your own life and in your faith community?

- Have you learned anything or gained fresh insights about your own life from observing the relationship and interacting with the couple?

Theological Reflection on Same-Sex Relationships: A Summary of "Faith, Hope, and Love"

Baptism, Eucharist, and the Paschal Mystery

All Christians are called to bear witness to the good news of God's love and grace in Jesus Christ, through the power of the Holy Spirit. We are empowered for such witness by our covenantal relationship with God. Baptism initiates us into that covenant, making us Christ's own forever and members of Christ's Body, the Church. The eucharist sustains us in that covenantal life and strengthens us to be Christ's witnesses in the world.

Our covenantal life with God can shape and be expressed in our relationships of commitment and faithfulness with others. Our committed relationships can thus reflect a *sacramental character* (making divine grace visible) and evoke *eschatological hope* (our ultimate union with God). These relationships thus invite further reflection on the mission of the Church, what it means "to bless," and the distinguishing marks of a covenantal relationship.

Themes for Theological Reflection

A sacramental framework for covenantal relationships suggests several other key theological themes for reflection and shared discernment, including the following:

- *Vocation*: God calls people into various kinds of relationship, whether as single people, in monastic communities, or as intimate couples. These vocational callings can empower our witness to the gospel. The decision to enter into a covenantal union is likewise a vocation marked by these characteristics: "fidelity; monogamy; mutual affection and respect; careful, honest communication; and the holy love which enables those in such relationships to see in each other the image of God."

- *Households*: Covenantal relationships are often lived in households in which we practice daily the giving of ourselves for the good of another. While households take many different forms, they create a space of mutual trust and accountability. The joy, intimacy, and shared vulnerability of households can thus help us learn the spiritual disciplines of compassion, forgiveness, and reconciliation in lives of committed monogamy and fidelity.

- *Fruitfulness*: The divine grace that sustains a covenantal relationship bears fruit in countless ways, not only for the couple but for the wider community as well. Covenanted couples manifest this grace in their shared gifts for ministry and in lives of service, generosity, and hospitality.

- *Mutual Blessing*: A blessed relationship is set apart for a divine purpose: to bear witness to the creating, redeeming, and sanctifying love of God in the world. As the Spirit empowers the couple for this witness, the Church is likewise blessed and strengthened for its mission and ministry.

In all of these ways and more, the blessing of a same-sex relationship invites covenantal couples and the whole Church to renew our commitment to the Baptismal Covenant. That commitment is expressed by *faith* in the good news of Jesus Christ, in the *hope* for union with God that Christ promised, and with the *love* that knits us together as the Body of Christ. As the apostle Paul reminds us, we live our life together as God's people with faith, hope, and love. And the greatest of these is love (1 Corinthians 13:13).

Principles for Evaluating Liturgical Materials

Materials proposed for blessing same-sex relationships must above all be consistent with the implicit theology and ecclesiology of the 1979 *Book of Common Prayer*. This would suggest, for example, that they must reflect the Prayer Book's underlying assumption that the entire life of the Church finds its origin in baptism.

Nearly as important is that the proposed liturgical materials embody a classically Anglican liturgical ethos and style. Recognizing the varying notions of what makes public prayer recognizably Anglican, the task group identified these qualities:

- It resonates with Scripture and proclaims the gospel.

- It is rooted in Anglican theological tradition.

- It has high literary value; it is beautiful according to accepted and respected standards.

- It uses the recurring structures, linguistic patterns, and metaphors of the 1979 *Book of Common Prayer*.

- It is formal, not casual, conversational, or colloquial.

- It is dense enough to bear the weight of the sacred purpose for which it is intended.

- It is metaphoric without being obtuse.

- It is performative: that is, it effects what it says.

At the same time, these rites must resonate as natural speech in contemporary ears. A religious or sacred tone must be achieved without the use of arcane or antiquated words or patterns of speech.

The rites should provide explanatory notes and rubrics. The material must be considered as the script for an event, not merely a collection of texts.

Any rite of blessing must be an expression primarily of the entire Church, not of the couple seeking a blessing. These rites must allow for robust communal participation, reflecting the baptismal ecclesiology of the Prayer Book. Related to this, since the eucharist is the symbol of the unity of the Church through unity with Christ, these services of blessing should normatively take place within a celebration of the eucharist.

Such rites must enact the notion of sacramental reciprocity by suggesting that, even as the Church blesses the relationship of the couple, the relationship of the couple is a blessing to the Church.

Options for various elements of the rites, particularly Scripture and the Prayers of the People, must be provided so that this action of the entire Church—this common prayer—does not degenerate into a generic rite.

Any rite of blessing a couple must hold up the two people making the covenant as the primary ministers within this action of God and of the entire Church. Such rites should give expression to the Church's understanding that the couple is freely assuming a vocation that can be expected to yield the fruits of mutual fidelity for the couple, for the Church, and for the entire world, and that points ultimately toward the fulfillment of all human relationships and unity in the eschatological Reign of God, when God will be all-in-all.

The rites must be what they purport to be—liturgical prayer—not didactic or polemical statements in the guise of liturgy.

Standing Commission on Liturgy
and Music 2010

VII. Appendices

232

Contents

1. A History of the Marriage Canon

This essay is from the report submitted to the 78th General Convention by the Task Force on the Study of Marriage, which was formed by the 77th General Convention (2012).

Canonical history in the Episcopal Church is consistent in one respect: canons follow practice. That is, the Church changes and evolves its practice and then amends the canons to reflect the current practice.[99] Sometimes this happens relatively quickly (for example, in the case of the ordination of women); sometimes this happens slowly (as in the case of the Church's practices regarding divorce and remarriage). In either case, a review of the journals of General Convention and White and Dykman's *The Annotated Constitution and Canons* shows that oftentimes the discussion has taken place over a number of years before the amendment passes General Convention. The marriage canon has followed this norm.

It should be noted that the term "Holy Matrimony" may appear to be used interchangeably with marriage. Holy Matrimony is not defined but in usage refers to the sacramental rite of the Church, and some prefer its use in the context of the Church's relationship to weddings and marriage. The connotation of "Holy Matrimony" is something more than marriage as defined by civil law. That "something more" is expressed in covenant language: the exchange of vows in the presence of a priest and at least two witnesses and blessed in the Name of God. Yet the marriage rite in the *Book of Common Prayer* 1979 is titled "The Celebration and Blessing of a Marriage." And both civil and Church law talks of "solemnizing" marriage. Even if Holy Matrimony is understood as "something more," that understanding is more aspirational than real, as marriage in the Church is no guarantee of the success of the relationship.

The canons addressing marriage or Holy Matrimony first addressed not the making of the marriage but its dissolution. The first mention

---

99 There are other instances when amending the canons was intended to change the practice. A recent example is the serial revisions of Title IV between 1994 and 2009.

of marriage in the canons[100] of the Episcopal Church appears in the Convention of 1808. The House of Deputies referred a communication to the House of Bishops, then consisting of the two bishops in attendance, White and Claggett, making a request. The communication asked the bishops to consider adopting the English canon regarding marriage and inserting it into future editions of the Prayer Book. The bishops responded by deferring the matter to consideration and action by a future convention, pointing to the absence of some of their members, as well as absences among the deputies. The 1808 convention instead passed a joint resolution stating "the sense of this Church" regarding the remarriage of the divorced, declaring "it is inconsistent with the law of God, and the Ministers of this Church, therefore, shall not unite in matrimony any person who is divorced, unless it be on account of the other party having been guilty of adultery."[101]

This joint resolution of 1808 remained the only statement of the General Convention on the subject of marriage until 1868, when the first canon was enacted as Canon II.13:

> No minister of this Church shall solemnize Matrimony in any case where there is a divorced wife or husband of either party still living; but this Canon shall not be held to apply to the innocent party in a divorce for the cause of adultery, or to parties once divorced seeking to be united again.

The new canon restated what the joint resolution of 1808 had put forward: remarriage of a divorced person is allowed only when the divorce occurs because of the adultery of one of the partners and then only of the innocent partner. It also adds a clarifying statement that allows a divorced couple to reunite and remarry in the Church. This statement regarding divorce and remarriage relied on what is commonly called "the Matthean exception," referring to Matthew 5:32: "But I say to you that anyone who divorces his wife, except on the ground of unchastity, causes her to commit adultery; and whoever marries a divorced woman commits adultery." Allowing this exception to the general prohibition of remarriage of a divorced person while the other partner lived was an Episcopal Church step away from the Church of England's blanket ban on remarriage of divorced persons.[102]

---

100 The Constitution of the Episcopal Church has not historically addressed marriage. The discussion here is confined to the canons.
101 Edwin A. White and Jackson A. Dykman, eds., *Annotated Constitution and Canons for the Government of the Protestant Episcopal Church* (New York: Church Publishing, Inc., 1979), 398.
102 White & Dykman, 398–399.

The 1877 convention repealed Canon II.13 as it was enacted in 1868 and enacted a new version entitled "Of Marriage and Divorce":

> Section 1 declared unlawful any marriage "otherwise than as God's Word doth allow."

> Section 2 prohibited ministers from knowingly solemnizing, after due inquiry, the marriage of any divorced person whose spouse is alive, if divorced for cause arising after marriage, and retains the exception for the innocent spouse or divorced spouses seeking to reunite.

> Section 3 prevented reception of a person not married according to the Word of God and the discipline of this Church into Baptism, Confirmation, or Holy Communion without the "godly judgment" of the bishop. But no minister could refuse the sacraments to a penitent person in imminent danger of death.

> Section 4 required referral of the facts of any case arising under section 2 to the bishop of the diocese or missionary jurisdiction in which the case arose, or, in the absence of such a bishop, to a bishop designated by the Standing Committee. The bishop was empowered to make inquiry into the matter as he found expedient and then deliver a judgment. No guidelines are given to serve as the basis for entering judgment.

> Section 5 applies the new canon only prospectively as to any penalties that may attach.[103]

The House of Bishops had concurred with the amendments in 1874 but the House of Deputies deferred consideration until the next convention in 1877. The 1868 amendments applied only to clergy, while the 1877 revision added penalties for laity by excluding from the sacraments those who married outside the Church.

Divorce rates remained low in the 1800s because secular law and social norms made divorce difficult. Spouses had to prove fault in some manner to obtain a divorce. Women, alone or with children, had few options for economic survival, a deterrent to seeking divorce. Divorce statistics were not even recorded prior to 1867. Less than 10 percent of marriages ended in divorce between 1867 and 1900. Nonetheless, the Church wrestled with how it should respond to its members who divorced. The idea of divorce ran counter to Church values and ideas about marriage, but it played out in how the Church

---

103 White & Dykman, 400–401.

responded to its divorced members. The Church's response came in the language of punishment: of clergy for knowingly officiating at the marriage of a person who was divorced from a living spouse, and of laity who divorced and remarried.

The convention of 1883 appointed a joint committee of bishops and deputies "to consider the duty of the Church in relation to the whole subject of Marriage, including the impediments to the contract thereof, the manner of its solemnization, and the conditions of its dissolution, and to report to the next General Convention."[104] In their report to the 1886 convention the committee contrasted the traditional view held by the Church with the prevailing secular sentiment seeking easier separation. The cause was identified as the ease with which first marriages were contracted, noting that children as young as twelve could marry without parental consent and without witnesses. The committee's response was a proposed canon that featured:

> Setting eighteen as the minimum age to marry without parental consent.
>
> Requiring solemnization to occur in the presence of at least two witnesses personally acquainted with both parties.
>
> Requiring clergy to keep a register of marriages, recording certain facts, and signed by the parties, at least two witnesses and the minister.
>
> Setting the law of the Church concerning divorce as that contained in Matthew 5:32 and 19:9, Mark 10:1, and Luke 16:18.
>
> Prohibiting divorce except for adultery or fornication, with the unfaithful spouse prohibited from marrying again during the lifetime of the innocent spouse.
>
> Subjecting clergy who violate the canon to ecclesiastical trial and admonition for a first offense and suspension or deposition for repeat offenses.
>
> Barring spouses from receiving Holy Communion for violating the canon except upon repentance and after separation from the new spouse.

The House of Deputies declined to concur in the adoption of the proposed canon, which was referred to the next conventions of 1889, 1892, 1895, and 1901 with similar results.[105]

---

104 White & Dykman, 402.
105 White & Dykman, 402–403.

The convention of 1904 took up the proposal to revise the marriage canon and passed Canon 38, "Of Solemnization of Matrimony," by a narrow majority after four days of debate in the House of Deputies meeting as a committee of the whole. Canon 38 set the following requirements:

> Section 1 required ministers to observe the law of the state governing the civil contract of marriage in the place where the marriage was performed.

> Section 2 required the presence of at least two witnesses to the solemnization and the recording in the proper register of the name, age, and residence of each party, signed by the parties, the minister, and at least two witnesses.

> Section 3 prohibited minister, knowingly and after due inquiry, from officiating at the marriage any person who was divorced from a living spouse, except the innocent party to a divorce for adultery. It added the new requirements in the latter case of a one-year waiting period and presentation of the divorce decree and record with "satisfactory evidence touching on the facts of the case" to the ecclesiastical authority along with evidence that the opposing spouse was personally served or appeared in court. The ecclesiastical authority, after taking legal advice on the evidence, declared in writing that in his judgment the case of the applicant conformed to the requirements of the canon. It further allowed any minister as a matter of discretion to decline to solemnize any marriage.

> Section 4 authorized any minister to refuse the ordinances of Holy Baptism, Confirmation, or Holy Communion to anyone who has been married "otherwise than as the Word of God and discipline of this Church allow" until the case was presented to the ecclesiastical authority for his godly judgment. But no minister was to refuse the sacraments to a penitent person in danger of death.

As adopted, the canon represented a compromise, one that had eluded the General Convention for fifteen years, between those who would prohibit remarriage of persons divorced from a still-living former spouse, and those who advocated the limited adultery exception, previously enacted in 1868, for the so-called innocent spouse in a divorce for adultery.[106]

---

106 White & Dykman, 403–404.

Efforts to drop the adultery exception continued without success in
the conventions of 1910 and 1913, when the question was referred
to a joint committee on marriage. The committee's report to the 1916
convention argued for the exercise of discretion in excluding persons
from the sacraments, recognizing that a subsequent marriage may have
been entered into in good faith and in ignorance of the Church's law
or while not subject to the Church's discipline, or may result in the
break-up of a family. This discretion would lie with the minister of the
congregation and the bishop of the diocese. The proposed canonical
amendments failed in 1916 and 1919.

A number of changes in American social and economic structures from
1850 to 1920 kept the Church's discussions of the role of divorce and
remarriage going. The Industrial Revolution drew men and women
from rural communities to the cities, from kinship community to
a community of peers, and began to redefine the roles of men and
women. Women organized to advocate for their civil rights in 1848
after the all-male Liberty Party added suffrage for women to its
national platform. A month later, the Seneca Falls Convention met and
adopted a "Declaration of Sentiments" demanding rights for women
so that they could protect their homes and families. Among the rights
sought were equal treatment before the law, participation in the
government of both State and Church, the right to own, inherit, and
dispose of their property, and fair treatment in divorce. The Women's
Christian Temperance Union (WCTU) organized in 1874, seeking to
ban alcohol, and later tobacco and other drugs, in order to protect the
home. Women protested their lack of civil rights and sought the rights
that would treat them as adults in the eyes of the law, as opposed
to the legal protections that kept them dependent on their fathers,
husbands, and sons. Unable to vote, women, especially married
women, lacked legal rights to retain custody of children and control
of their own property in a divorce, legal protection against rape and
other assaults, including domestic violence, and access to the economy
to become self-supporting when they were widowed or divorced. The
institutions of that time were controlled by white men. Legislatures
were all male. Women faced juries of men in civil and criminal cases.
The Church reflected its times: only men could be ordained as clergy
and only men could serve on vestries and as deputies to General
Convention. The WCTU obtained passage of Prohibition with the
18th Amendment to the federal Constitution in 1920, subsequently
repealed in 1933 in response to the uneven application of the law
across economic class and in the face of widespread and open
disregard for a law with a raft of unintended consequences. In short,
Prohibition was unworkable. But women obtained the right to vote in
1920 with ratification of the 19th Amendment.

Women's roles in society continued to change with the Depression and
World War II. Divorce rates increased in the early twentieth century,
doubling from 8 percent in 1900 to 16 percent in 1930. Divorce
continued to be fault-based divorce codes which required proof of
abuse, adultery, or abandonment. Divorce rates dropped slightly
during the Great Depression, in part because couples could not afford
the economic consequences of divorce on top of unemployment. As
the unemployment rate dropped, divorce rates began to rise gradually.
By 1940, 20 percent of marriages ended in divorce. Fertility rates
increased immediately following World War I, but then resumed
a fifty-year decline which was slowed only by the unreliability of
available birth control.[107]

The General Convention of 1922 amended section 3 of Canon 38,
making it unlawful for any member of the Church to enter into
a marriage when either of the parties was divorced from a living
husband or wife. The convention of 1925 considered and rejected
an amendment to section 3 of Canon 38 that restricted remarriage
to cases where the bishop, acting with legal advice, found on the
record that the divorce was granted for cause arising before marriage,
essentially annulling the marriage, allowing remarriage of either party.
The House of Bishops considered a separate amendment that allowed
remarriage of either party of any divorce, abolishing the Matthean
exception. The proposal failed, and the Matthean exception survived.

The Joint Commission on Marriage and Divorce presented an
extensive revision of the marriage canon that was adopted in 1931.
Compared with the previous limited measures to regulate the
solemnization of marriage by the Church, the new Canon 41, "Of
the Solemnization of Holy Matrimony," enacted far more detailed
regulation of Church marriage:

> Section 1 for the first time stated an affirmative duty
> that clergy instruct their congregations, both publicly
> and privately, on the nature and responsibilities of Holy
> Matrimony, and the mutual love and forbearance required.

> Section 2 retained the 1904 admonition that ministers
> conform to the laws of the State governing civil marriage, and
> added a parallel admonition to conform to the laws of the
> Church regarding the solemnization of Holy Matrimony.

> Section 3 expanded to five the list of conditions that the
> minister must discern before solemnizing a marriage. Among

---

107 Stephanie Coontz, *Marriage, A History: How Love Conquered Marriage* (New York:
Penguin, 2005).

the new conditions were verifying that the parties had a right to contract a marriage under Church law; instructing the parties on "the nature of Holy Matrimony, its responsibilities, and the means of grace which God has provided through His Church"; and requiring the parties to give the minister at least three days' notice of their intent to marry. Requirements for at least two witnesses and entry into the parish register were retained.

Section 4 added a new requirement that the parties to an imperiled marriage must present the matter to the minister who has "the duty ... to labor that the parties may be reconciled."

Section 5 retained the 1904 process and expectations for the remarriage of the divorced.

Section 6 added new provisions and conditions for the annulment or dissolution of a marriage by reason of the presence of one of the listed impediments to the marriage: relationship by blood within the prohibited degree (consanguinity within first cousins); absence of free consent; mistake as to the identity of either party; mental deficiency affecting exercise of intelligent choice; insanity of either party; failure of a party to reach puberty; undisclosed impotence, venereal disease, or facts making the marriage bigamous. Section 6 added a role for the ecclesiastical court in the exercise of judgments on annulment or dissolution petitions as an alternative to presentation to the bishop. A further provision stated that no judgment was to be construed as addressing the legitimacy of children or the civil validity of the relationship.

Section 7 retained the 1904 provision for excluding from the sacraments persons not married "according to the word of God and discipline of this Church" and the process for review by the bishop. Section 7 added an additional process for admitting persons married by civil authority or "otherwise than as this Church provides" to the sacraments. The process involved judgment by the bishop or ecclesiastical court.

Two of the 1931 proposals were subject to debate and amendment. The Joint Commission's proposal did not include continuing recognition of the Matthean exception, which was added back by the convention. The second major change, removing the right of determining nullity of a marriage from the local clergy to the bishop or ecclesiastical court, has an unclear basis but a best guess is that clergy were thought to be too lenient with their congregants. Requiring the bishop to make the determination opened the door to more uniform results and more objective consideration. One additional significant change was the omission of the section 3 clause that permitted any minister in his own discretion to decline to solemnize any marriage.[108]

The 1934 convention modified the three days' notice requirement to allow the minister to waive "for weighty cause," when one of the parties was a member of the minister's congregation or was well known to the minister, facts which had to be reported immediately to the ecclesiastical authority.[109]

The report of the Joint Commission on Marriage and Divorce to the 1937 General Convention lamented that the Church's views on divorce and marriage were increasingly ignored by the Church as well as the public at large. To remedy this concern, the Commission made observations about the points of tension, noting that "almost everyone agrees that the present Canon is inadequate, but there is a wide difference of opinion as to the course that should be followed."[110] The report went on to identify three issues:

> Some are slow to make changes, foreseeing difficulties and dangers and hence voting for the status quo.

> Others want to prohibit remarriage or the blessing of a remarriage of divorced persons, a strategy that has failed.

> Still others want to adopt annulment as done in the Eastern Orthodox and Roman churches, observing that "to most Anglicans and Protestants this seems nothing but divorce under another name. In either case it 'puts asunder' those whom, to all appearances and understanding 'God hath joined together.'"

The Commission proposed only two minor changes to the impediments section of the canon which were adopted, adding "lack of free *and legal* consent of either party" and "impotence *or sexual perversion of either party* undisclosed to the other."[111] Sexual perversion would include homosexuality.

The Commission proposed more extensive revisions of the marriage canon in 1940 and 1943 without success, receiving unfavorable action in the House of Deputies in a vote by orders. The 1943 convention

---

108 White & Dykman, 406–408.
109 White & Dykman, 408.
110 Joint Commission on Marriage and Divorce, quoted in White & Dykman, 409.
111 White & Dykman, 410; emphasis added.

passed successfully a reorganization of canons related to marriage by transferring section 7 (1931), governing the access of divorced persons to the sacraments, to Canon 15, "Of Regulations Respecting the Laity." Section 4, the duty to seek counseling; section 5, the Matthean exception to the prohibition of remarriage after divorce; and section 6, annulment, dissolution, and the impediments to marriage, became a new Canon 17, "Of Regulations Respecting Holy Matrimony and the Impediments Thereto." And sections 1–3, telling ministers their duties and obligations in solemnizing marriage, became the new Canon 16, "Of the Solemnization of Holy Matrimony."

After nearly eighty years of struggle, the 1946 convention eliminated the prohibition of the remarriage of divorced persons, including the Matthean exception. Applying solely to active members in good standing, the revised and renumbered Canon 18, "Of the Regulations Respecting Holy Matrimony," allowed a person whose marriage was annulled or dissolved by a civil court to petition the bishop or ecclesiastical authority of the diocese of canonical residence for a judgment of status or permission to be married by a minister of this Church. A one-year waiting period after issuance of the civil judgment was required and petition had to be made at least thirty days before the planned date of marriage. In considering such a petition, the bishop was required to be "satisfied that the parties intend a true Christian marriage," and, if so finding, refer the petition to his council of advisers or the court if the diocese has established one. The bishop or ecclesiastical authority was to base the judgment on and conform with the doctrine of the Church, "that marriage is a physical, spiritual, and mystical union of a man and a woman created by their mutual consent of heart, mind and will thereto and is a Holy Estate instituted of God and is in intention lifelong." Canon 18 references the list of conditions in Canon 17 as forming the basis for the judgment of the ecclesiastical authority. The result of the judgment is that no marriage bond recognized by the Church was established and may be so declared by the proper authority. However, the judgment was held not to say anything about the legitimacy of children or the civil viability of the former relationship. Judgments were to be rendered in writing and kept as a permanent record of the diocese. Any person granted such a judgment could then be married by a minister of the Church.[112] Essentially the convention accepted remarriage of divorced members as determined by civil law.

Controversy lingered over a perceived ambiguity in Canon 18, Section 2(b), whether the impediments listed in Canon 17, section 2(b), "are

112 White & Dykman, 416–418.

shown to exist or to have existed which manifestly establish that no marriage bond [existed]." Some bishops were only willing to consider granting petitions to remarry if the marriage impediment arose before the marriage, a concept of contract law known as *nullity ab initio*, meaning that some defect occurred in the formation of the marriage contract. Others were willing to recognize that for causes arising after marriage the marriage bond dissolved. A special committee of the House of Bishops reported to the 1949 convention on this split of opinion by taking the middle way opposing further clarification, stating: "But as a matter of fact there is no ambiguity here. The Canon recognized two points of view as legitimate; one, that if one or more impediments existed before the marriage, no marital bond was created; the other, that if one of the impediments arises after marriage, the marital bond is broken." The bishops could have it both ways.[113]

The 1946 revision changed the requirement that both parties have received Holy Baptism to requiring that only one party be baptized. The change addressed a disagreement in interpretation that had arisen. Some clergy felt that the nature of Holy Matrimony implied its availability only to baptized persons. This interpretation pushed unbaptized parties to seek instruction and Holy Baptism before being married in the Church, as some clergy refused to solemnize the marriage otherwise. This view is rejected by requiring at least one party to have been baptized.[114]

The 1949 convention nonetheless made two changes:

> Removed the referral by the bishop to his council of advisers or to a court formed for that purpose.

> Added the requirement that, if the remarriage was to be solemnized in a different jurisdiction than where the judgment is granted, the bishop or ecclesiastical authority of the second jurisdiction had to give approval as well.

These changes left the granting of permission to remarry to the bishop or ecclesiastical authority, without requiring consultation with attorneys, psychologists, a council of advice, or an ecclesiastical court, as had been required in prior times.

Proposals to return to the principle of *nullity ab initio* (1958) and to shorten the one-year waiting period (1970) were defeated.

From 1945 to 1947, a distinct spike in divorce rates was evident in the

---

113 White & Dykman, 419, quoting the 1949 *Journal*, 439.
114 White & Dykman, 414.

aftermath of World War II, reaching 43 percent when compared to the number of marriages in 1946. There may have been many reasons for this rise: hasty marriages immediately before deployment to the war, newfound independence among wives on the home front, and inability to undertake the burden of sustaining marriages to returning war veterans who were injured physically or psychologically as a result of their service. Divorce rates leveled off in the 1950s and 1960s, averaging about 24 percent over the two decades.

As General Convention prepared to convene in 1973, bishops and deputies submitted from 30 to 40 resolutions calling for amending or repealing the canons on Holy Matrimony. Both houses appointed special committees that met jointly during the first week of the convention, came to agreement on major issues, and drew up proposed amendments to the canons which were adopted by considerable majorities without significant floor changes.

Canon I.16, "Of Regulations Respecting the Laity," was amended to repeal section 7 addressing a Minister's withholding of the sacraments from a person "married otherwise than as the word of God and discipline of this Church allow".

Canon I.17, "Of the Solemnization of Holy Matrimony," was repealed and a new canon adopted in its place.

Section 1 was retained, requiring clergy to conform to state law governing civil marriage and the laws of this Church governing Holy Matrimony.

Sections 2 and 3 required clergy to meet the conditions and follow the procedures in solemnizing any marriage. The list of impediments to marriage was eliminated in an effort to move clergy from a legalistic evaluation of the marriage to a more pastoral approach emphasizing the nature of Christian marriage. The clergy were required to instruct and ascertain the understanding of the parties that marriage is a physical and spiritual union entered into in the community of faith by mutual consent of heart, mind, and will intending to be a lifelong commitment. Further, the parties must satisfy the minister that they are entering into marriage without fraud, coercion, mistaken identity, or mental reservation. Section 3 procedures requiring thirty days' notice to the minister, presence of at least two witnesses, and recording the marriage in the proper register were retained, as was the requirement that the couple sign the "Declaration of Intent" contained in section 3(d), which was first introduced into the canon in 1949. The Declaration of Intent was connected to the required instruction, but it sounded, in fact, more like a confessional statement expressed as the couple's "understanding" of Christian marriage.

Section 4 retained the clergy's discretion to decline to perform any marriage.

Canon I.18, "Of Regulations Respecting Holy Matrimony: Concerning Preservation of Marriage, Dissolution of Marriage, and Remarriage," was repealed and a new canon adopted:

Section 1 addressed the duty of the parties and the minister to attempt reconciliation in the face of imperiled marriage unity before filing legal action.

Section 2 allowed a party who wished to remarry after receiving a civil decree of annulment or dissolution to petition the bishop or ecclesiastical authority for a judgment of nullity or termination. The requirements for this permission were streamlined from earlier versions. Reliance on a civil decree of annulment or dissolution continued.

Section 3 set out procedures for the minister to follow in preparation for solemnizing the marriage of a party who was previously married to a living spouse. As revised, section 3 made clear that divorced persons could remarry in the Church and set out the simplified procedures for ministers to follow and obtain the bishop's consent.

Section 4 makes Canon I.17 applicable to all remarriages.[115]

No-fault divorce arrived in the 1970s as states changed their laws to move away from the necessity of proving a grievous wrong to the marriage and toward recognition that marital relationships simply do not work out or meet the expectations of both parties. In the 1980s equitable distribution of marital property became the law, reducing the battles between divorcing spouses over property as a means of punishing the other or reducing an offending spouse to abject poverty. Divorce rates jumped from 33 percent in 1970 to 50 percent in 1985 as these two legal trends took hold nationwide. Divorce rates continue to run to about 50 percent of marriages in 2014.

The 1973 rewrites of Canons I.16, I.17 and I.18, renumbered as Canons I.17, I.18 and I.19 in 1985, settled the canons on marriage

---

115 White & Dykman, 413–415.

and remarriage for the next thirty years. There have been a few relatively minor changes adopted subsequently:

> In 1979, Canon I.18.3 (now I.19.3) was amended to clarify which bishop would be consulted when a member of the clergy canonically resident in one diocese was licensed to perform a remarriage in another diocese. The canon required consulting with and reporting to the minister's bishop.

> In 2000, Canon I.19.1 was amended to clarify the duty of clergy when consulted by the parties to an imperiled marriage. The prior canon emphasized reconciliation as the purpose of the consultation. Some clergy apparently took this charge literally, encouraging women in abusive relationships to work matters out without regard to the physical safety of the woman and/or children. Societal, legal, and law enforcement norms regarding domestic violence, spousal abuse, and child abuse changed significantly during the 1980s and 1990s. The amendment changed the charge to reconcile if possible and imposed an additional duty on the clergy to "act first to protect and promote the physical and emotional safety of those involved and only then, if possible, to labor that the parties be reconciled."

> In 2000, General Convention further amended Canon I.19.3 to add reporting to the bishop of the diocese where the member of the clergy is canonically resident or the bishop where the member of the clergy is licensed to officiate and report to that bishop on the remarriage.

Even though the marriage canons did not change dramatically, discussion of issues related to marriage continued in General Convention in parallel with secular society. These discussions occurred under the umbrella of human sexuality and across interim bodies of the General Convention, debating what the Church should say and do about premarital sex and adultery; infertility and emerging technologies to allow infertile couples to conceive and bear children and surrogacy; abortion and birth control; couples cohabiting without marriage; marriage across religious denominations; interracial marriage; and full inclusion of gay and lesbian, later widened to include bisexual and transgender persons (LGBT), in community. Calls continue for revision of the canons to permit same-sex marriage or some form of recognition for same-sex relationships; to remove clergy from acting as agents of the state in solemnizing marriage; to allow blessings for same-sex couples, heterosexual couples who choose not to marry for financial reasons, and immigrants living illegally in the United States. These issues will be considered further in the critique of the present canons.

Bibliography

The Constitution and Canons of the Episcopal Church. New York: Church Publishing Inc., 2012.

Coontz, Stephanie. *Marriage, A History: How Love Conquered Marriage.* New York: Penguin, 2005.

Jones, Audrey M. "Historical Divorce Rate Statistics," on website Love to Know Divorce. http://divorce.lovetoknow.com/Historical_Divorce_Rate_Statistics.

National Conference of State Legislatures. "Same-Sex Marriage Laws." November 20, 2014. http://www.ncsl.org/research/human-services/same-sex-marriage-laws.aspx#2.

White, Edwin A., and Jackson A. Dykman, eds. *Annotated Constitution and Canons for the Government of the Protestant Episcopal Church.* New York: Church Publishing, Inc., 1979.

Women's Christian Temperance Union website. "Early History." http://www.wctu.org/earlyhistory.html.

2. Marriage Canons

From The Episcopal Church, *Constitution and Canons*, 2015

In Resolution 2015-A036, the General Convention revised Canon I.18, effective on the First Sunday of Advent 2015.

TITLE I: ORGANIZATION AND ADMINISTRATION

CANON 18: Of the Celebration and Blessing of Marriage

Sec. 1. Every Member of the Clergy of this Church shall conform to the laws of the State governing the creation of the civil status of marriage, and also these canons concerning the solemnization of marriage. Members of the Clergy may solemnize a marriage using any of the liturgical forms authorized by this Church.

Sec. 2. The couple shall notify the Member of the Clergy of their intent to marry at least thirty days prior to the solemnization; Provided, that if one of the parties is a member of the Congregation of the Member of the Clergy, or both parties can furnish satisfactory evidence of the need for shortening the time, this requirement can be waived for weighty cause; in which case the Member of the Clergy shall immediately report this action in writing to the Bishop.

Sec. 3. Prior to the solemnization, the Member of the Clergy shall determine:

(a) that both parties have the right to marry according to the laws of the State and consent to do so freely, without fraud, coercion, mistake as to the identity of either, or mental reservation; and

(b) that at least one of the parties is baptized; and

(c) that both parties have been instructed by the Member of the Clergy, or a person known by the Member of the Clergy to be competent and responsible, in the nature, purpose, and meaning, as well as the rights, duties and responsibilities of marriage.

Sec. 4. Prior to the solemnization, the parties shall sign the following Declaration of Intention:

> We understand the teaching of the church that God's purpose for our marriage is for our mutual joy, for the help and comfort we will give to each other in prosperity and adversity, and, when it is God's will, for the gift and heritage of children and their nurture in the knowledge and love of God. We also understand that our marriage is to be unconditional, mutual, exclusive, faithful, and lifelong; and we engage to make the utmost effort to accept these gifts and fulfill these duties, with the help of God and the support of our community.

Sec. 5. At least two witnesses shall be present at the solemnization, and together with the Member of the Clergy and the parties, sign the record of the solemnization in the proper register; which record shall include the date and place of the solemnization, the names of the witnesses, the parties and their parents, the age of the parties, Church status, and residence(s).

Sec. 6. A bishop or priest may pronounce a blessing upon a civil marriage using any of the liturgical forms authorized by this Church.

Sec. 7. It shall be within the discretion of any Member of the Clergy of this Church to decline to solemnize or bless any marriage.

CANON 19: Of Regulations Respecting Holy Matrimony: Concerning Preservation of Marriage, Dissolution of Marriage, and Remarriage

Sec. 1. When marital unity is imperiled by dissension, it shall be the duty, if possible, of either or both parties, before taking legal action, to lay the matter before a Member of the Clergy; it shall be the duty of such Member of the Clergy to act first to protect and promote the physical and emotional safety of those involved and only then, if it be possible, to labor that the parties may be reconciled.

Sec. 2 (a) Any member of this Church whose marriage has been annulled or dissolved by a civil court may apply to the Bishop or Ecclesiastical Authority of the Diocese in which such person is legally or canonically resident for a judgment as to his or her marital status in the eyes of the Church. Such judgment may be a recognition of the nullity, or of the termination of the said marriage; *Provided*, that no such judgment shall be construed as affecting in any way the legitimacy of children or the civil validity of the former relationship.

(b) Every judgment rendered under this Section shall be in writing and shall be made a matter of permanent record in the Archives of the Diocese.

Sec. 3. No Member of the Clergy of this Church shall solemnize the marriage of any person who has been the husband or wife of any other person then living, nor shall any member of this Church enter into a marriage when either of the contracting parties has been the husband or the wife of any other person then living, except as hereinafter provided:

(a) The Member of the Clergy shall be satisfied by appropriate evidence that the prior marriage has been annulled or dissolved by a final judgment or decree of a civil court of competent jurisdiction.

(b) The Member of the Clergy shall have instructed the parties that continuing concern must be shown for the well-being of the former spouse, and of any children of the prior marriage.

(c) The Member of the Clergy shall consult with and obtain the consent of the Bishop of the Diocese wherein the Member of the Clergy is canonically resident or the Bishop of the Diocese in which the Member of the Clergy is licensed to officiate prior to, and shall report to that Bishop, the solemnization of any marriage under this Section.

(d) If the proposed marriage is to be solemnized in a jurisdiction other than the one in which the consent has been given, the consent shall be affirmed by the Bishop of that jurisdiction.

Sec. 4. All provisions of Canon I.18 shall, in all cases, apply.

3. A Review of General Convention Legislation

Introduction

The legislative history here shows the development of General Convention deliberations about the place of gay men and lesbians in the life of the Church, particularly with regard to the blessing of their faithful, monogamous, lifelong relationships. Successive conventions have both acknowledged the work of their predecessors and reached new decisions.

Resolution texts are from the website of the Archives of the Episcopal Church: http://www.episcopalarchives.org/e-archives/acts/.

Minneapolis, 1976: For the first time, General Convention adopted a resolution that acknowledged and affirmed the presence of persons of homosexual orientation in the Church.

> Resolution 1976-A069:
> *Resolved*, the House of Bishops concurring, That it is the sense of this General Convention that homosexual persons are children of God who have a full and equal claim with all other persons upon the love, acceptance, and pastoral concern and care of the Church.

Anaheim, 1985: General Convention reaffirmed the 1976 resolution and encouraged dioceses to deepen understanding.

> Resolution 1985-D082:
> *Resolved*, the House of Bishops concurring, That the 68th General Convention urge each diocese of this Church to find an effective way to foster a better understanding of homosexual persons, to dispel myths and prejudices about homosexuality, to provide pastoral support, and to give life to the claim of homosexual persons "upon the love, acceptance,

and pastoral care and concern of the Church" as recognized by the General Convention in 1976.

Indianapolis, 1994: General Convention added sexual orientation, along with marital status, sex, disabilities, and age as categories to which non-discrimination in Church membership is assured.

Resolution 1994-C020:
Resolved, the House of Bishops concurring, That Title I, Canon 17, Section 5 be amended as follows:

No person shall be denied rights, status [in], or [access to] an equal place in the life, worship, and governance of this Church because of race, color, [or] ethnic origin, national origin, marital status, sex, sexual orientation, disabilities or age, except as otherwise specified by [this] Canon.

Indianapolis, 1994: General Convention called for a study of "the theological foundations and pastoral considerations involved in the development of rites honoring love and commitment between persons of the same sex."

Resolution 1994-C042:
Resolved, the House of Deputies concurring, That the 71st General Convention direct the Standing Liturgical Commission and the Theology Committee of the House of Bishops to prepare and present to the 72nd General Convention, as part of the Church's ongoing dialogue on human sexuality, a report addressing the theological foundations and pastoral considerations involved in the development of rites honoring love and commitment between persons of the same sex; and be it further

Resolved, That no rites for the honoring of love and commitment between persons of the same sex be developed unless and until the preparation of such rites has been authorized by the General Convention; and be it further

Resolved, That the sum of $8,600 be appropriated to support this work, subject to funding considerations.

Philadelphia, 1997: General Convention reaffirmed the traditional understanding of marriage and called for continuing study.

Resolution 1997-C003:
Resolved, That this 72nd General Convention affirm the sacredness of Christian marriage between one man and one woman with intent of life-long relationship; and be it further

Resolved, That this Convention direct the Standing Liturgical
Commission to continue its study of theological aspects of
committed relationships of same-sex couples, and to issue a
full report including recommendations of future steps for the
resolution of issues related to such committed relationships
no later than November 1999 for consideration at the 73rd
General Convention.

Denver, 2000: General Convention acknowledged relationships other
than marriage.

Resolution 2000-D039:
Resolved, That the members of the 73rd General Convention
intend for this Church to provide a safe and just structure
in which all can utilize their gifts and creative energies for
mission; and be it further

Resolved, That we acknowledge that while the issues of
human sexuality are not yet resolved, there are currently
couples in the Body of Christ and in this Church who are
living in marriage and couples in the Body of Christ and
in this Church who are living in other life-long committed
relationships; and be it further

Resolved, That we expect such relationships will be
characterized by fidelity, monogamy, mutual affection and
respect, careful, honest communication, and the holy love
which enables those in such relationships to see in each other
the image of God; and be it further

Resolved, That we denounce promiscuity, exploitation, and
abusiveness in the relationships of any of our members; and
be it further

Resolved, That this Church intends to hold all its members
accountable to these values, and will provide for them the
prayerful support, encouragement, and pastoral care necessary
to live faithfully by them; and be it further

Resolved, That we acknowledge that some, acting in good
conscience, who disagree with the traditional teaching of the
Church on human sexuality, will act in contradiction to that
position; and be it further

Resolved, That in continuity with previous actions of the
General Convention of this Church, and in response to the
call for dialogue by the Lambeth Conference, we affirm that
those on various sides of controversial issues have a place
in the Church, and we reaffirm the imperative to promote

conversation between persons of differing experiences and perspectives, while acknowledging the Church's teaching on the sanctity of marriage.

Minneapolis, 2003: Acknowledging continuing differences, General Convention recognized "that local faith communities are operating within the bounds of our common life as they explore and experience liturgies celebrating and blessing same-sex unions."

Resolution 2003-C051:
Resolved, That the 74th General Convention affirm the following:

1. That our life together as a community of faith is grounded in the saving work of Jesus Christ and expressed in the principles of the Chicago-Lambeth Quadrilateral: Holy Scripture, the historic Creeds of the Church, the two dominical Sacraments, and the Historic Episcopate.

2. That we reaffirm Resolution A069 of the 65th General Convention (1976) that "homosexual persons are children of God who have a full and equal claim with all other persons upon the love, acceptance, and pastoral concern and care of the Church."

3. That, in our understanding of homosexual persons, differences exist among us about how best to care pastorally for those who intend to live in monogamous, non-celibate unions; and what is, or should be, required, permitted, or prohibited by the doctrine, discipline, and worship of The Episcopal Church concerning the blessing of the same.

4. That we reaffirm Resolution D039 of the 73rd General Convention (2000), that "We expect such relationships will be characterized by fidelity, monogamy, mutual affection and respect, careful, honest communication, and the holy love which enables those in such relationships to see in each other the image of God," and that such relationships exist throughout the church.

5. That we recognize that local faith communities are operating within the bounds of our common life as they explore and experience liturgies celebrating and blessing same-sex unions.

6. That we commit ourselves, and call our church, in the spirit of Resolution A104 of the 70th General Convention (1991), to continued prayer, study, and discernment on the pastoral care for gay and lesbian persons, to include the compilation and

development by a special commission organized and appointed by the Presiding Bishop, of resources to facilitate as wide a conversation of discernment as possible throughout the church.

7. That our baptism into Jesus Christ is inseparable from our communion with one another, and we commit ourselves to that communion despite our diversity of opinion and, among dioceses, a diversity of pastoral practice with the gay men and lesbians among us.

8. That it is a matter of faith that our Lord longs for our unity as his disciples, and for us this entails living within the boundaries of the Constitution and Canons of The Episcopal Church. We believe this discipline expresses faithfulness to our polity and that it will facilitate the conversation we seek, not only in The Episcopal Church, but also in the wider Anglican Communion and beyond.

Anaheim, 2009: The General Convention directed the Standing Commission on Liturgy and Music to "collect and develop theological and liturgical resources" for blessing same-gender relationships.

<u>Resolution 2009-C056:</u>
Resolved, the House of Deputies concurring, That the 76th General Convention acknowledge the changing circumstances in the United States and in other nations, as legislation authorizing or forbidding marriage, civil unions or domestic partnerships for gay and lesbian persons is passed in various civil jurisdictions that call forth a renewed pastoral response from this Church, and for an open process for the consideration of theological and liturgical resources for the blessing of same gender relationships; and be it further

Resolved, That the Standing Commission on Liturgy and Music, in consultation with the House of Bishops, collect and develop theological and liturgical resources, and report to the 77th General Convention; and be it further

Resolved, That the Standing Commission on Liturgy and Music, in consultation with the House of Bishops, devise an open process for the conduct of its work inviting participation from provinces, dioceses, congregations, and individuals who are engaged in such theological work, and inviting theological reflection from throughout the Anglican Communion; and be it further

Resolved, That bishops, particularly those in dioceses within civil jurisdictions where same-gender marriage, civil unions, or domestic partnerships are legal, may provide generous pastoral response to meet the needs of members of this Church; and be it further

Resolved, That this Convention honor the theological diversity of this Church in regard to matters of human sexuality; and be it further

Resolved, That the members of this Church be encouraged to engage in this effort.

Indianapolis, 2012: In Resolution A049, the General Convention commended the resource "I Will Bless You and You Will Be a Blessing" for study and use, authorized the liturgy for provisional use, and called for a process of review and further development of the theological resources. In addition, in Resolution A050, the General Convention called for a task force to explore understandings of marriage, including attention to legislation authorizing or forbidding same-sex marriage.

Resolution 2012-A049:

Resolved, the House of Deputies concurring, That the 77th General Convention commend "Liturgical Resources I: I Will Bless You and You Will Be a Blessing" for study and use in congregations and dioceses of The Episcopal Church, with the following revisions:

Throughout "I Will Bless You and You Will Be a Blessing" change "same-gender" to "same-sex";

BB p. 184 (Te bendecire pdf, p.1): change "Resources for Blessing Same-Gender Relationships" to "Resources for The Witnessing and Blessing of a Lifelong Covenant in a same-sex relationship"

BB p. 240 (Te bendecire pdf, p. 83): Add rubric after first rubric, stating: "At least one of the couple must be a baptized Christian."

BB p. 240 (Te bendecire pdf, p. 83): In paragraph 2, line 1, delete "at least one of whom is baptized,"

BB p. 241 (Te bendecire pdf, p. 85): In Presider's address to the assembly, delete "come what may," (paragraph 1, line 9)

BB pp. 241-242 (Te bendecire pdf, p. 85): In Presider's address to the assembly, delete all of paragraph 2 ("Ahead of them...calls us all to share.")

BB p. 242 (Te bendecire pdf, p. 85): In Presider's address to the assembly, change "let us pray, then," (paragraph 3, line 1) to "Therefore, in the name of Christ, let us pray"

BB p. 245 (Te bendecire pdf, p. 90): After the bidding for peace in their home and love in their family, add the following bidding: "For the grace, when they hurt each other, to recognize and acknowledge their fault, and to seek each other's forgiveness and yours: Lord, in your mercy (or Lord, in your goodness) Hear our prayer."

BB p. 246 (Te bendecire pdf, p. 91): Change rubric that begins "After a time of silence" to the following: "The leader may add one or more of the following biddings"

BB p. 247 (Te bendecire pdf, p. 93): In Commitment (both forms) line 7, change "I will honor and keep you" to "I will honor and love you"

BB p. 248 (Te bendecire pdf, p. 94): In first form of blessing rings, change line 2 to "as signs of the enduring covenant"

BB p. 248 (Te bendecire pdf, p. 95): In Blessing of the Couple, add rubric between first and second paragraphs: "The Presider continues with one of the following"

BB p. 248 (Te bendecire pdf, p. 95): In Blessing of the Couple, add third paragraph after the "Amen": "or this / God, the holy and undivided Trinity, bless, preserve, and keep you, and mercifully grant you rich and boundless grace, that you may please God in body and soul. God make you a sign of the loving-kindness and steadfast fidelity manifest in the life, death, and resurrection of our Savior, and bring you at last to the delight of the heavenly banquet, where he lives and reigns for ever and ever. Amen."

BB p. 257 (Te bendecire pdf, p. 104): In paragraph under E. Vocation, change "1 Samuel 18" to "1 Samuel 3";

and be it further

Resolved, That the 77th General Convention authorize for provisional use "The Witnessing and Blessing of a Lifelong Covenant" from "Liturgical Resources I: I Will Bless You and You Will Be a Blessing" beginning the First Sunday of Advent 2012, under the direction and subject to the permission of the bishop exercising ecclesiastical authority; and be it further

Resolved, That bishops, particularly those in dioceses within civil jurisdictions where same-*sex* marriage, civil unions, or domestic partnerships are legal, may provide generous pastoral response to meet the needs of members of this Church; and be it further

Resolved, That bishops may authorize adaptation of these materials to meet the needs of members of this Church: and be it further

Resolved, that the provision of Canon I.18.4 applies by extension to "Theological Resources for Blessing Same-Sex Relationships," namely, "It shall be within the discretion of any Member of the Clergy of this Church to decline to" preside at any rite of blessing defined herein; and be it further

Resolved, That this convention honor the theological diversity of this church in regard to matters of human sexuality, and that no bishop, priest, deacon or lay person should be coerced or penalized in any manner, nor suffer any canonical disabilities, as a result of his or her conscientious objection to or support for the 77th General Convention's action with regard to the Blessing of Same-Sex Relationships; and be it further

Resolved, That the theological resource for the blessing of a life-long covenant be further developed by the Standing Commission on Liturgy and Music over the 2013-2015 triennium with specific attention to further engagement with scripture and the relevant categories and sources of systematic theology (e.g., creation, sin, grace, salvation, redemption, human nature); and be it further

Resolved, That the Standing Commission on Liturgy and Music include the work of diverse theological perspectives in the further development of the theological resource; and be it further

Resolved, That the Standing Commission on Liturgy and Music develop an open process to review "I Will Bless You and You Will Be a Blessing," inviting responses from provinces, dioceses, congregations, and individuals from throughout The Episcopal Church and the Anglican Communion, and from our ecumenical partners, and report to the 78th General Convention.

Resolution 2012-A050

Resolved, the House of Deputies concurring, That the 77th General Convention direct the Presiding Bishop and President of the House of Deputies to appoint a task force of not more than twelve people, consisting of theologians, liturgists, pastors, and educators, to identify and explore biblical, theological, historical, liturgical, and canonical dimensions of marriage; and be it further,

Resolved, That the task force consult with the Standing Commission on Constitution and Canons and The Standing Commission on Liturgy and Music to address the pastoral need for priests to officiate at a civil marriage of a same-sex couple in states that authorize such; and be it further

Resolved, That the task force consult with couples living in marriage and in other lifelong committed relationships and with single adults, and be it further,

Resolved, that the task force consult with other churches in the Anglican Communion and with our ecumenical partners, and be it further

Resolved, That the task force consider issues raised by changing societal and cultural norms and legal structures, including legislation authorizing or forbidding marriage, civil unions, or domestic partnerships between two people of the same sex, in the U.S. and other countries where The Episcopal Church is located; and be it further

Resolved, That the task force develop tools for theological reflection and norms for theological discussion at a local level; and be it further

Resolved, That the task force report its progress to the 78th General Convention; and be it further

Resolved, That the General Convention request the Joint Standing Committee on Program, Budget and Finance to consider a budget allocation of $30,000 for the implementation of this resolution.

Salt Lake City, 2015: In Resolution A054, the General Convention authorized two liturgies for marriage for trial use and the use of "The Witnessing and Blessing of a Lifelong Covenant," thus allowing the marriage of same-sex couples in civil jurisdictions where such marriages are legal. In addition, Resolution A036 revised the marriage canon (Canon I.18; the revised text appears above in Appendix 2), and Resolution A037 requested dioceses and parishes to use the study materials produced by the Task Force on the Study of Marriage established by the 2012 Convention, and called for an expanded task force to continue to study marriage.

Resolution 2015-A036:
Resolved, the House of Deputies concurring, That Canon I.18 is hereby amended to read as follows:

~~CANON 18: Of the Solemnization of Holy Matrimony~~

Canon 18: Of the Celebration and Blessing of Marriage

Sec. 1. Every Member of the Clergy of this Church shall conform to the laws of the State governing the creation of the civil status of marriage, and also ~~to the laws of this Church governing~~ *these canons concerning* the solemnization of *marriage* ~~Holy Matrimony~~. *Members of the Clergy may solemnize a marriage using any of the liturgical forms authorized by this Church.*

~~Sec. 2. Before solemnizing a marriage the Member of the Clergy shall have ascertained:~~

~~(a) That both parties have the right to contract a marriage according to the laws of the State.~~

~~(b) That both parties understand that Holy Matrimony is a physical and spiritual union of a man and a woman, entered into within the community of faith, by mutual consent of heart, mind, and will, and with intent that it be lifelong.~~

~~(c) That both parties freely and knowingly consent to such marriage, without fraud, coercion, mistake as to identity of a partner, or mental reservation.~~

~~(d) That at least one of the parties has received Holy Baptism.~~

~~(e) That both parties have been instructed as to the nature, meaning, and purpose of Holy Matrimony by the Member of the Clergy, or that they have both received such instruction from persons known by the Member of the Clergy to be competent and responsible.~~

Sec. 2. The couple shall notify the Member of the Clergy of their intent to marry at least thirty days prior to the solemnization; Provided, that if one of the parties is a member of the Congregation of the Member of the Clergy, or both parties can furnish satisfactory evidence of the need for shortening the time, this requirement can be waived for weighty cause; in which case the Member of the Clergy shall immediately report this action in writing to the Bishop.

~~Sec. 3. No Member of the Clergy of this Church shall solemnize any marriage unless the following procedures are complied with:~~

~~(a) The intention of the parties to contract marriage shall have been signified to the Member of the Clergy at least thirty days before the service of solemnization; Provided, that for weighty~~

~~cause, this requirement may be dispensed with if one of the parties is a member of the Congregation of the Member of the Clergy, or can furnish satisfactory evidence of responsibility. In case the thirty days' notice is waived, the Member of the Clergy shall report such action in writing to the Bishop immediately.~~

~~(b) There shall be present at least two witnesses to the solemnization of marriage.~~

~~(c) The Member of the Clergy shall record in the proper register the date and place of the marriage, the names of the parties and their parents, the age of the parties, their residences, and their Church status the witnesses and the Member of the Clergy shall sign the record.~~

~~(d) The Member of the Clergy shall have required that the parties sign the following declaration:~~

~~(e) "We, A.B. and C.D., desiring to receive the blessing of Holy Matrimony in the Church, do solemnly declare that we hold marriage to be a lifelong union of husband and wife as it is set forth in the Book of Common Prayer.~~

~~(f) "We believe that the union of husband and wife, in heart, body, and mind, is intended by God for their mutual joy; for the help and comfort given one another in prosperity and adversity; and, when it is God's will, for the procreation of children and their nurture in the knowledge and love of the Lord.~~

~~(g) "And we do engage ourselves, so far as in us lies, to make our utmost effort to establish this relationship and to seek God's help thereto."~~

Sec. 3. Prior to the solemnization, the Member of the Clergy shall determine:

(a) that both parties have the right to marry according to the laws of the State and consent to do so freely, without fraud, coercion, mistake as to the identity of either, or mental reservation; and

(b) that at least one of the parties is baptized; and

(c) that both parties have been instructed by the Member of the Clergy, or a person known by the Member of the Clergy to be competent and responsible, in the nature, purpose, and meaning, as well as the rights, duties and responsibilities of marriage.

Sec. 4. Prior to the solemnization, the parties shall sign the following Declaration of Intention:

We understand the teaching of the church that God's purpose for our marriage is for our mutual joy, for the help and comfort we will give to each other in prosperity and adversity, and, when it is God's will, for the gift and heritage of children and their nurture in the knowledge and love of God. We also understand that our marriage is to be unconditional, mutual, exclusive, faithful, and lifelong; and we engage to make the utmost effort to accept these gifts and fulfill these duties, with the help of God and the support of our community.

Sec. 5. At least two witnesses shall be present at the solemnization, and together with the Member of the Clergy and the parties, sign the record of the solemnization in the proper register; which record shall include the date and place of the solemnization, the names of the witnesses, the parties and their parents, the age of the parties, Church status, and residence(s).

Sec. 6. A bishop or priest may pronounce a blessing upon a civil marriage using any of the liturgical forms authorized by this Church.

~~Sec. 4~~ S *ec. 7. It shall be within the discretion of any Member of the Clergy of this Church to decline to solemnize or bless any marriage.*

and be it further

Resolved that this canon shall become effective on the First Sunday of Advent, 2015.

Resolution 2015-A037:

Resolved, the House of Deputies concurring, That the 78th General Convention requests dioceses and parishes use the study materials on marriage provided in the last triennium by the Task Force on the Study of Marriage, namely the "Dearly Beloved" toolkit and the appended essays in their Blue Book report to this Convention; and be it further

Resolved, That the 78th General Convention directs the Presiding Bishop and President of the House of Deputies to appoint jointly an expanded Task Force on the Study of Marriage to continue this work, consisting of not more than 15 people, including theologians, ethicists, pastors, liturgists, and educators, who represent the cultural and theological diversity in the Church; membership should include some of the Task Force on the Study of Marriage appointed in 2012, some from dioceses outside the United States, and young adults; and be it further

Resolved, That the Task Force explore further those contemporary trends and norms identified by the Task Force on the Study of Marriage in the previous triennium, specifically regarding those who choose to remain single; unmarried persons in intimate relationships; couples who cohabitate either in preparation for, or as an alternative to, marriage; couples who desire a blessing from the Church but not marriage; parenting by single or and/or unmarried persons; differing forms of family and household such as those including same-sex parenting, adoption, and racial diversity; and differences in marriage patterns between ethnic and racial groups; and be it further

Resolved, That the Task Force consult with (i) individuals and couples within these groups about their experience of faith and church life; and (ii) the results of diocesan and parochial study of "Dearly Beloved" toolkit; and be it further

Resolved, That the Task Force explore biblical, theological, moral, liturgical, cultural, and pastoral perspectives on these matters, and develop written materials about them which represent the spectrum of understanding in our Church and which include responses from theologians, ethicists, pastors, liturgists, social scientists, and educators who are not members of the expanded Task Force, and whose perspectives represent the spectrum of understandings on these matters in our Church; and be it further

Resolved, That the Task Force study and monitor, in consultation with the Standing Commission on Liturgy and Music, the impact of same-sex marriage and rites of blessing on our Church; the continuing debate about clergy acting as agents of the state in officiating at marriages; and any other matters related to marriage by action of or referral by this Convention; and be it further

Resolved, That the Task Force report and make recommendations to the 79th General Convention; and be it further

Resolved, That the Task Force provide educational and pastoral resources for congregational use on these matters that represents the spectrum of understandings on these matters in our Church; and be it further

Resolved, That the General Convention request the Joint Standing Committee on Program, Budget and Finance to consider a budget allocation of $90,000 for the implementation of this resolution.

Resolution 2015-A054:

Resolved, the House of Deputies concurring, That the 78th General Convention commend "Liturgical Resources I: I Will Bless You and You Will Be a Blessing, Revised and Expanded 2015," as found in the Blue Book, Liturgy Supplemental Materials: Appendices of the Report of the Standing Commission on Liturgy and Music (BBLSM), pp. 2-151, with the following revisions:

BBLSM p. 84: In The Commitment, change the rubric to read "Each member of the couple, in turn, takes the right hand of the other and says"

BBLSM p.84: After "I N., give myself to you, N." add ", and take you to myself."

BBLSM p. 85: At the Pronouncement, change the rubric to read "The Presider joins the right hands and says"

BBLSM p. 87: In Concerning the Service, change the second paragraph to read "At least one of the couple must be a baptized Christian, and the marriage shall conform to the laws of the state and canons of this church."

BBLSM p. 88: Under Gathering, change the rubric to read "The couple joins the assembly."

BBLSM p. 89: Change "In marriage according to the laws of the state [or civil jurisdiction] of X" to "In marriage [according to the laws of the state or civil jurisdiction of X]"

BBLSM p. 89: Change "Solemnize their marriage according to the laws of the state [or civil jurisdiction] of X" to "are married [according to the laws of the state or civil jurisdiction of X]"

BBLSM p.94: After "I N., give myself to you, N." add ", and take you to myself."

BBLSM p. 95: At the Pronouncement, change the rubric to read "The Presider joins the right hands of the couple and says"

BBLSM p. 95: Replace "I pronounce that they are married according to the laws of the state [or civil jurisdiction] of X" to "I pronounce that they are married [according to the laws of the state or civil jurisdiction of X]"

BBLSM p. 100: At The Marriage, change the rubric to read "Each member of the couple, in turn, takes the right hand of the other and says"

for study and use in congregations and dioceses of The Episcopal Church; and be it further

Resolved, That the 78th General Convention authorize for use "The Witnessing and Blessing of a Lifelong Covenant" from "Liturgical Resources I: I Will Bless You and You Will Be a Blessing, Revised and Expanded 2015" (as found in Supplemental Materials: Appendices of the Report of the Standing Commission on Liturgy and Music, pp. 77-86, as amended) beginning the First Sunday of Advent 2015; under the direction and with the permission of the bishop exercising ecclesiastical authority; and be it further

Resolved, That the 78th General Convention authorize for trial use in accordance with Article X of the Constitution and Canon II.3.6 "The Witnessing and Blessing of a Marriage," and "The Celebration and Blessing of a Marriage 2," from "Liturgical Resources I: I Will Bless You and You Will Be a Blessing, Revised and Expanded 2015" (as found in Supplemental Materials: Appendices of the Report of the Standing Commission on Liturgy and Music, pp. 87-105) beginning the First Sunday of Advent 2015. Bishops exercising ecclesiastical authority or, where appropriate, ecclesiastical supervision will make provision for all couples asking to be married in this Church to have access to these liturgies. Trial use is only to be available under the direction and with the permission of the Diocesan Bishop; and be it further

Resolved, That bishops may continue to provide generous pastoral response to meet the needs of members of this Church; and be it further

Resolved, That the provision of Canon I.18.4* applies by extension to "Liturgical Resources I: I Will Bless You and You Will Be a Blessing, Revised and Expanded 2015," namely, "It shall be within the discretion of any Member of the Clergy of this Church to decline to" preside at any rite contained herein; and be it further

Resolved, That the provisions of Canon I.19.3 regarding marriage after divorce apply equally to all the rites of "Liturgical Resources I: I Will Bless You and You Will Be a Blessing, Revised and Expanded 2015," in accordance with guidelines established by each diocese; and be it further

Resolved, That this convention honor the theological diversity of this Church in regard to matters of human sexuality; and that no bishop, priest, deacon or lay person should be coerced or penalized in any manner, nor suffer any canonical disabilities, as a result of his or her theological objection to or support for the 78th General Convention's action contained in this resolution; and be it further

Resolved, That the Standing Commission on Liturgy and Music continue to monitor the use of this material and report to the 79th General Convention; and be it further

Resolved, That the 78th General Convention direct the Secretary of General Convention, and the Custodian of the Standard Book of Common Prayer in consultation with the outgoing Chair of the Standing Commission on Liturgy and Music and the Chairs of the Legislative Committees to whom this legislation is referred, to finalize and arrange for the publication with Church Publishing of the material (in English and Spanish) contained in "Liturgical Resources 1: I Will Bless You and You Will Be a Blessing, Revised and Expanded 2015" as approved by the 78th General Convention, no later than the first Sunday of Advent 2015, these materials to be available electronically at no cost.

*Canon I.18.4 refers to the 2012 Constitution and Canons; a comparable provision is contained in Canon I.18.7 of the 2015 Constitution and Canons.

4. Consultation on Same-Sex Marriage: Executive Summary of Evaluations

The Consultation on Same-Sex Marriage invited participants from several dioceses in states where marriage equality is legally recognized to share their experiences and contexts and also to provide responses to the resources that the SCLM subcommittee had developed. Additionally, the Consultation also invited participants from other Anglican Communion Provinces having marriage equality as well as representatives from other mainline Protestant denominations, which added both international and ecumenical dimensions to the discussion.

The intensive two-day consultation (held in Kansas City, Missouri on June 3–5, 2014, Tuesday evening through Thursday evening) included both an *indaba*-style conversation, with the objective of structured mutual listening to diverse contexts and concerns on the topic of marriage equality, and a focused workshop to provide responses to the work of the SCLM subcommittee on the resources. Recorders for small groups captured the key points of the resources discussion.

At the end of the Consultation, a short evaluative questionnaire was distributed to solicit feedback from participants on their experience and personal responses to the meeting. Although the survey response rate was over 50 percent (N=36) and provided some helpful feedback, other questions remained that needed following up.

The objective of this follow-up evaluation report for the SCLM Consultation on Same-Sex Marriage is to probe for further insights and reflections on the resources discussed in the Consultation, on the value of the *indaba*-style conversation to the overall process, and on the inclusion of other Anglican Communion and ecumenical participants in the Consultation, and to gather suggestions for next steps. The report is based on a sample of seven in-depth participant interviews bringing together perspectives from within The Episcopal Church (TEC), from other Anglican Communion Provinces, and from an ecumenical standpoint.

Respondents highly valued the Consultation experience, including both the content that was presented and shared and the opportunity to hear and learn from other contexts. The Consultation also served to reinforce the interconnections among those deeply involved with this topic yet deeply embedded within their own congregational, diocesan, provincial, or denominational contexts.

The resources were broadly affirmed. For TEC participants, they were seen as fully answering why the Episcopal Church is blessing same-sex relationships. The absence of a blessing substantively similar to that used in the BCP Marriage Rite was the only concern raised over the liturgy. International and ecumenical responses were complimentary, but they also noted some need for local adaptation. The resources addressing biblical and theological issues were viewed as usable as-is across a range of differing contexts. A request was made to translate the resources for use in another Province.

All respondents found the mixture of TEC, international, and ecumenical participants highly informative and deeply moving. The Consultation's inclusion of those voices also demonstrated the Episcopal Church's interest in engaging other Anglican Communion Provinces and seriously listening to their contexts. This step also helped to dispel stereotypical assumptions held by some participants about other contexts, and it helped some to realize that the Provinces could talk to each other in less formal ways about topics of mutual interest.

The *indaba*-style conversation at first appeared to suffer from a lack of diversity in viewpoints, but participants also found value in being able to explore other facets, which allowed subtle but important nuances to emerge. The *indaba* approach was particularly effective in helping participants move to a deeper level of conversation and understanding. International participants also hoped to apply aspects of this experience to future *indabas* in their own Provinces.

Suggested next steps focused on two themes: 1) rethinking marriage overall in the context and life of the Church, and 2) immediate advocacy as a social justice issue. Other suggestions included supplementary materials for deputations along with more publicly visible actions.

In conclusion, respondents felt hopeful about the work of the SCLM and for the Episcopal Church's leadership on this topic, which was described as "cutting edge." Both interview responses and a review of the questionnaire data suggest that the Consultation was an invaluable step for participants personally and for working within the Church interactively for broad social change.

The Rev. Paula D. Nesbitt, Ph.D.

5. Glossary of Legal and Canonical Terms

This glossary of legal and canonical terms, along with other terms often used in discussing same-sex blessings, is intended to inform and enhance discussions of the theological and liturgical resources, as well as preparation for and use of any liturgy authorized by General Convention. Most of these terms are discussed in greater depth in the essay "Faith, Hope, and Love: Theological Resources for Blessing Same-Sex Relationships."

Blessing. "The active outgoing of divine grace."[116] When a blessing is given, for example, at a Celebration and Blessing of a Marriage or during a rite for blessing a same-sex relationship, the Church understands that God's blessing has been recognized in the lives of the couple and also imparted in a new way because of the Church's action. The marital blessing involves three distinct but interdependent aspects: we (the Church) bless God in thanksgiving for God's grace already evident in the lives of the couple; we pronounce God's blessing upon those in covenantal relationships to strengthen their covenantal bonds; and we commission couples as witnesses of God's love for the world.

Blessing of a Civil Marriage. The Book of Common Prayer rite by which a husband and wife who were previously married by competent civil authority, with appropriate documentation, have their civil marriage blessed by the Church.

Canon. The Canons of the Episcopal Church are the laws which set out the enactments of the ecclesiastical polity of the Church as governed by the Episcopal Church's Constitution and revised by General Convention. Each diocese of the Episcopal Church has its own canons, which must be consistent with the Canons of the Episcopal Church.

---

116 Alan Richardson, ed., *A Theological Word Book of the Bible* (New York: Macmillan, 1960), 33.

Civil marriage. A civil marriage is a marriage obtained by following the legal requirements of the state or jurisdiction in which the marriage is created. A civil marriage is often described as a special form of legal contract, established and regulated by each state and entered into by two consenting parties. A civil marriage carries both legal benefits and responsibilities under both state and federal law. A state's civil marriage statutes specify which couples are permitted to marry or are prohibited from marrying and who is authorized to officiate at a civil marriage.

Civil union. A civil union was a state-recognized legal contract alternative authorized under the laws of some states. The enacting statutes typically granted couples, including same-sex couples, in a civil union the rights, benefits, and obligations of married couples under state law. These benefits and responsibilities varied from state to state and in some cases did not replicate all of the benefits of civil marriage. The statutes specified who was eligible to enter into a civil union and who was authorized to officiate at a civil union.

Under the federal law known as the Defense of Marriage Act (DOMA) and the laws of at least thirty-five states, civil unions were either not recognized at all or were not recognized as the equivalent of civil marriage. DOMA withheld federal recognition of civil unions as marriages so couples in a civil union could not have access to the same federal benefits. On June 26, 2013, the U. S. Supreme Court ruled that DOMA's restriction of federal benefits to married couples consisting of one man and one woman was unconstitutional, depriving married same-sex couples of equal protection and due process under the U. S. Constitution.[117]

Common-law marriage. A common-law marriage is established when a man and a woman live together and identify themselves as husband and wife for a sufficient time, with the express mutual intent of establishing a marriage. Some states require seven years of continuous cohabitation, but others do not specify the number of years. In states that recognize common-law marriage, the status of common-law marriage is generally accorded all of the benefits and obligations of a civil marriage. Fewer than twenty states recognize common-law marriages.

Constitution. Unless otherwise noted, this word refers to the Constitution of the Protestant Episcopal Church in the United States of America, otherwise known as the Episcopal Church, as adopted by the General Convention in October 1789 and amended in subsequent General Conventions.

---

117 http://www.ncsl.org/research/human-services/same-sex-marriage-laws.aspx.

Covenant. The fundamental relationship between God and God's people. The concept has a long and varied history, biblical and otherwise. Christians understand covenantal relationship to derive primarily from the gracious covenant God has made with us in Christ. We enact this covenant in baptism and sustain it in the eucharist. For the Church, a covenant is a relationship initiated by God through Jesus Christ to which a body of people responds in faith; in which God promises that the people will be God's; and in which God requires God's people to be faithful, to do justice, to love mercy, and to walk humbly with God; and to whom, through the Holy Spirit, God gives the grace to do so. As Christians, we respond to God's gracious covenant in Christ by living faithfully in all of our various relationships. Scripture and Christian history bear witness to these essential elements of covenantal relationship: taking vows, intending lifelong commitment, and bearing the fruit of God's grace in the relationship.

Covenant of marriage. The Book of Common Prayer proclaims that "Christian marriage is a solemn and public covenant between a man and a woman in the presence of God" (BCP, 422). In the Catechism (BCP, 861), in response to the question "What is Holy Matrimony?" we read: "Holy Matrimony is Christian Marriage, in which the woman and man enter into a life-long union, make their vows before God and the Church, and receive the grace and blessing of God to help them fulfill their vows."

Defense of Marriage Act (DOMA). See above, "civil union."

Divorce. The legal process under state law by which a marriage is ended and through which the court determines the parties' future legal and financial obligations to each other and to their children. In states with civil unions, the termination process generally is known as "dissolution," or some term other than "divorce."

Domestic partnership. Some states and cities have enacted domestic partnership laws or ordinances, granting same-sex and different-sex couples a bundle of specific rights, less than those granted under marriage or civil-union laws. These laws vary considerably in their scope.

Holy Matrimony. Holy Matrimony is Christian marriage, as defined above under "Covenant of Marriage," using The Celebration and Blessing of a Marriage or An Order for Marriage from the *Book of Common Prayer*.

Judgment of marital status. Under Canon I.19.2, a "member of the Church whose marriage has been annulled or dissolved by a civil court may apply to the Bishop or Ecclesiastical Authority of the Diocese in which such person is legally or canonically resident for a judgment as to his or her marital status in the eyes of the Church. Such judgment may be a recognition of the nullity, or of the termination of the said marriage." A judgment of marital status may be requested at any time, not just when contemplating remarriage. Many Church members find support and comfort, after the termination of a civil marriage, in seeking this judgment, which establishes the unmarried status in the eyes of the Church. Such a judgment is also useful if the person seeks to remarry and, under Canon I.19.3(a), must provide evidence of the end of the prior marriage through annulment or divorce. This process is distinct from the consultation with the Bishop Diocesan regarding remarriage after divorce, found in Canon I.19.3(c).

Same-sex marriage. On June 26, 2015, the Supreme Court of the United States ruled that the Fourteenth Amendment requires a state to license a marriage between two people of the same sex and to recognize a marriage between two people of the same sex when that marriage has been lawfully licensed and performed outside of the state. These marriages are accorded all of the rights and obligations of civil marriage under state law.

Vow. A solemn and voluntary promise. Marital vows are voluntary pledges instituted and accepted by the Church, by which the woman and man give and bind themselves to each other. Vows exchanged in Holy Matrimony or in the liturgy for blessing a same-sex couple represent commitment, fidelity, and witness.

As Christians have come to understand covenantal relationship, especially in the light of God's gracious covenant with us in Christ, a "vow" signifies permanence and inviolability. The Church affirms and supports this definition of a vowed relationship for all couples entering into marriage as well as for same-sex couples entering into covenantal relationship using the liturgy in this resource. The Church also recognizes that human covenants will sometimes, perhaps often, fall short of the model established in the covenant God makes with us in baptism. Nonetheless, Christians strive to enter into a vowed relationship with God's help and in the power of the Holy Spirit.